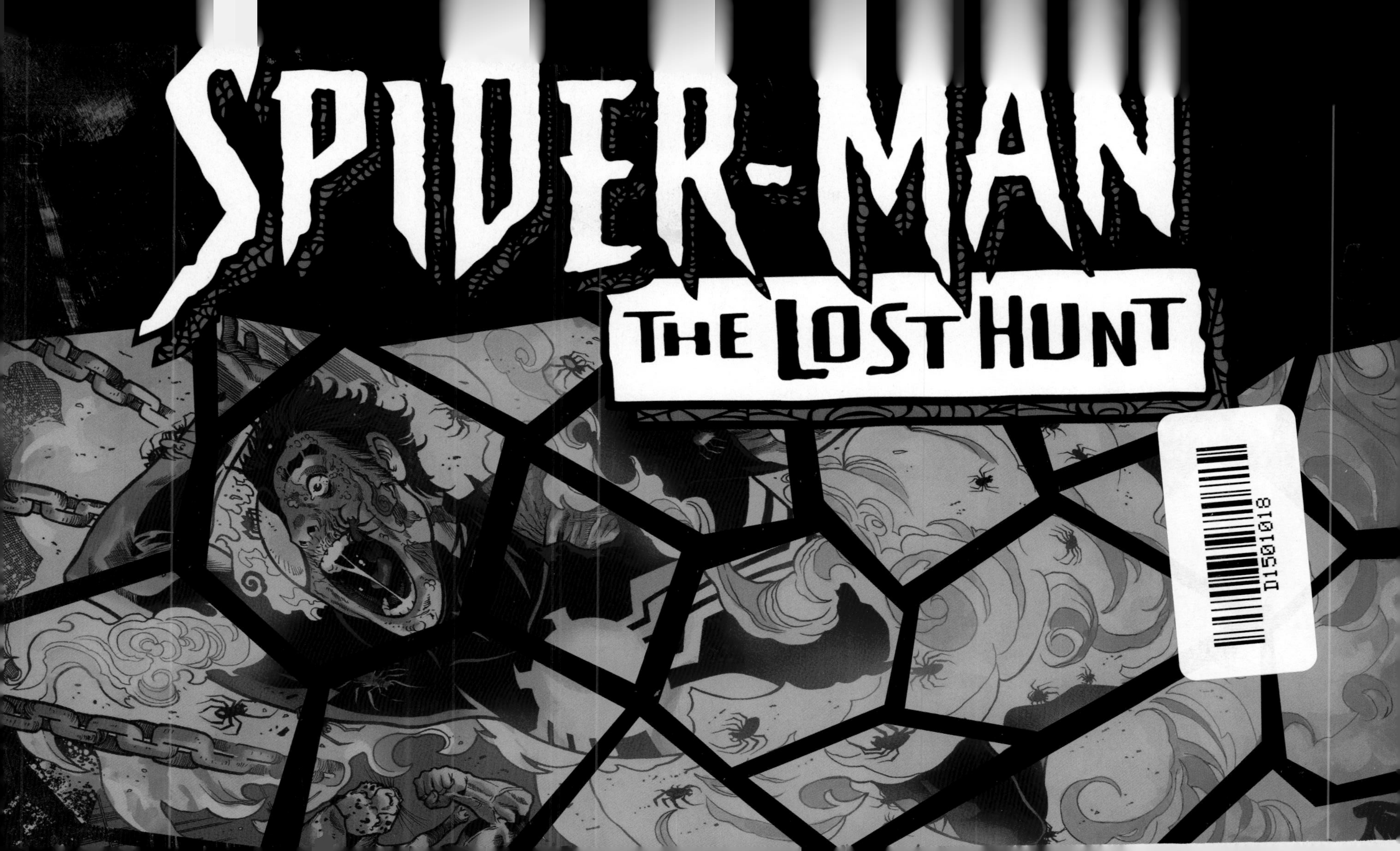
SPIDER-MAN
THE LOST HUNT

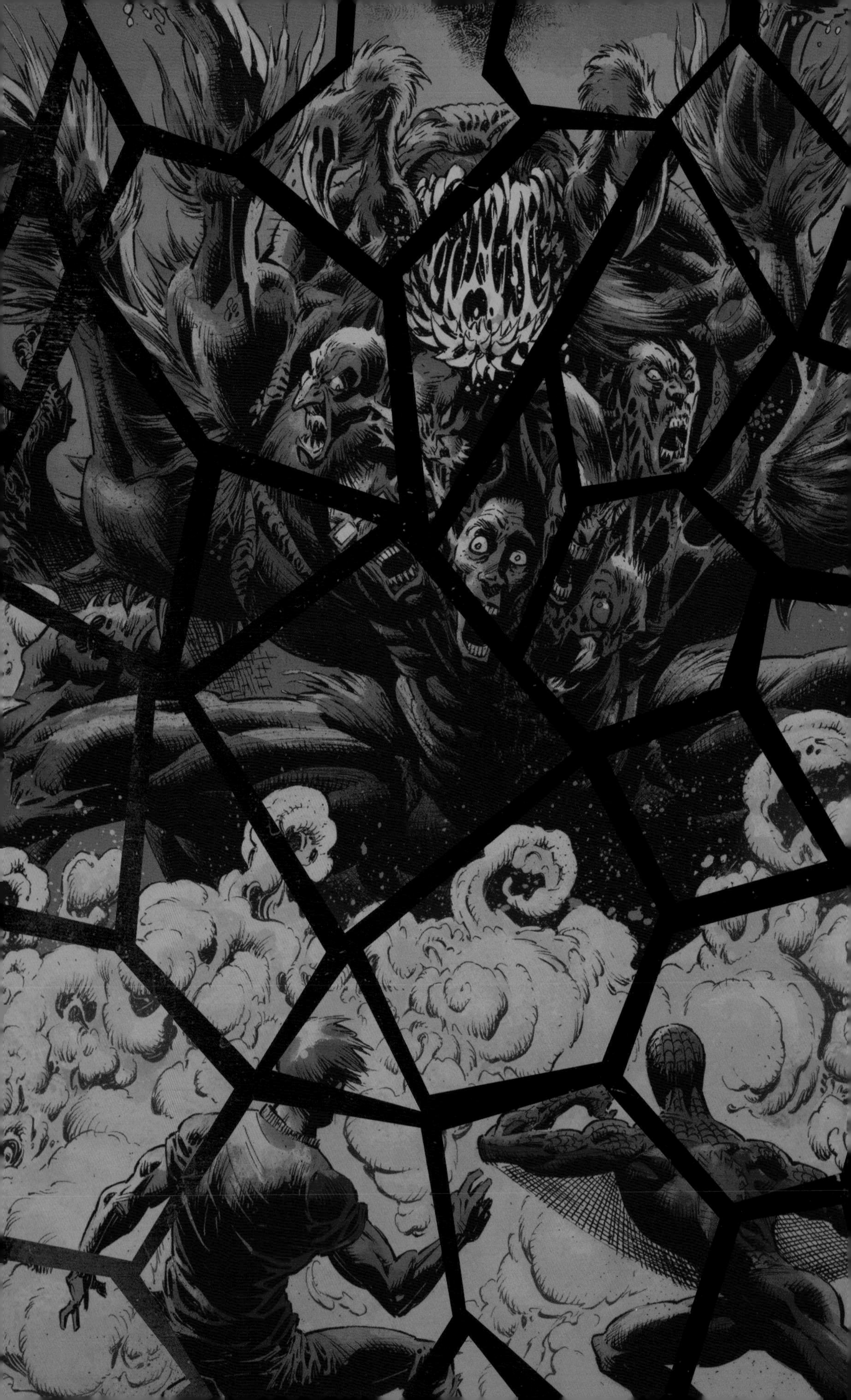

PETER PARKER was bitten by a radioactive spider and gained the proportional speed, strength and agility of a SPIDER, adhesive fingertips and toes and the unique precognitive awareness of danger called "SPIDER-SENSE"! After the tragic death of his Uncle Ben, Peter understood that with great power there must also come great responsibility. He became the crimefighting super hero called SPIDER-MAN!

Years later, after an altercation with the villain the JACKAL, Peter was cloned. At this time, Peter, believing he was the clone, left New York City and the mantle of SPIDER-MAN to BEN REILLY. Peter and a pregnant Mary Jane Watson-Parker looked to begin a new life in Portland, Oregon. Now powerless, Peter Parker learns to live his life without...

SPIDER-MAN
THE LOST HUNT

J.M. DeMATTEIS
WRITER

EDER MESSIAS WITH BRENT PEEPLES [#2], KYLE HOTZ [#3], MARGUERITE SAUVAGE [#4] & TRAVEL FOREMAN [#4]
PENCILERS

BELARDINO BRABO WITH BRENT PEEPLES [#2], KYLE HOTZ [#3], MARGUERITE SAUVAGE [#4], TRAVEL FOREMAN [#4] & WAYNE FAUCHER [#5]
INKERS

NEERAJ MENON [#1, #3-4], CRIS PETER [#1-2] & JAVA TARTAGLIA [#5] WITH DEE CUNNIFFE [#4] & MARGUERITE SAUVAGE [#4]
COLORISTS

VC's JOE CARAMAGNA
LETTERER

RYAN BROWN
COVER ART

DANNY KHAZEM
EDITOR

NICK LOWE
EXECUTIVE EDITOR

SPIDER-MAN CREATED BY STAN LEE & STEVE DITKO

COLLECTION EDITOR JENNIFER GRÜNWALD • ASSISTANT EDITOR DANIEL KIRCHHOFFER • ASSISTANT MANAGING EDITOR MAIA LOY
ASSOCIATE MANAGER, TALENT RELATIONS LISA MONTALBANO • VP PRODUCTION & SPECIAL PROJECTS JEFF YOUNGQUIST
BOOK DESIGNER STACIE ZUCKER • MANAGER & SENIOR DESIGNER ADAM DEL RE • LEAD DESIGNER JAY BOWEN
SVP PRINT, SALES & MARKETING DAVID GABRIEL • EDITOR IN CHIEF C.B. CEBULSKI

SPIDER-MAN: THE LOST HUNT. Contains material originally published in magazine form as SPIDER-MAN: THE LOST HUNT (2022) #1-5. First printing 2023. ISBN 978-1-302-94807-8. Published by MARVEL WORLDWIDE, INC., a subsidiary of MARVEL ENTERTAINMENT, LLC. OFFICE OF PUBLICATION: 1290 Avenue of the Americas, New York, NY 10104.

Printed in the U.S.A. KEVIN FEIGE, Chief Creative Officer; DAN BUCKLEY, President, Marvel Entertainment; DAVID BOGART, Associate Publisher & SVP of Talent Affairs; TOM BREVOORT, VP, Executive Editor; NICK LOWE, Executive Editor, VP of Content, Digital Publishing; DAVID GABRIEL, VP of Print & Digital Publishing; SVEN LARSEN, VP of Licensed Publishing; MARK ANNUNZIATO, VP of Planning & Forecasting; JEFF YOUNGQUIST, VP of Production & Special Projects; ALEX MORALES, Director of Publishing Operations; DAN EDINGTON, Director of Editorial Operations; RICKEY PURDIN, Director of Talent Relations; JENNIFER GRÜNWALD, Director of Production & Special Projects; SUSAN CRESPI, Production Manager; STAN LEE, Chairman Emeritus. For information regarding advertising in Marvel Comics or on Marvel.com, please contact Vit DeBellis, Custom Solutions & Integrated ... Manufactured between 4/14/2023 and 5/16/2023 by SEAWAY PRINTING, GREEN BAY, WI, USA.

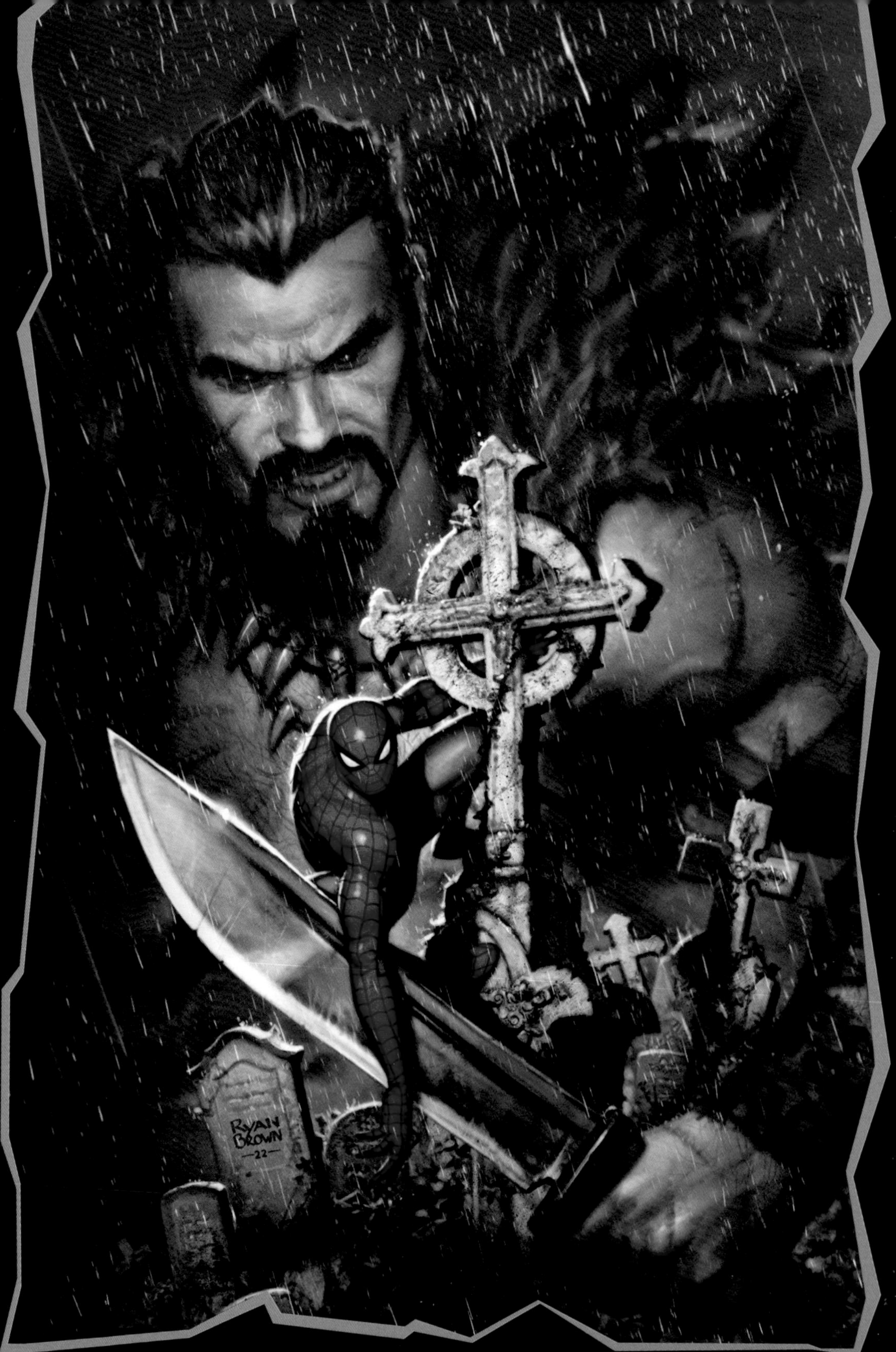
RYAN
BROWN
—22—

1

I KILLED SERGEI KRAVINOFF.

KRAAAAAK

A GOOD DEATH. A *NECESSARY* DEATH.

AND AFTER I BURIED HIS LIFELESS BODY IN THE GROUND...

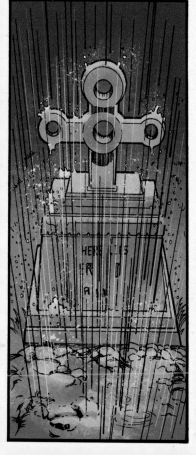

HERE LIES
ER
A

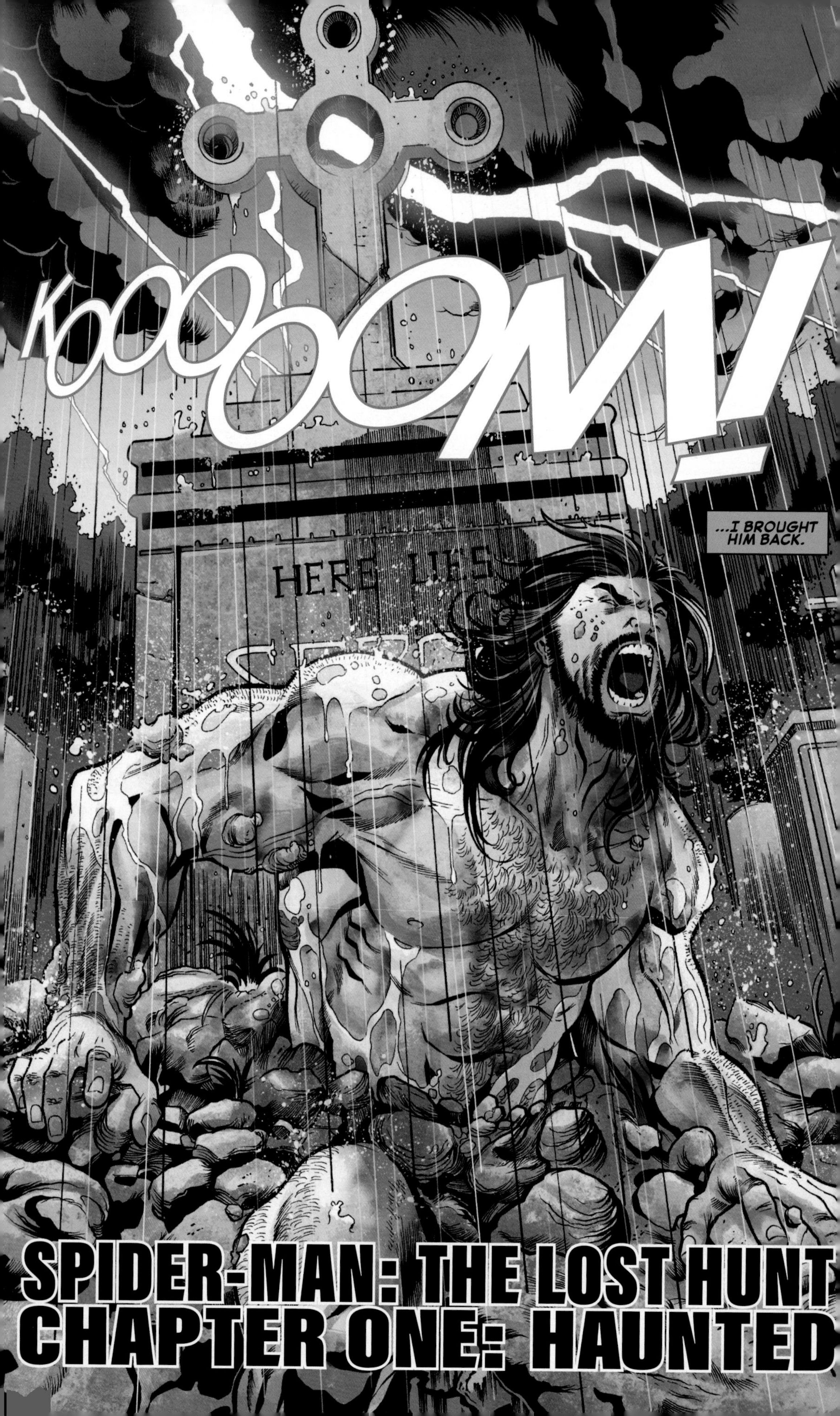
KOOOOOM!
...I BROUGHT HIM BACK.
HERE LIES
SPIDER-MAN: THE LOST HUNT
CHAPTER ONE: HAUNTED

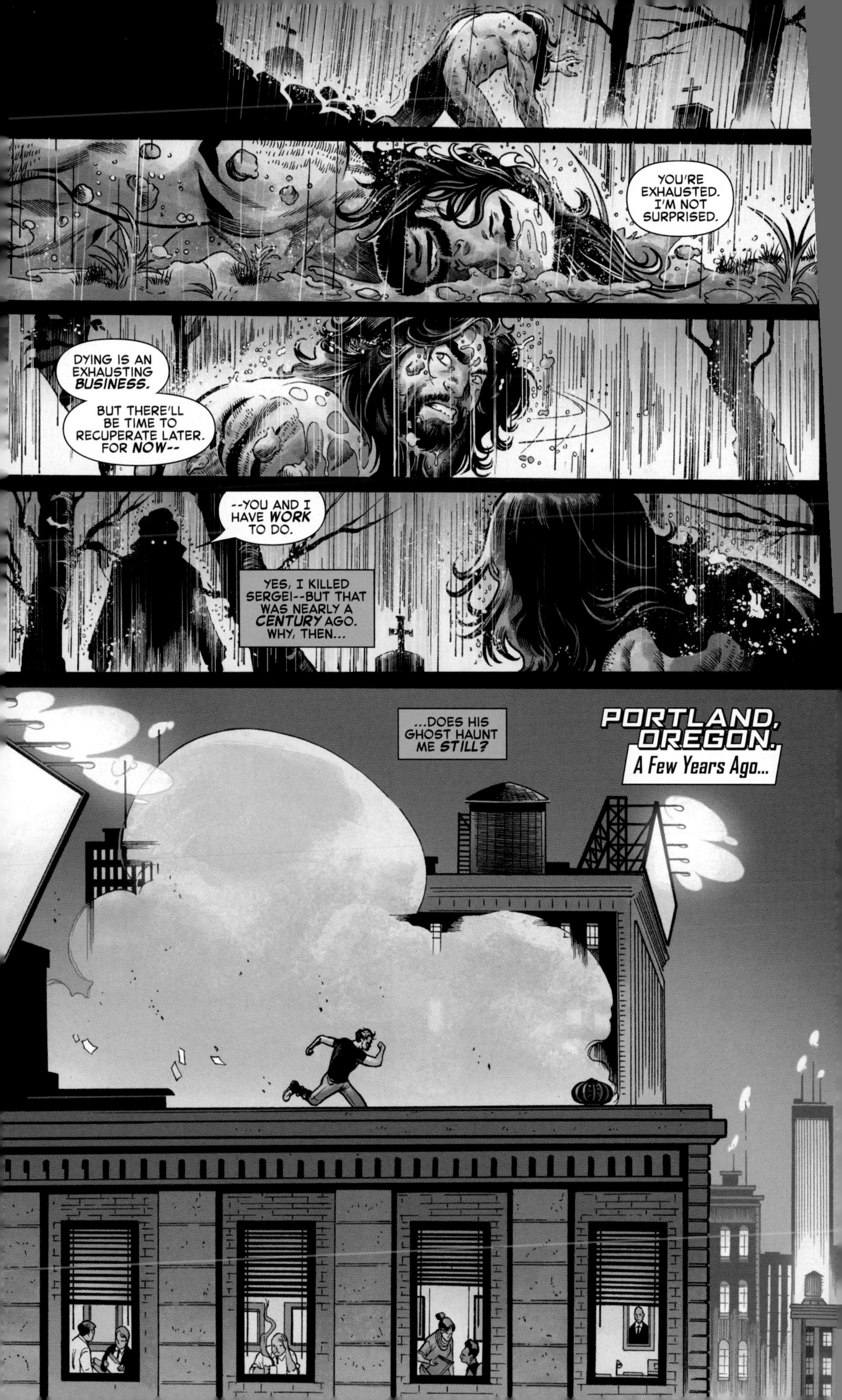

YOU'RE EXHAUSTED. I'M NOT SURPRISED.
DYING IS AN EXHAUSTING BUSINESS.
BUT THERE'LL BE TIME TO RECUPERATE LATER. FOR NOW--
--YOU AND I HAVE WORK TO DO.
YES, I KILLED SERGEI--BUT THAT WAS NEARLY A CENTURY AGO. WHY, THEN...
...DOES HIS GHOST HAUNT ME STILL?
PORTLAND, OREGON.
A Few Years Ago...

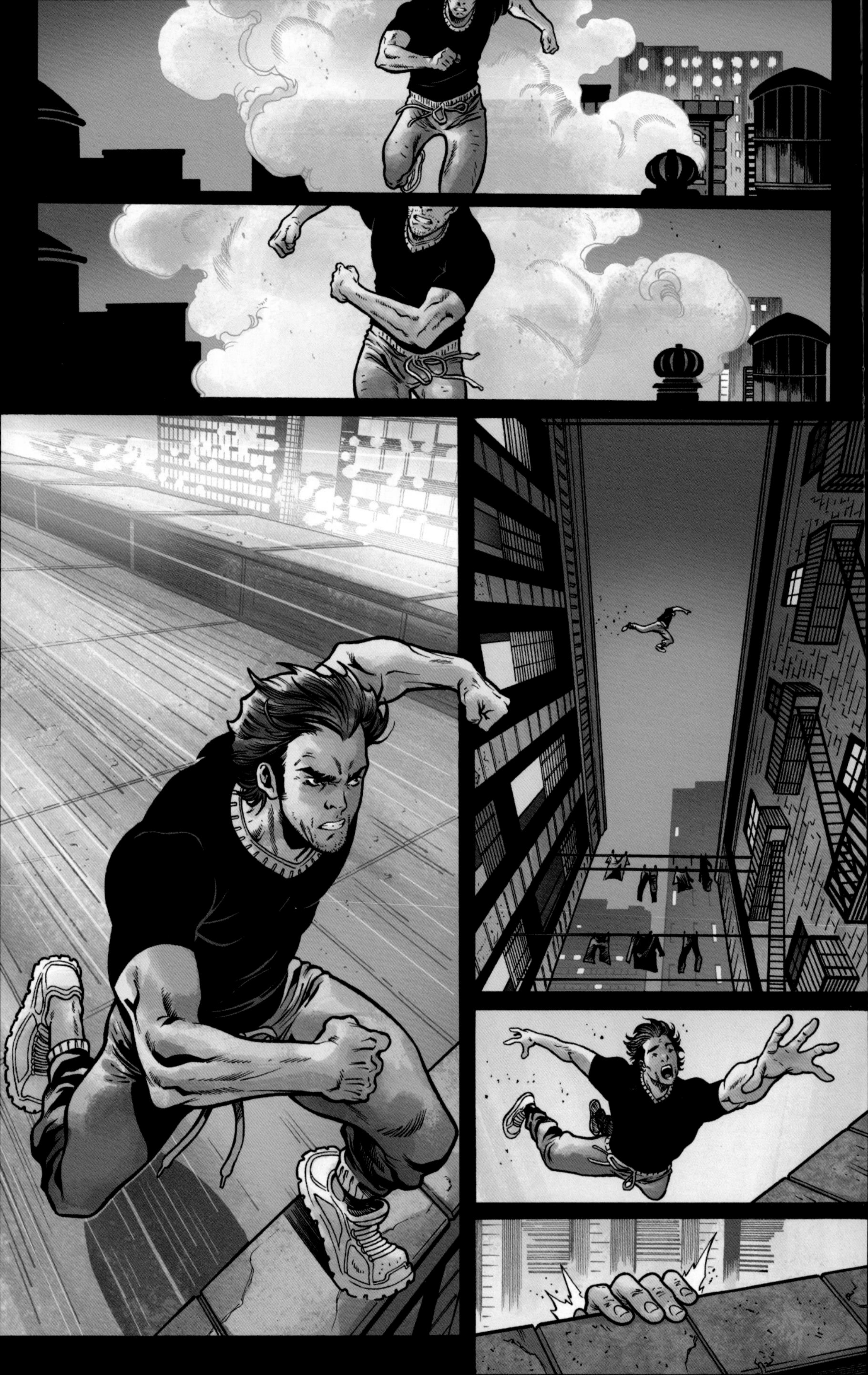

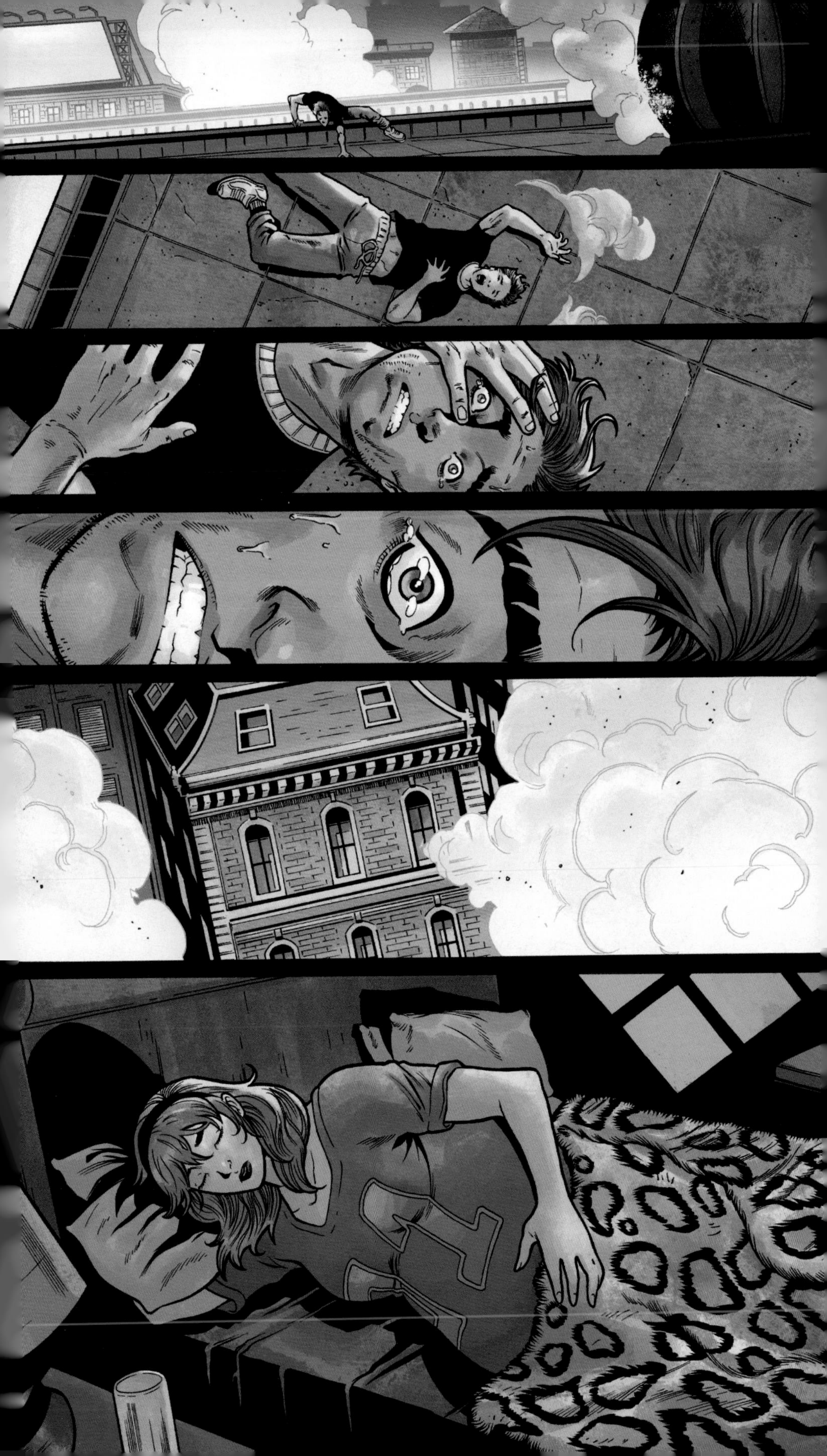

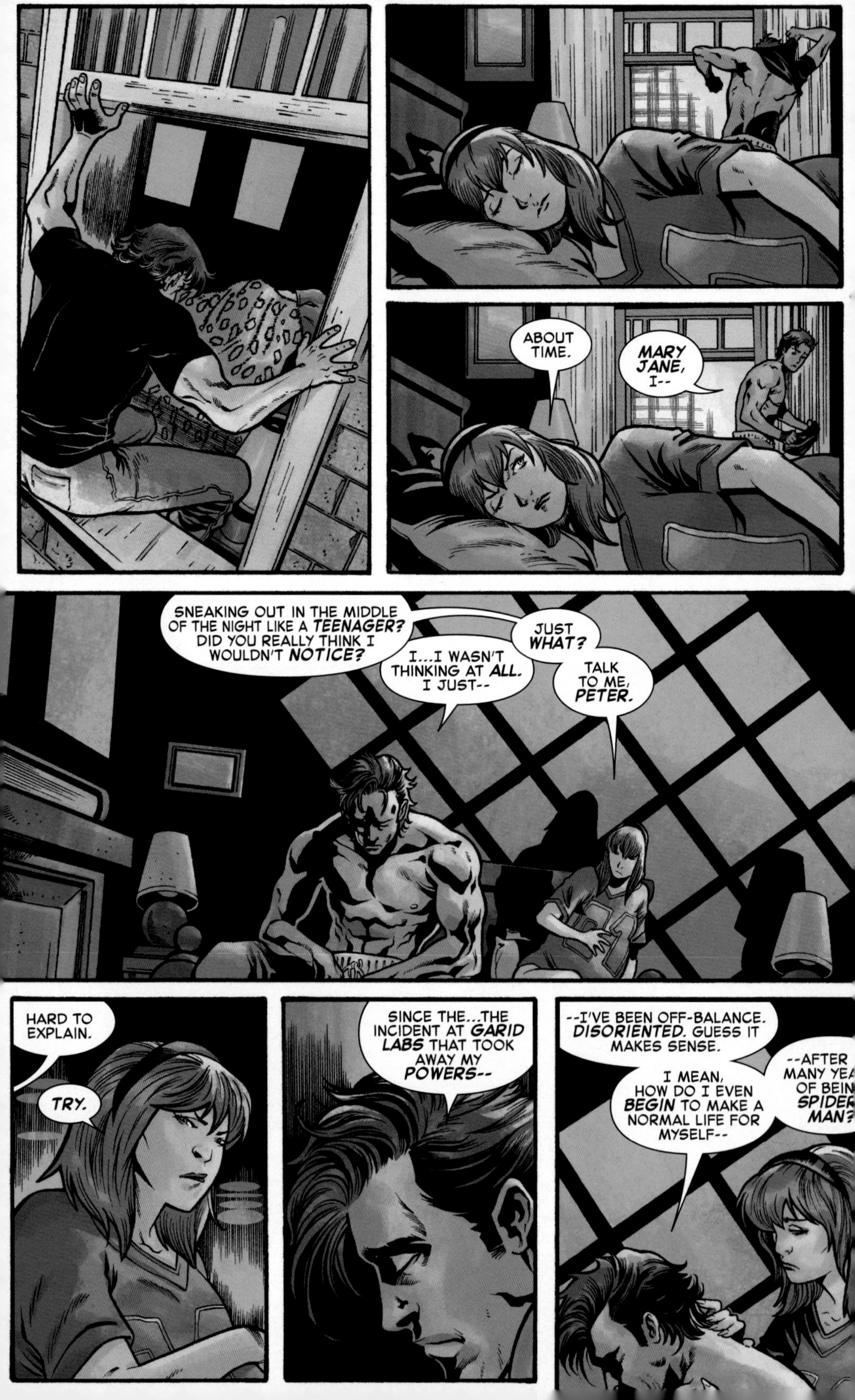

ABOUT TIME.
MARY JANE, I--
SNEAKING OUT IN THE MIDDLE OF THE NIGHT LIKE A TEENAGER? DID YOU REALLY THINK I WOULDN'T NOTICE?
I...I WASN'T THINKING AT ALL. I JUST--
JUST WHAT?
TALK TO ME, PETER.
HARD TO EXPLAIN.
TRY.
SINCE THE...THE INCIDENT AT GARID LABS THAT TOOK AWAY MY POWERS--
--I'VE BEEN OFF-BALANCE. DISORIENTED. GUESS IT MAKES SENSE.
I MEAN, HOW DO I EVEN BEGIN TO MAKE A NORMAL LIFE FOR MYSELF--
--AFTER MANY YEA OF BEIN SPIDER MAN?

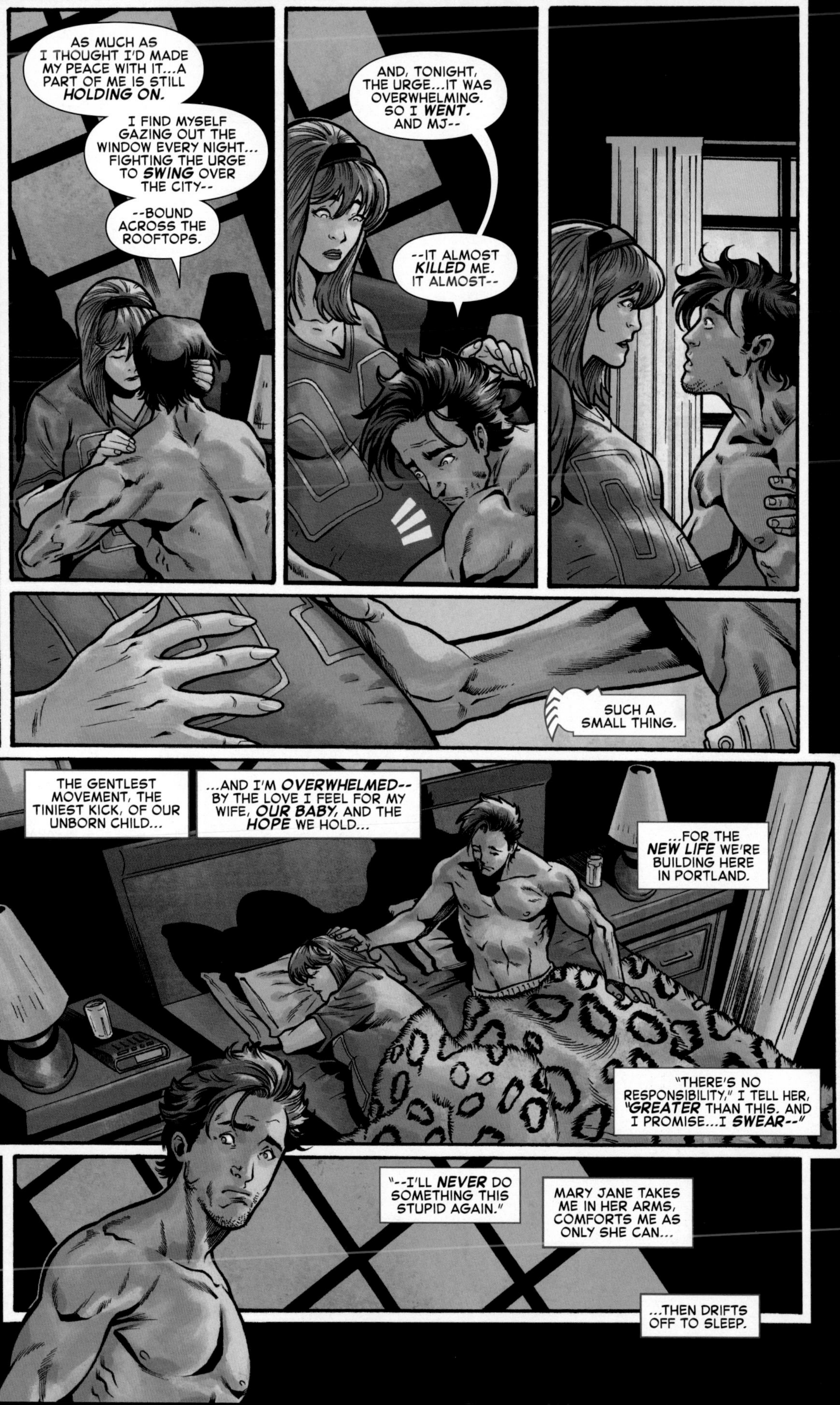

AS MUCH AS I THOUGHT I'D MADE MY PEACE WITH IT...A PART OF ME IS STILL HOLDING ON.
I FIND MYSELF GAZING OUT THE WINDOW EVERY NIGHT... FIGHTING THE URGE TO SWING OVER THE CITY--
--BOUND ACROSS THE ROOFTOPS.
AND, TONIGHT, THE URGE...IT WAS OVERWHELMING. SO I WENT. AND MJ--
--IT ALMOST KILLED ME. IT ALMOST--
SUCH A SMALL THING.
THE GENTLEST MOVEMENT, THE TINIEST KICK, OF OUR UNBORN CHILD...
...AND I'M OVERWHELMED-- BY THE LOVE I FEEL FOR MY WIFE, OUR BABY, AND THE HOPE WE HOLD...
...FOR THE NEW LIFE WE'RE BUILDING HERE IN PORTLAND.
"THERE'S NO RESPONSIBILITY," I TELL HER, "GREATER THAN THIS. AND I PROMISE...I SWEAR--"
"--I'LL NEVER DO SOMETHING THIS STUPID AGAIN."
MARY JANE TAKES ME IN HER ARMS, COMFORTS ME AS ONLY SHE CAN...
...THEN DRIFTS OFF TO SLEEP.

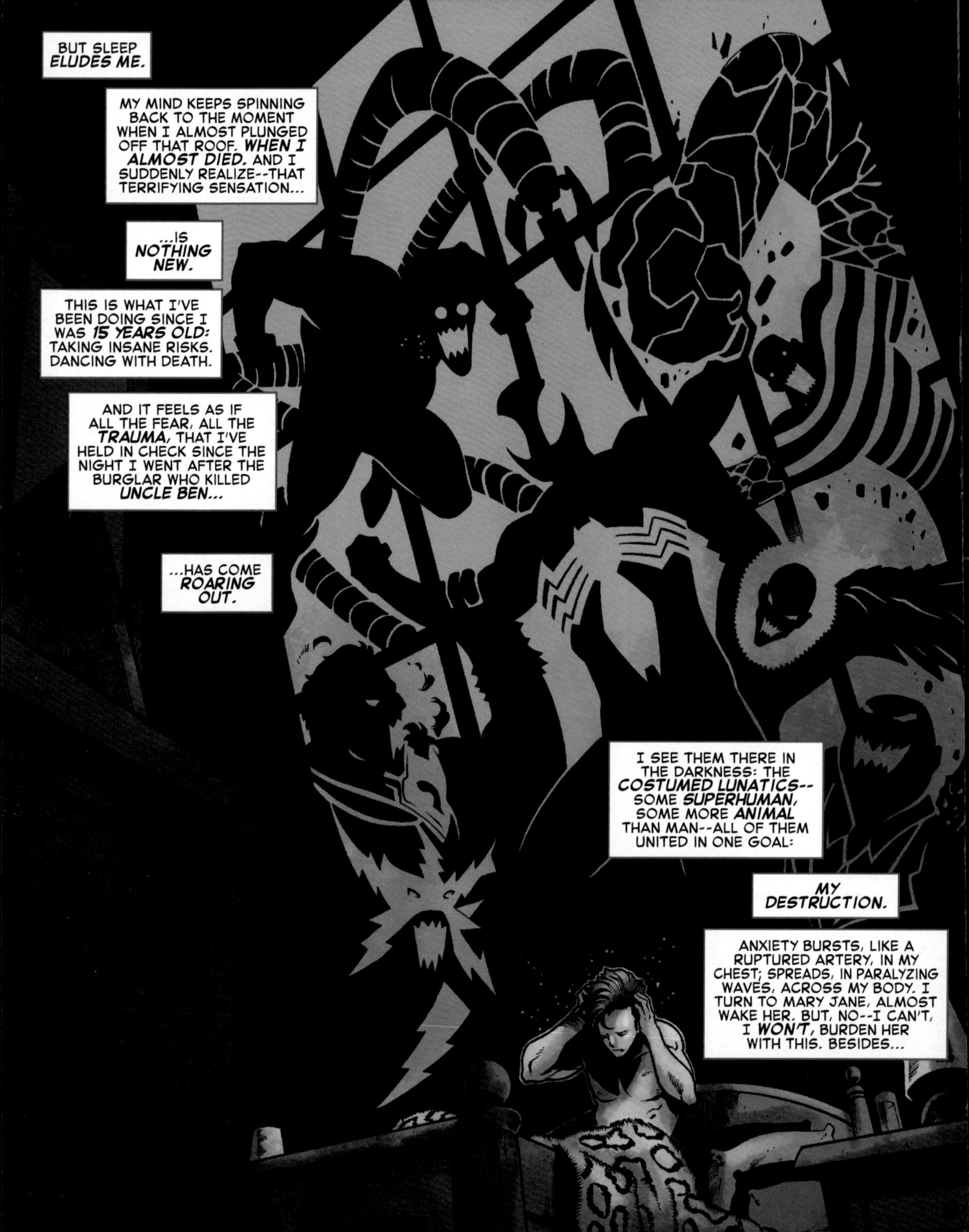

BUT SLEEP ELUDES ME.
MY MIND KEEPS SPINNING BACK TO THE MOMENT WHEN I ALMOST PLUNGED OFF THAT ROOF. WHEN I ALMOST DIED. AND I SUDDENLY REALIZE--THAT TERRIFYING SENSATION...
...IS NOTHING NEW.
THIS IS WHAT I'VE BEEN DOING SINCE I WAS 15 YEARS OLD: TAKING INSANE RISKS. DANCING WITH DEATH.
AND IT FEELS AS IF ALL THE FEAR, ALL THE TRAUMA, THAT I'VE HELD IN CHECK SINCE THE NIGHT I WENT AFTER THE BURGLAR WHO KILLED UNCLE BEN...
...HAS COME ROARING OUT.
I SEE THEM THERE IN THE DARKNESS: THE COSTUMED LUNATICS--SOME SUPERHUMAN, SOME MORE ANIMAL THAN MAN--ALL OF THEM UNITED IN ONE GOAL:
MY DESTRUCTION.
ANXIETY BURSTS, LIKE A RUPTURED ARTERY, IN MY CHEST; SPREADS, IN PARALYZING WAVES, ACROSS MY BODY. I TURN TO MARY JANE, ALMOST WAKE HER. BUT, NO--I CAN'T, I WON'T, BURDEN HER WITH THIS. BESIDES...

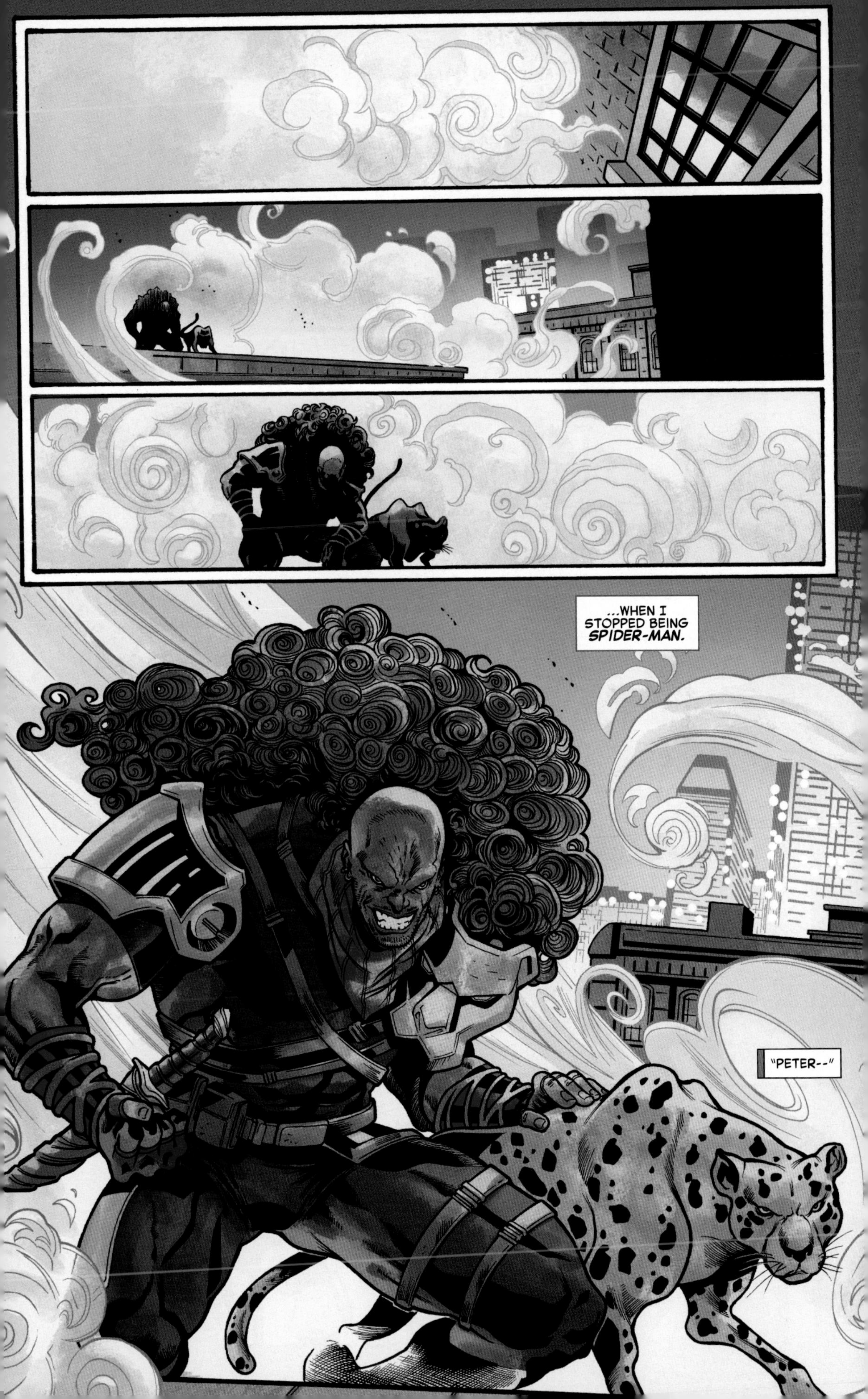
...WHEN I STOPPED BEING SPIDER-MAN.
"PETER--"

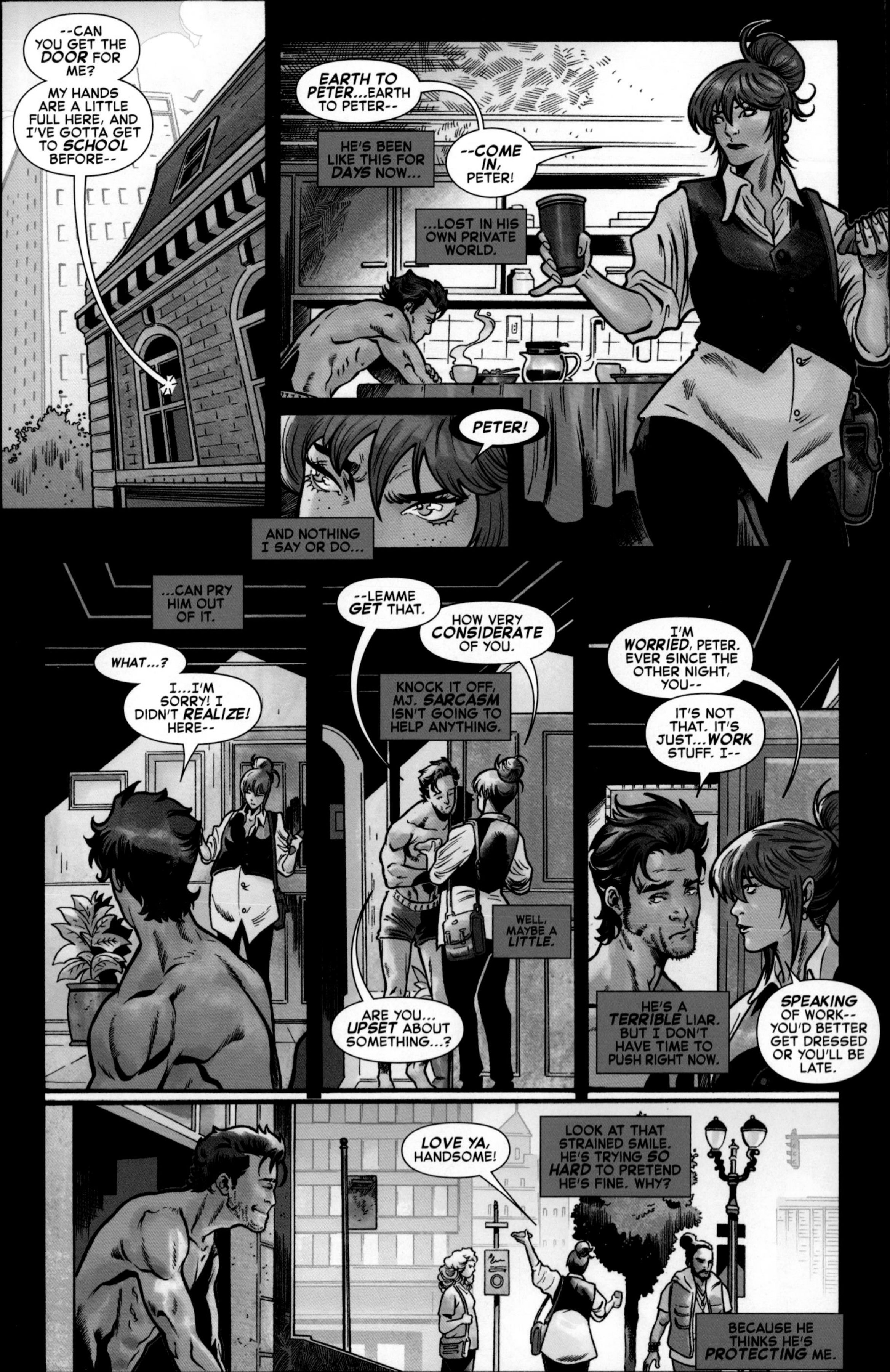

--CAN YOU GET THE DOOR FOR ME?
MY HANDS ARE A LITTLE FULL HERE, AND I'VE GOTTA GET TO SCHOOL BEFORE--
EARTH TO PETER...EARTH TO PETER--
HE'S BEEN LIKE THIS FOR DAYS NOW...
--COME IN, PETER!
...LOST IN HIS OWN PRIVATE WORLD.
PETER!
AND NOTHING I SAY OR DO...
...CAN PRY HIM OUT OF IT.
WHAT...?
I...I'M SORRY! I DIDN'T REALIZE! HERE--
--LEMME GET THAT.
HOW VERY CONSIDERATE OF YOU.
KNOCK IT OFF, MJ. SARCASM ISN'T GOING TO HELP ANYTHING.
WELL, MAYBE A LITTLE.
ARE YOU... UPSET ABOUT SOMETHING...?
I'M WORRIED, PETER. EVER SINCE THE OTHER NIGHT, YOU--
IT'S NOT THAT. IT'S JUST...WORK STUFF. I--
HE'S A TERRIBLE LIAR. BUT I DON'T HAVE TIME TO PUSH RIGHT NOW.
SPEAKING OF WORK-- YOU'D BETTER GET DRESSED OR YOU'LL BE LATE.
LOVE YA, HANDSOME!
LOOK AT THAT STRAINED SMILE. HE'S TRYING SO HARD TO PRETEND HE'S FINE. WHY?
BECAUSE HE THINKS HE'S PROTECTING ME.

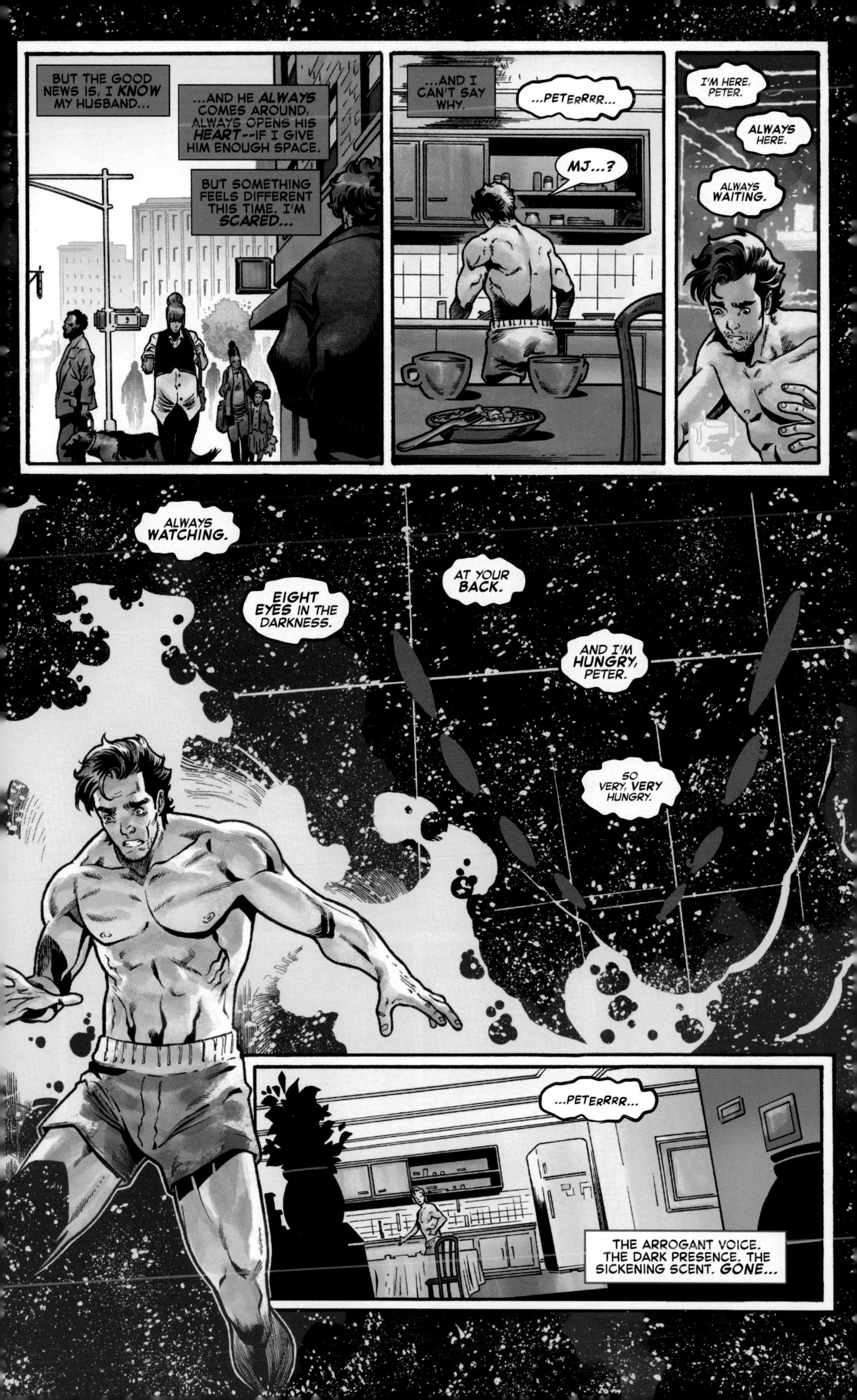
BUT THE GOOD NEWS IS, I KNOW MY HUSBAND...
...AND HE ALWAYS COMES AROUND, ALWAYS OPENS HIS HEART--IF I GIVE HIM ENOUGH SPACE.
BUT SOMETHING FEELS DIFFERENT THIS TIME. I'M SCARED...
...AND I CAN'T SAY WHY.
...PETERRRR...
MJ...?
I'M HERE, PETER.
ALWAYS HERE.
ALWAYS WAITING.
ALWAYS WATCHING.
EIGHT EYES IN THE DARKNESS.
AT YOUR BACK.
AND I'M HUNGRY, PETER.
SO VERY, VERY HUNGRY.
...PETERRRR...
THE ARROGANT VOICE. THE DARK PRESENCE. THE SICKENING SCENT. GONE...

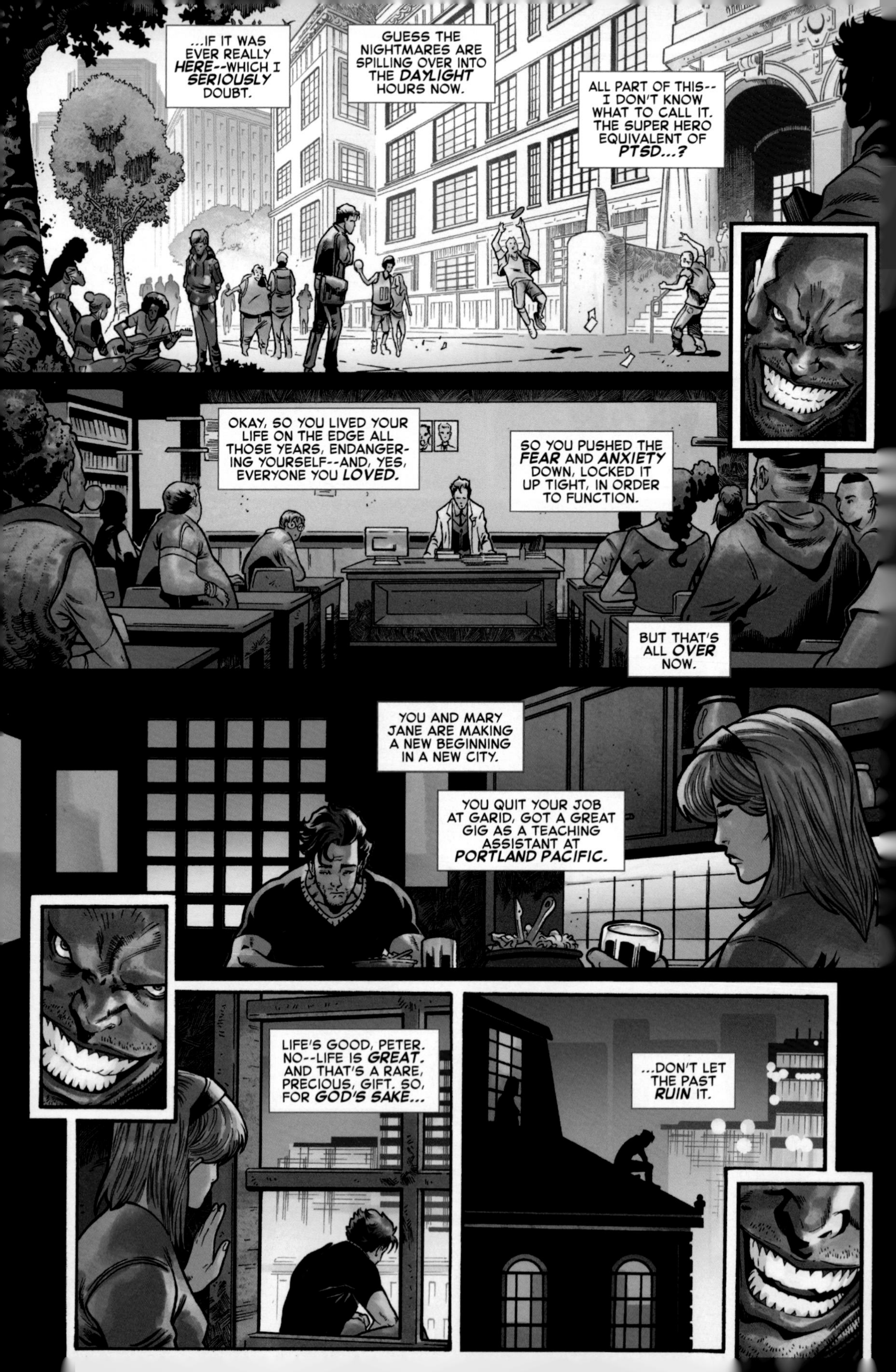
...IF IT WAS EVER REALLY HERE--WHICH I SERIOUSLY DOUBT.
GUESS THE NIGHTMARES ARE SPILLING OVER INTO THE DAYLIGHT HOURS NOW.
ALL PART OF THIS-- I DON'T KNOW WHAT TO CALL IT. THE SUPER HERO EQUIVALENT OF PTSD...?
OKAY, SO YOU LIVED YOUR LIFE ON THE EDGE ALL THOSE YEARS, ENDANGERING YOURSELF--AND, YES, EVERYONE YOU LOVED.
SO YOU PUSHED THE FEAR AND ANXIETY DOWN, LOCKED IT UP TIGHT, IN ORDER TO FUNCTION.
BUT THAT'S ALL OVER NOW.
YOU AND MARY JANE ARE MAKING A NEW BEGINNING IN A NEW CITY.
YOU QUIT YOUR JOB AT GARID, GOT A GREAT GIG AS A TEACHING ASSISTANT AT PORTLAND PACIFIC.
LIFE'S GOOD, PETER. NO--LIFE IS GREAT. AND THAT'S A RARE, PRECIOUS, GIFT. SO, FOR GOD'S SAKE...
...DON'T LET THE PAST RUIN IT.

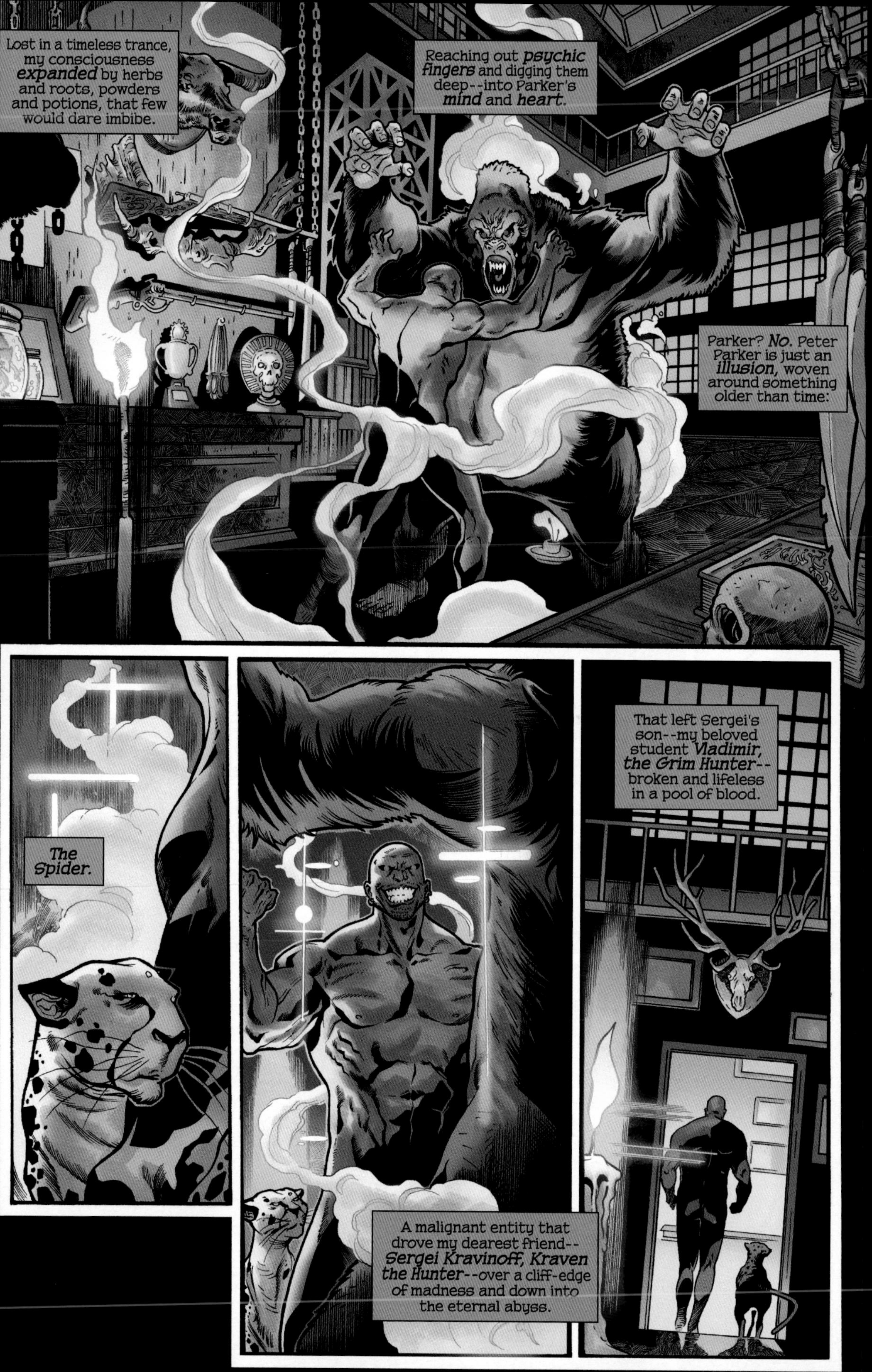

Lost in a timeless trance, my consciousness expanded by herbs and roots, powders and potions, that few would dare imbibe.
Reaching out psychic fingers and digging them deep--into Parker's mind and heart.
Parker? No. Peter Parker is just an illusion, woven around something older than time:
The Spider.
A malignant entity that drove my dearest friend--Sergei Kravinoff, Kraven the Hunter--over a cliff-edge of madness and down into the eternal abyss.
That left Sergei's son--my beloved student Vladimir, the Grim Hunter--broken and lifeless in a pool of blood.

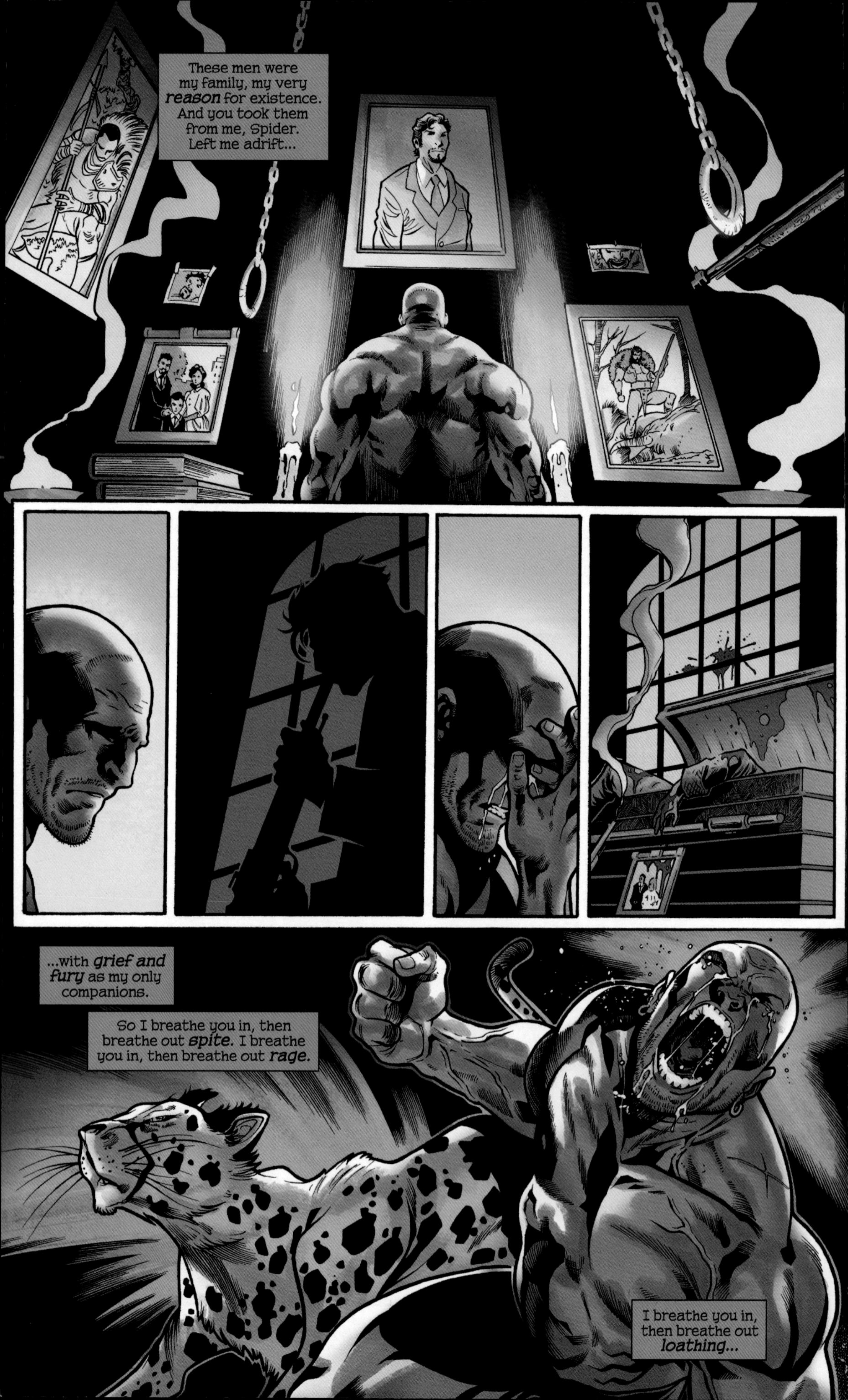
These men were my family, my very *reason* for existence. And you took them from me, Spider. Left me adrift...
...with *grief and fury* as my only companions.
So I breathe you in, then breathe out *spite*. I breathe you in, then breathe out *rage*.
I breathe you in, then breathe out *loathing*...

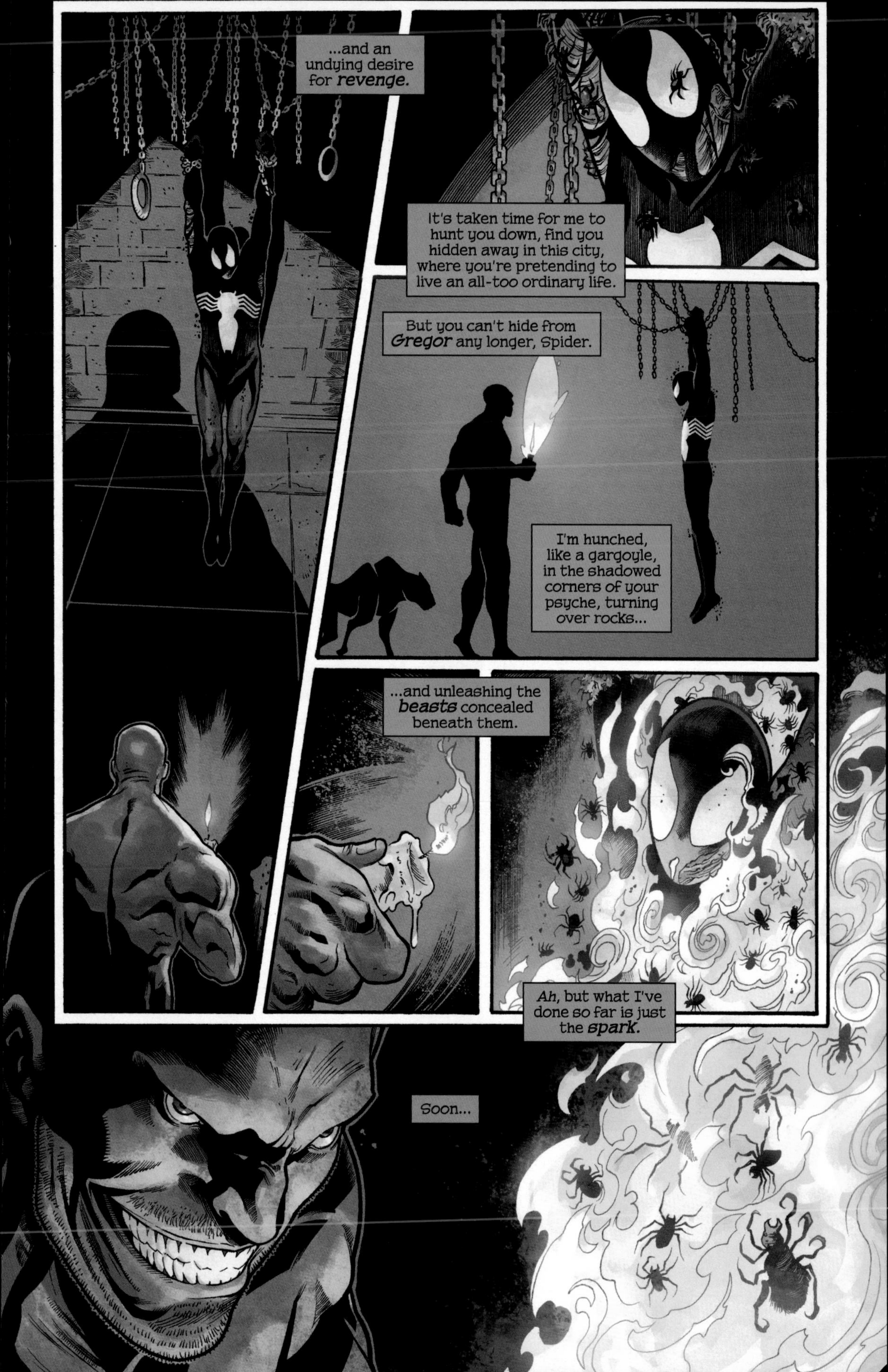

...and an undying desire for *revenge.*
It's taken time for me to hunt you down, find you hidden away in this city, where you're pretending to live an all-too ordinary life.
But you can't hide from *Gregor* any longer, Spider.
I'm hunched, like a gargoyle, in the shadowed corners of your psyche, turning over rocks...
...and unleashing the *beasts* concealed beneath them.
Ah, but what I've done so far is just the *spark.*
Soon...

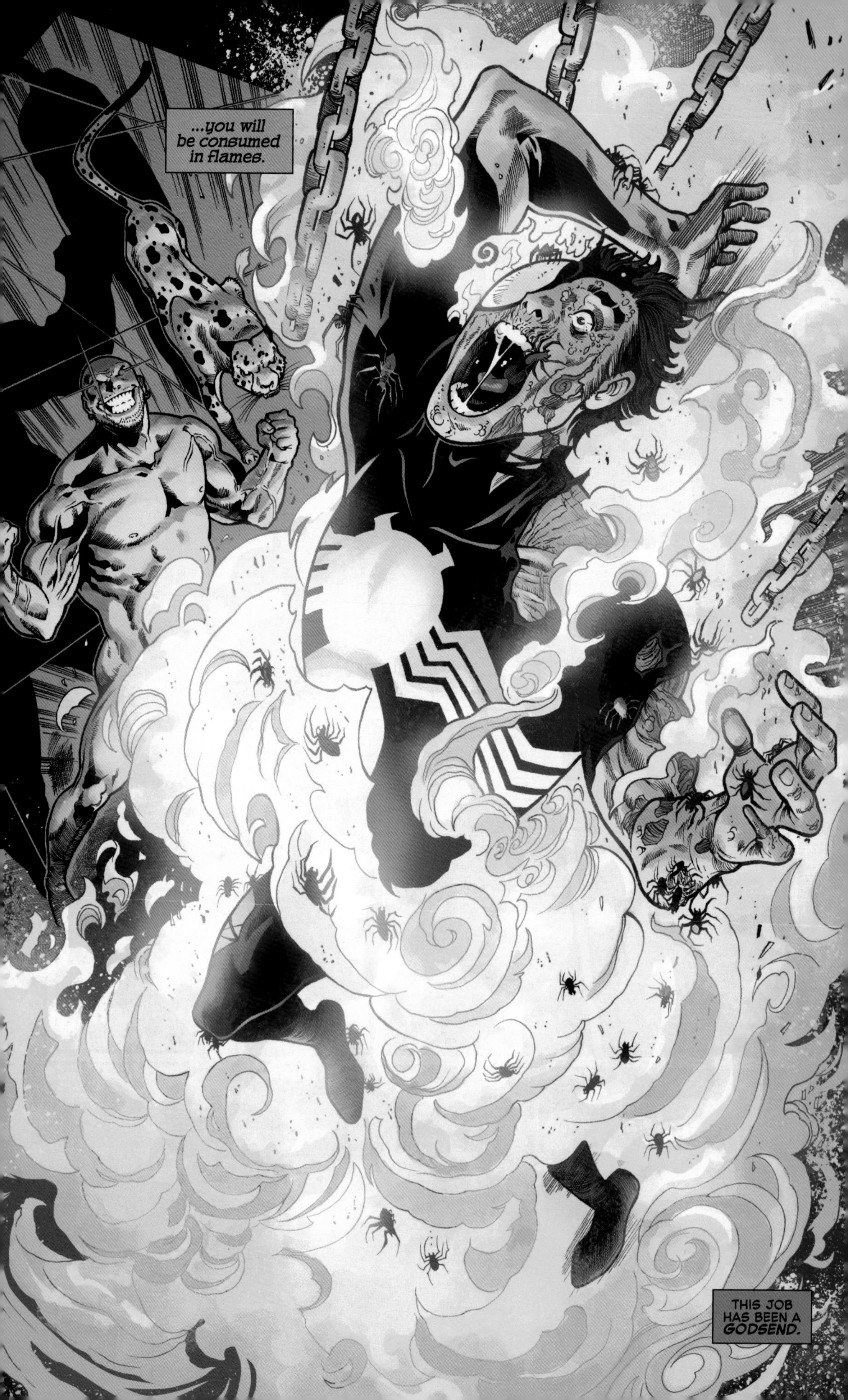
...you will be consumed in flames.
THIS JOB HAS BEEN A GODSEND.

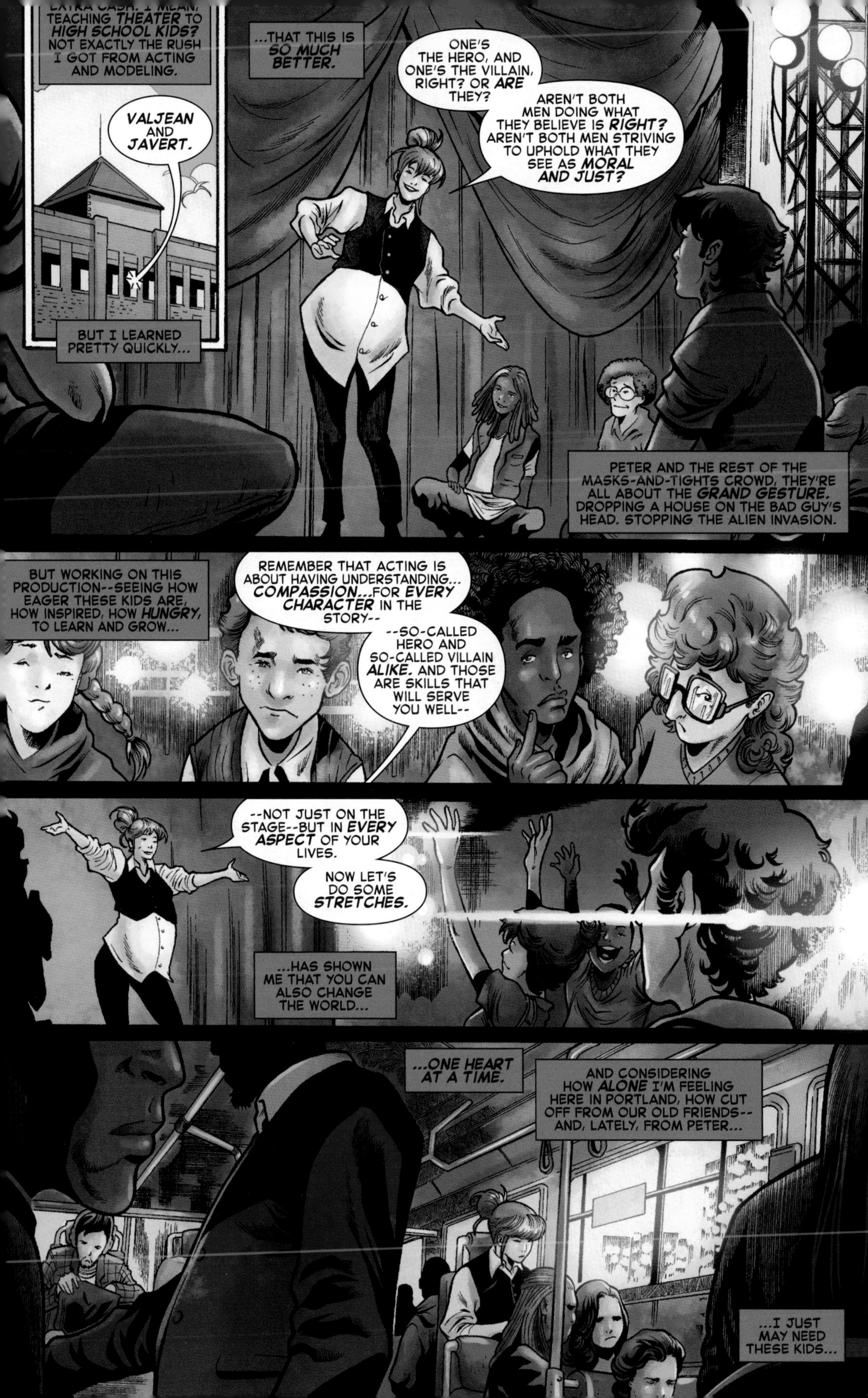

TEACHING THEATER TO HIGH SCHOOL KIDS? NOT EXACTLY THE RUSH I GOT FROM ACTING AND MODELING.
VALJEAN AND JAVERT.
BUT I LEARNED PRETTY QUICKLY...
...THAT THIS IS SO MUCH BETTER.
ONE'S THE HERO, AND ONE'S THE VILLAIN, RIGHT? OR ARE THEY?
AREN'T BOTH MEN DOING WHAT THEY BELIEVE IS RIGHT? AREN'T BOTH MEN STRIVING TO UPHOLD WHAT THEY SEE AS MORAL AND JUST?
PETER AND THE REST OF THE MASKS-AND-TIGHTS CROWD, THEY'RE ALL ABOUT THE GRAND GESTURE. DROPPING A HOUSE ON THE BAD GUY'S HEAD. STOPPING THE ALIEN INVASION.
BUT WORKING ON THIS PRODUCTION--SEEING HOW EAGER THESE KIDS ARE, HOW INSPIRED, HOW HUNGRY, TO LEARN AND GROW...
REMEMBER THAT ACTING IS ABOUT HAVING UNDERSTANDING... COMPASSION...FOR EVERY CHARACTER IN THE STORY--
--SO-CALLED HERO AND SO-CALLED VILLAIN ALIKE. AND THOSE ARE SKILLS THAT WILL SERVE YOU WELL--
--NOT JUST ON THE STAGE--BUT IN EVERY ASPECT OF YOUR LIVES.
NOW LET'S DO SOME STRETCHES.
...HAS SHOWN ME THAT YOU CAN ALSO CHANGE THE WORLD...
...ONE HEART AT A TIME.
AND CONSIDERING HOW ALONE I'M FEELING HERE IN PORTLAND, HOW CUT OFF FROM OUR OLD FRIENDS--AND, LATELY, FROM PETER...
...I JUST MAY NEED THESE KIDS...

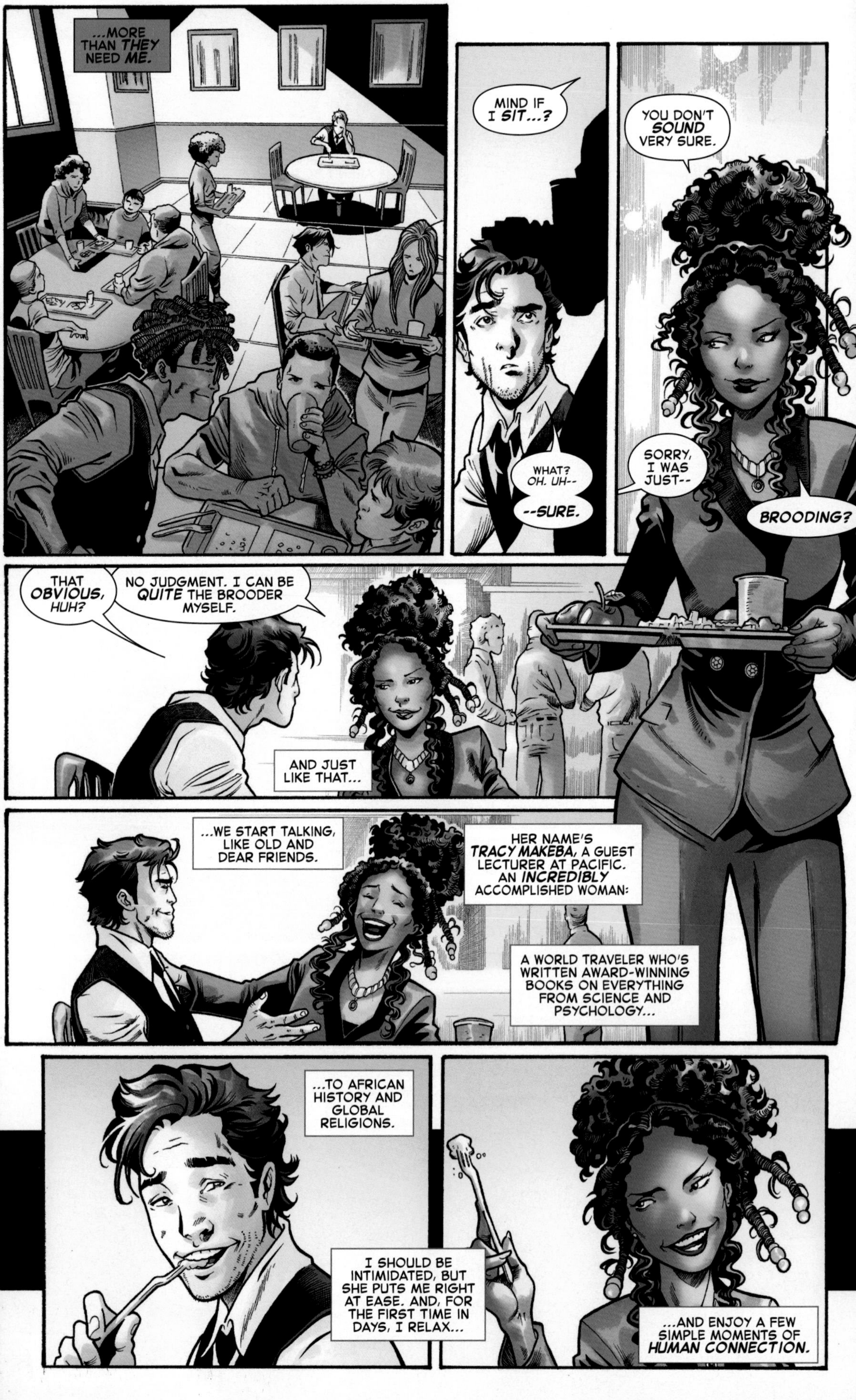
...MORE THAN THEY NEED ME.
MIND IF I SIT...?
WHAT? OH. UH--
--SURE.
YOU DON'T SOUND VERY SURE.
SORRY, I WAS JUST--
BROODING?
THAT OBVIOUS, HUH?
NO JUDGMENT. I CAN BE QUITE THE BROODER MYSELF.
AND JUST LIKE THAT...
...WE START TALKING, LIKE OLD AND DEAR FRIENDS.
HER NAME'S TRACY MAKEBA, A GUEST LECTURER AT PACIFIC. AN INCREDIBLY ACCOMPLISHED WOMAN:
A WORLD TRAVELER WHO'S WRITTEN AWARD-WINNING BOOKS ON EVERYTHING FROM SCIENCE AND PSYCHOLOGY...
...TO AFRICAN HISTORY AND GLOBAL RELIGIONS.
I SHOULD BE INTIMIDATED, BUT SHE PUTS ME RIGHT AT EASE. AND, FOR THE FIRST TIME IN DAYS, I RELAX...
...AND ENJOY A FEW SIMPLE MOMENTS OF HUMAN CONNECTION.

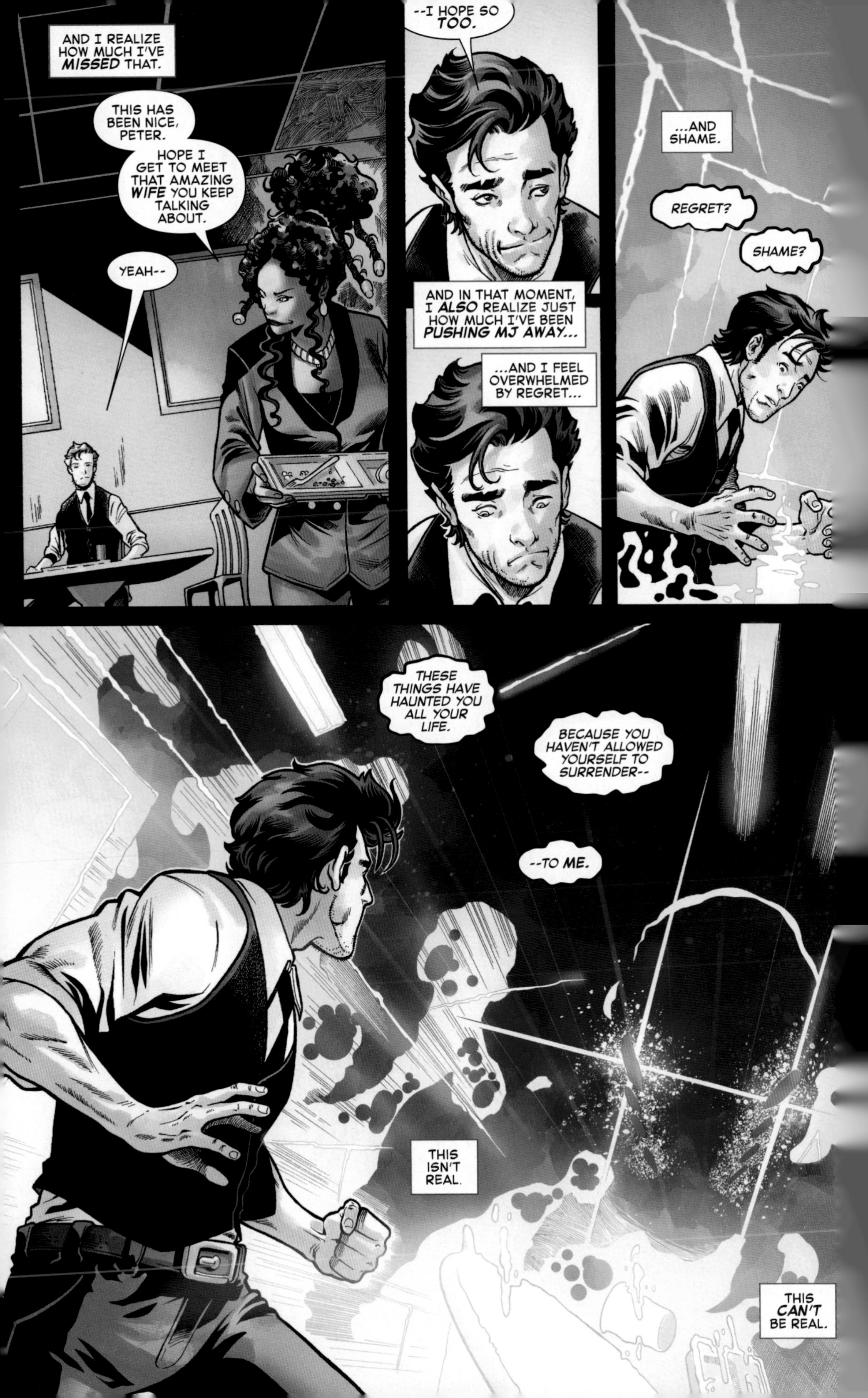
AND I REALIZE HOW MUCH I'VE MISSED THAT.
THIS HAS BEEN NICE, PETER.
HOPE I GET TO MEET THAT AMAZING WIFE YOU KEEP TALKING ABOUT.
YEAH--
--I HOPE SO TOO.
AND IN THAT MOMENT, I ALSO REALIZE JUST HOW MUCH I'VE BEEN PUSHING MJ AWAY...
...AND I FEEL OVERWHELMED BY REGRET...
...AND SHAME.
REGRET?
SHAME?
THESE THINGS HAVE HAUNTED YOU ALL YOUR LIFE.
BECAUSE YOU HAVEN'T ALLOWED YOURSELF TO SURRENDER--
--TO ME.
THIS ISN'T REAL.
THIS CAN'T BE REAL.

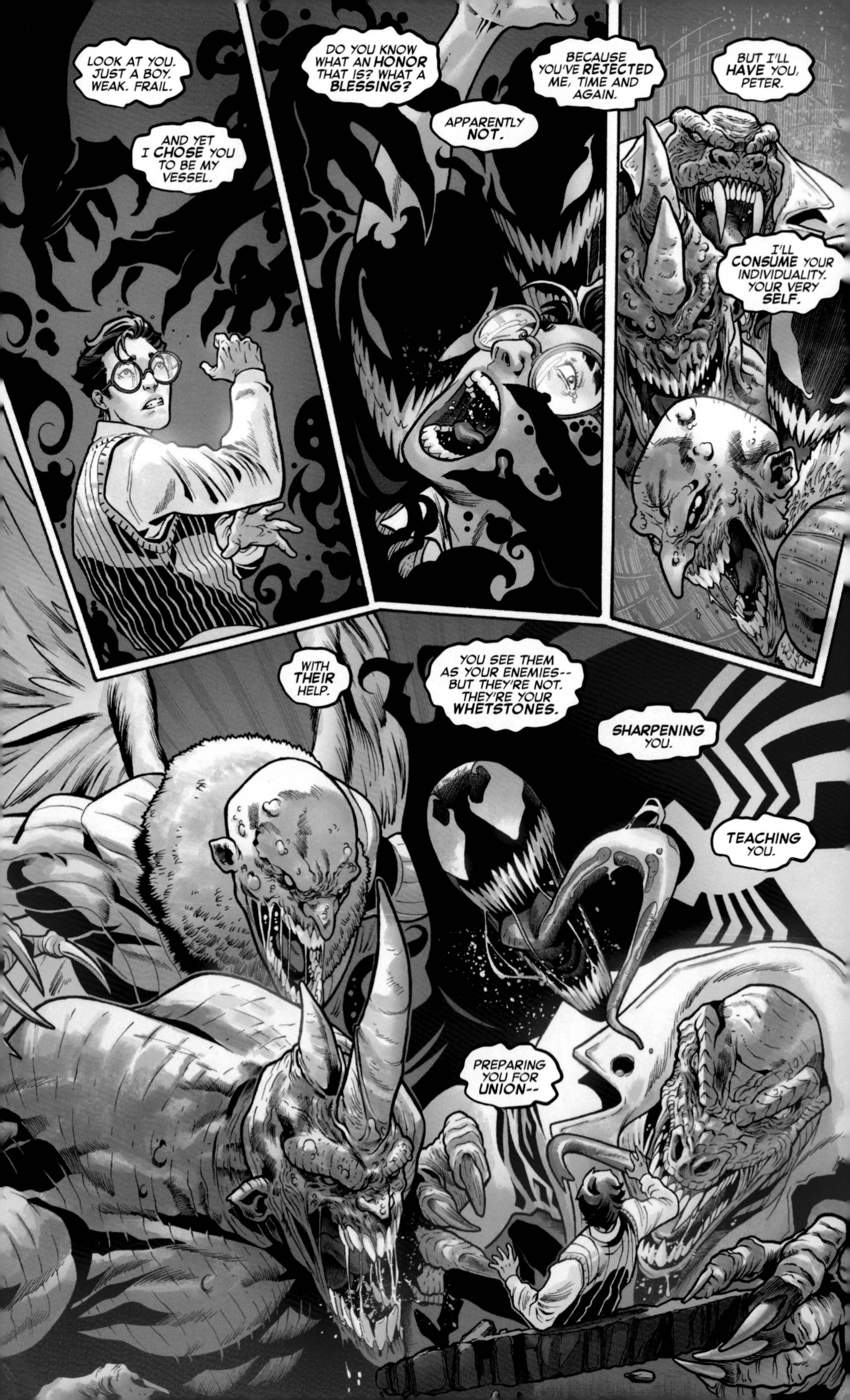

LOOK AT YOU. JUST A BOY. WEAK. FRAIL.
AND YET I CHOSE YOU TO BE MY VESSEL.
DO YOU KNOW WHAT AN HONOR THAT IS? WHAT A BLESSING?
APPARENTLY NOT.
BECAUSE YOU'VE REJECTED ME, TIME AND AGAIN.
BUT I'LL HAVE YOU, PETER.
I'LL CONSUME YOUR INDIVIDUALITY. YOUR VERY SELF.
WITH THEIR HELP.
YOU SEE THEM AS YOUR ENEMIES-- BUT THEY'RE NOT. THEY'RE YOUR WHETSTONES.
SHARPENING YOU.
TEACHING YOU.
PREPARING YOU FOR UNION--

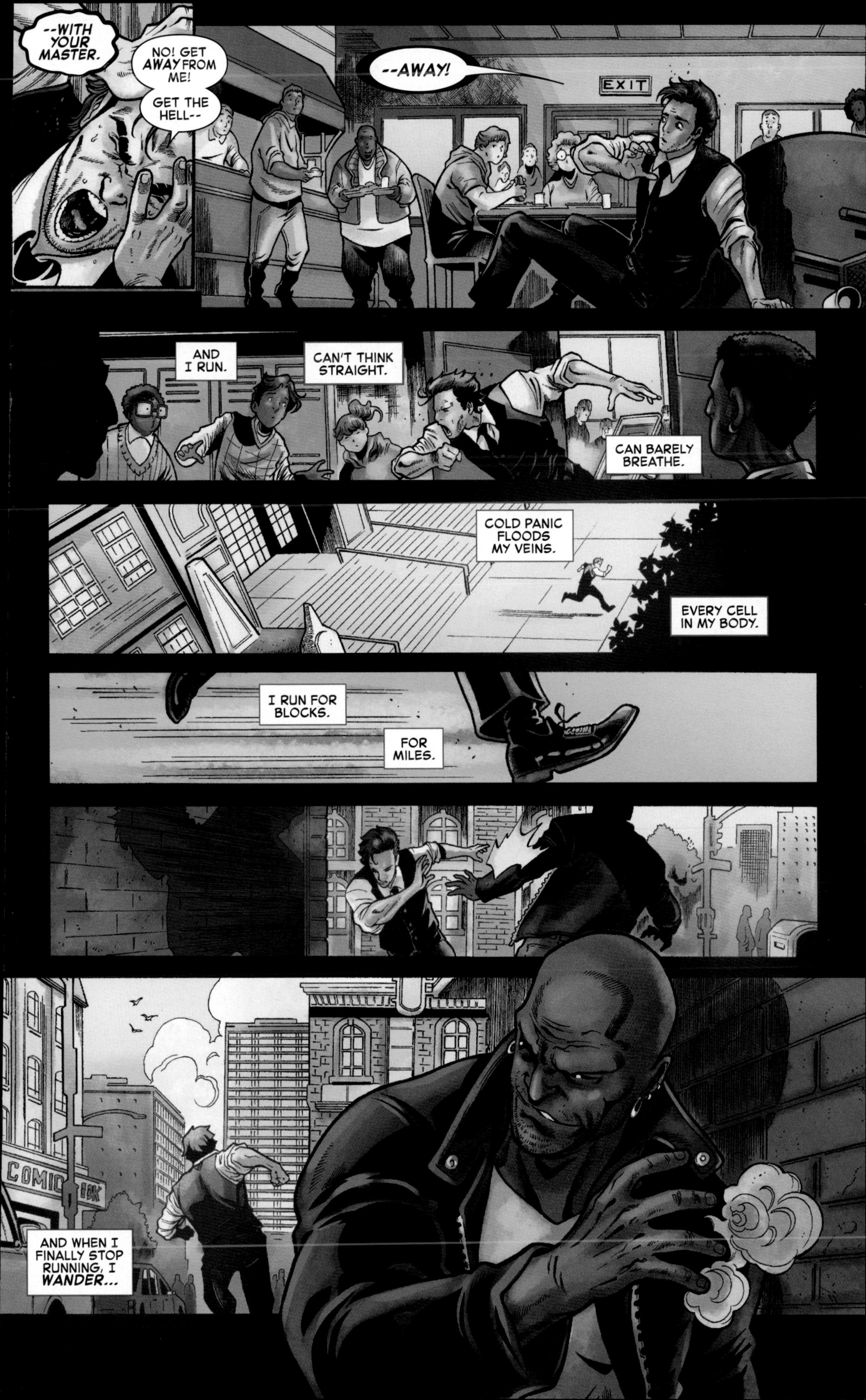
--WITH YOUR MASTER.
NO! GET AWAY FROM ME!
GET THE HELL--
--AWAY!
EXIT
AND I RUN.
CAN'T THINK STRAIGHT.
CAN BARELY BREATHE.
COLD PANIC FLOODS MY VEINS.
EVERY CELL IN MY BODY.
I RUN FOR BLOCKS.
FOR MILES.
COMIC
AND WHEN I FINALLY STOP RUNNING, I WANDER...

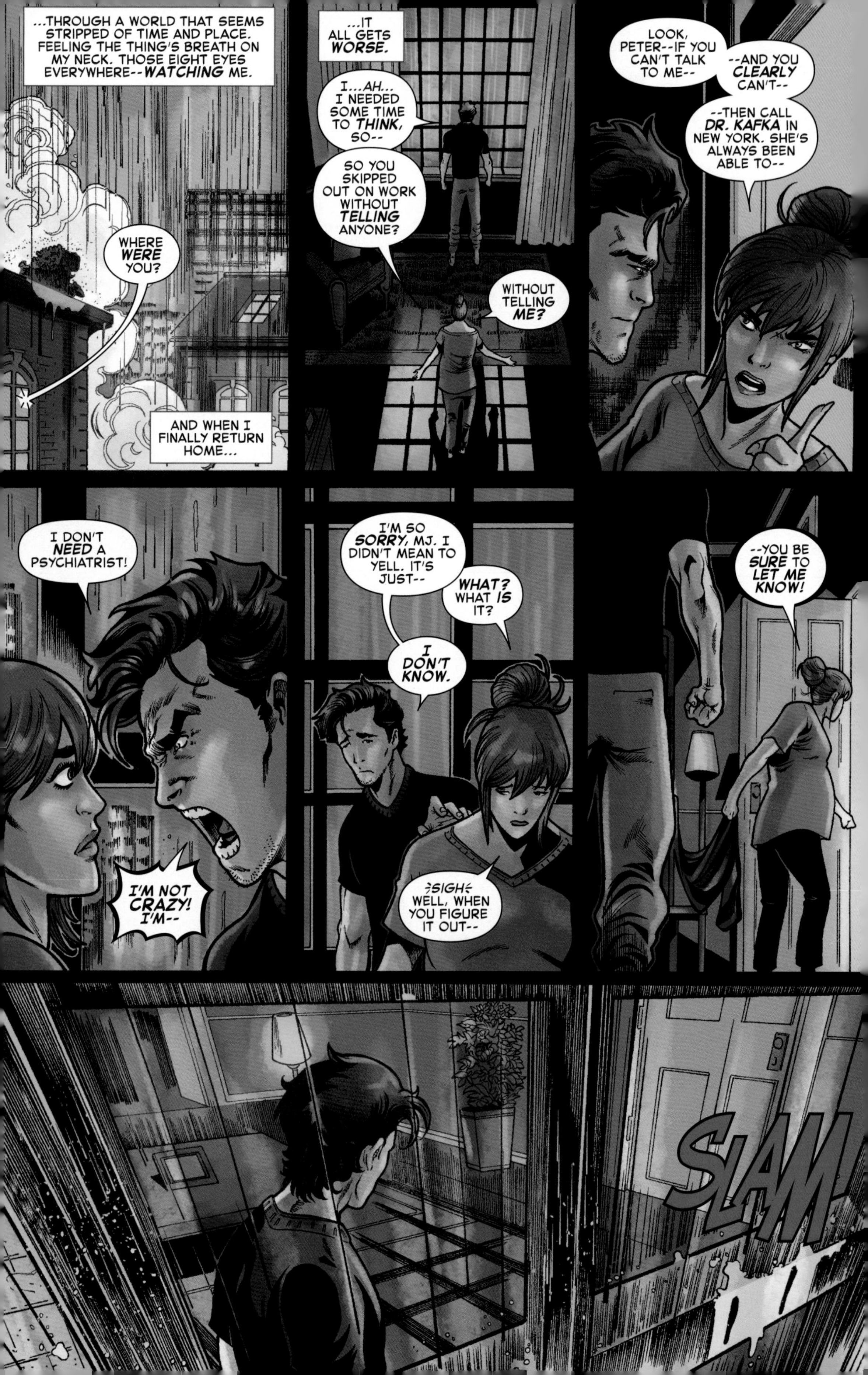
...THROUGH A WORLD THAT SEEMS STRIPPED OF TIME AND PLACE. FEELING THE THING'S BREATH ON MY NECK. THOSE EIGHT EYES EVERYWHERE--WATCHING ME.
WHERE WERE YOU?
AND WHEN I FINALLY RETURN HOME...
...IT ALL GETS WORSE.
I...AH... I NEEDED SOME TIME TO THINK, SO--
SO YOU SKIPPED OUT ON WORK WITHOUT TELLING ANYONE?
WITHOUT TELLING ME?
LOOK, PETER--IF YOU CAN'T TALK TO ME--
--AND YOU CLEARLY CAN'T--
--THEN CALL DR. KAFKA IN NEW YORK. SHE'S ALWAYS BEEN ABLE TO--
I DON'T NEED A PSYCHIATRIST!
I'M NOT CRAZY! I'M--
I'M SO SORRY, MJ. I DIDN'T MEAN TO YELL. IT'S JUST--
WHAT? WHAT IS IT?
I DON'T KNOW.
SIGH WELL, WHEN YOU FIGURE IT OUT--
--YOU BE SURE TO LET ME KNOW!
SLAM

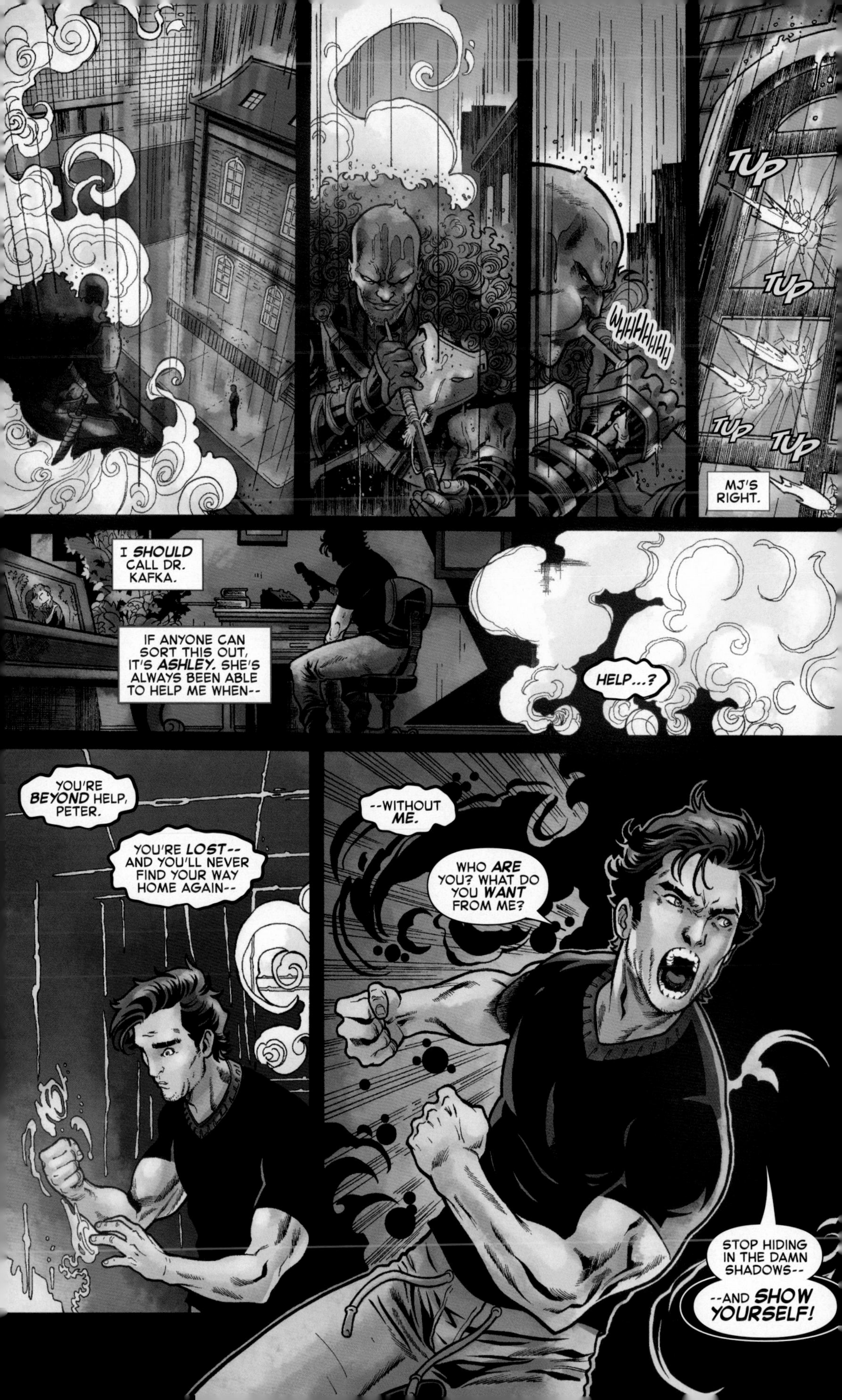
WHHHHHHH
TUP
TUP
TUP
TUP
MJ'S RIGHT.
I SHOULD CALL DR. KAFKA.
IF ANYONE CAN SORT THIS OUT, IT'S ASHLEY. SHE'S ALWAYS BEEN ABLE TO HELP ME WHEN--
HELP...?
YOU'RE BEYOND HELP, PETER.
YOU'RE LOST-- AND YOU'LL NEVER FIND YOUR WAY HOME AGAIN--
--WITHOUT ME.
WHO ARE YOU? WHAT DO YOU WANT FROM ME?
STOP HIDING IN THE DAMN SHADOWS--
--AND SHOW YOURSELF!

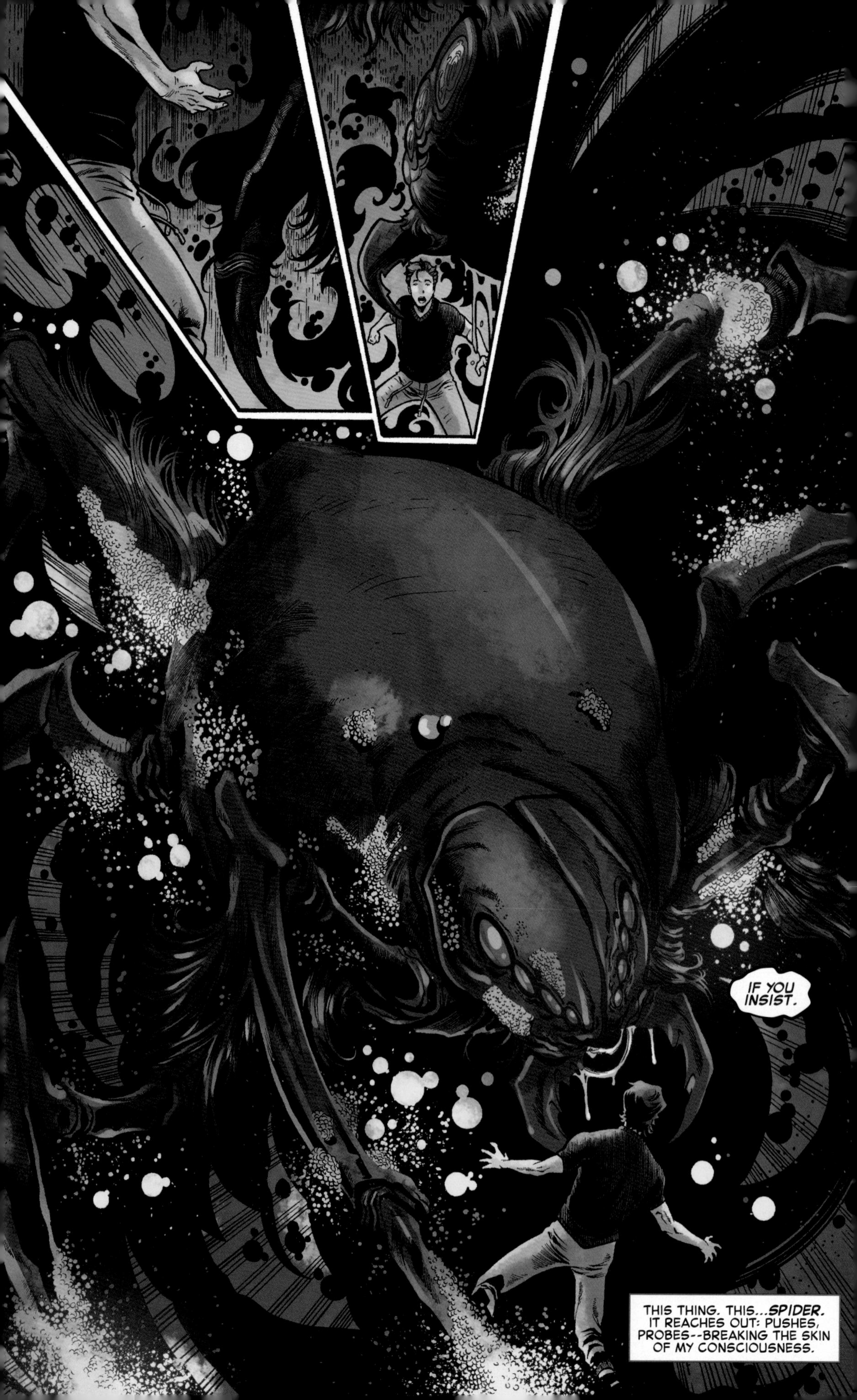
IF YOU INSIST.
THIS THING. THIS...SPIDER. IT REACHES OUT: PUSHES, PROBES--BREAKING THE SKIN OF MY CONSCIOUSNESS.

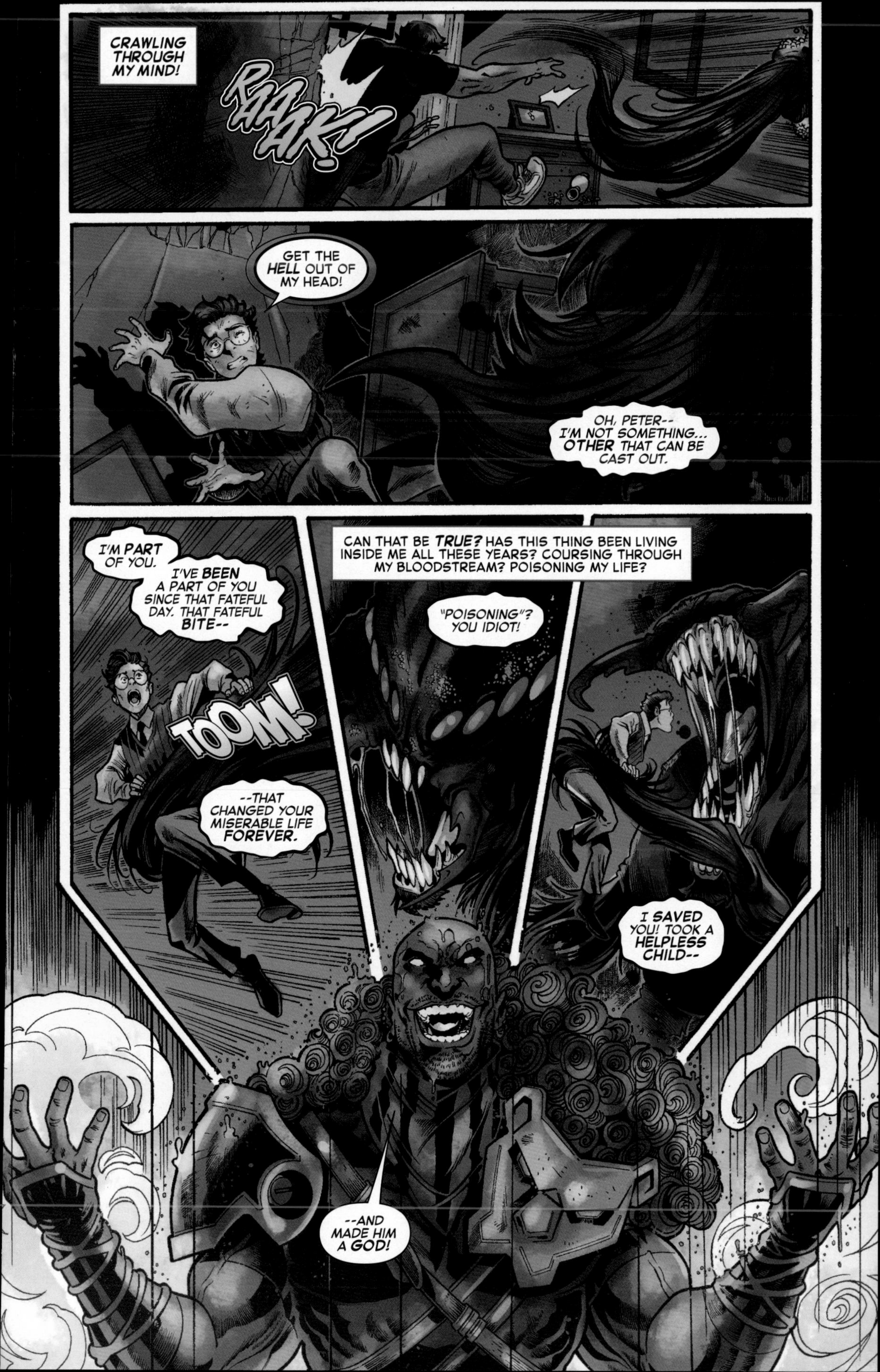
CRAWLING THROUGH MY MIND!
RAAAK!!
GET THE HELL OUT OF MY HEAD!
OH, PETER-- I'M NOT SOMETHING... OTHER THAT CAN BE CAST OUT.
I'M PART OF YOU.
I'VE BEEN A PART OF YOU SINCE THAT FATEFUL DAY. THAT FATEFUL BITE--
TOOM!
--THAT CHANGED YOUR MISERABLE LIFE FOREVER.
CAN THAT BE TRUE? HAS THIS THING BEEN LIVING INSIDE ME ALL THESE YEARS? COURSING THROUGH MY BLOODSTREAM? POISONING MY LIFE?
"POISONING"? YOU IDIOT!
I SAVED YOU! TOOK A HELPLESS CHILD--
--AND MADE HIM A GOD!

RELEASE YOUR ATTACHMENTS TO THE PERSON YOU *THINK* YOU ARE.

TO THE FLESHLINGS YOU SO DESPERATELY CLING TO.

THEY'RE NOTHING BUT OBSTACLES ON YOUR PATH TO GREATNESS. *OUR* PATH.

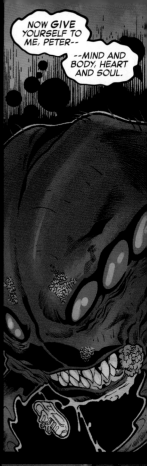

NOW *GIVE* YOURSELF TO ME, PETER--

--MIND AND BODY, HEART AND SOUL.

AND ONCE I'VE *DEVOURED* YOU, DIGESTED YOU, WE'LL--

--WE'LL--

WHAT ARE YOU DOING?

WHAT

ARE

YOU

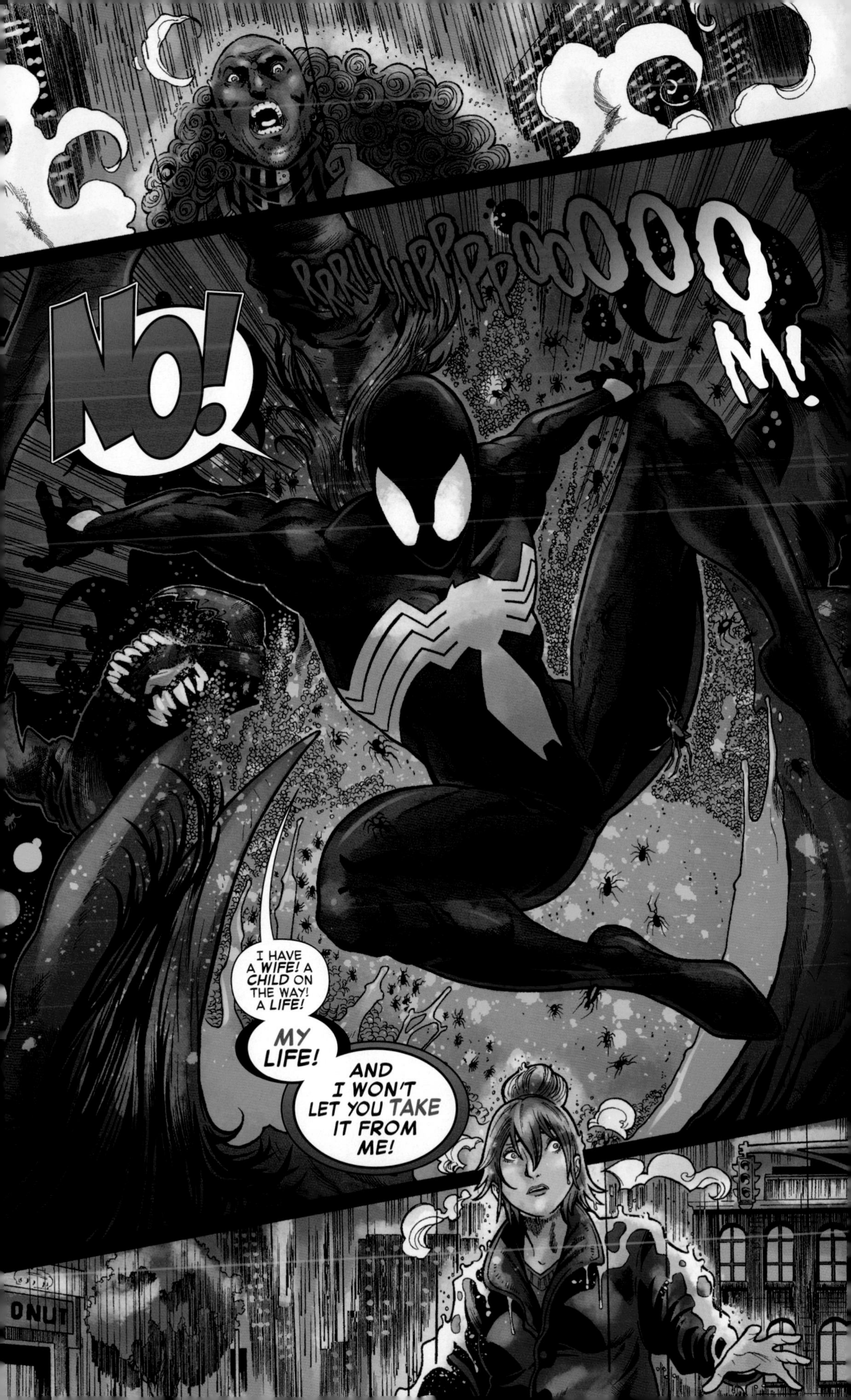
NO!
KRRLLLIPPPPOOOOOM!
I HAVE A WIFE! A CHILD ON THE WAY! A LIFE!
MY LIFE!
AND I WON'T LET YOU TAKE IT FROM ME!
DONUT

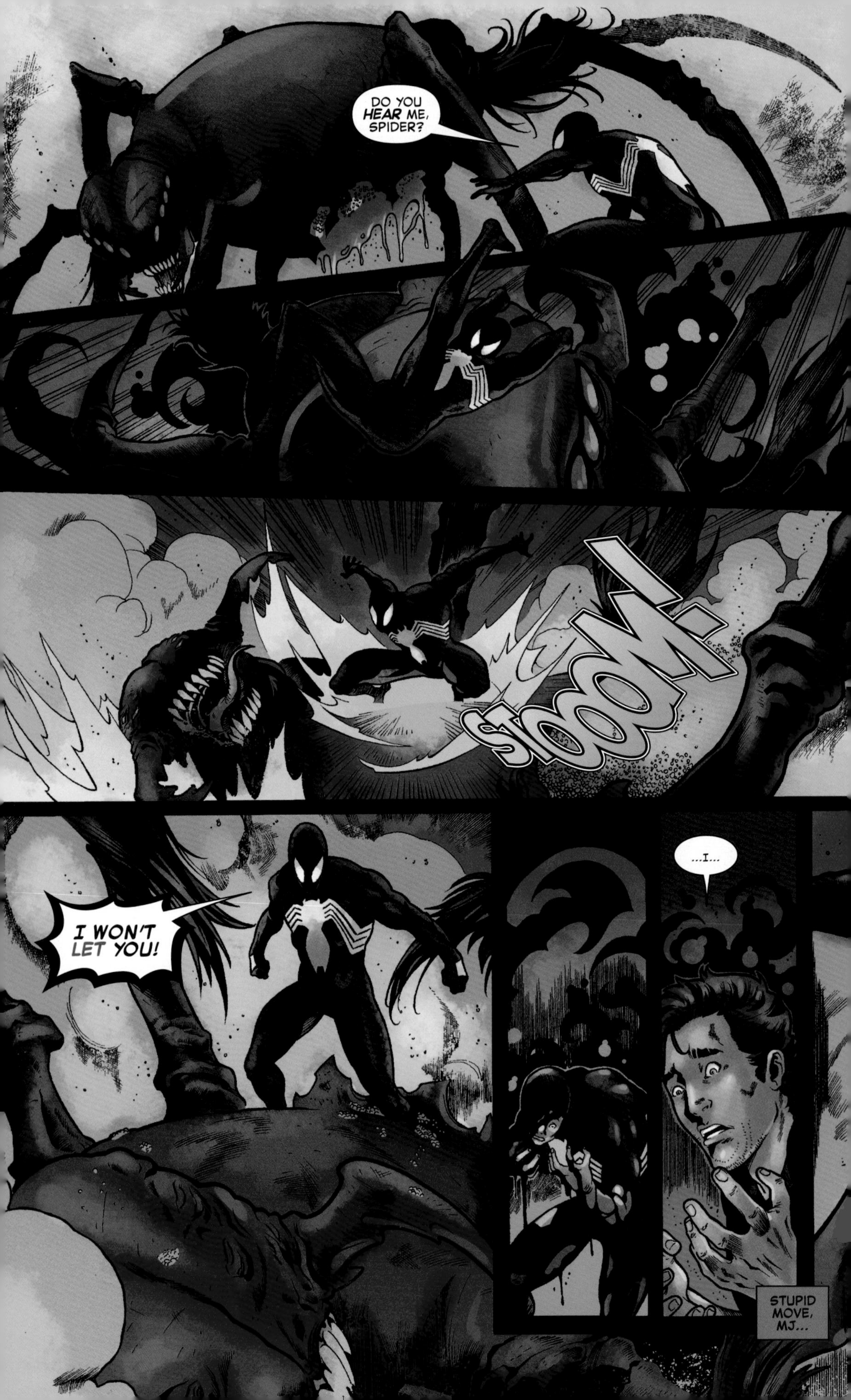
DO YOU HEAR ME, SPIDER?
SPOOOM!
I WON'T LET YOU!
...I...
STUPID MOVE, MJ...

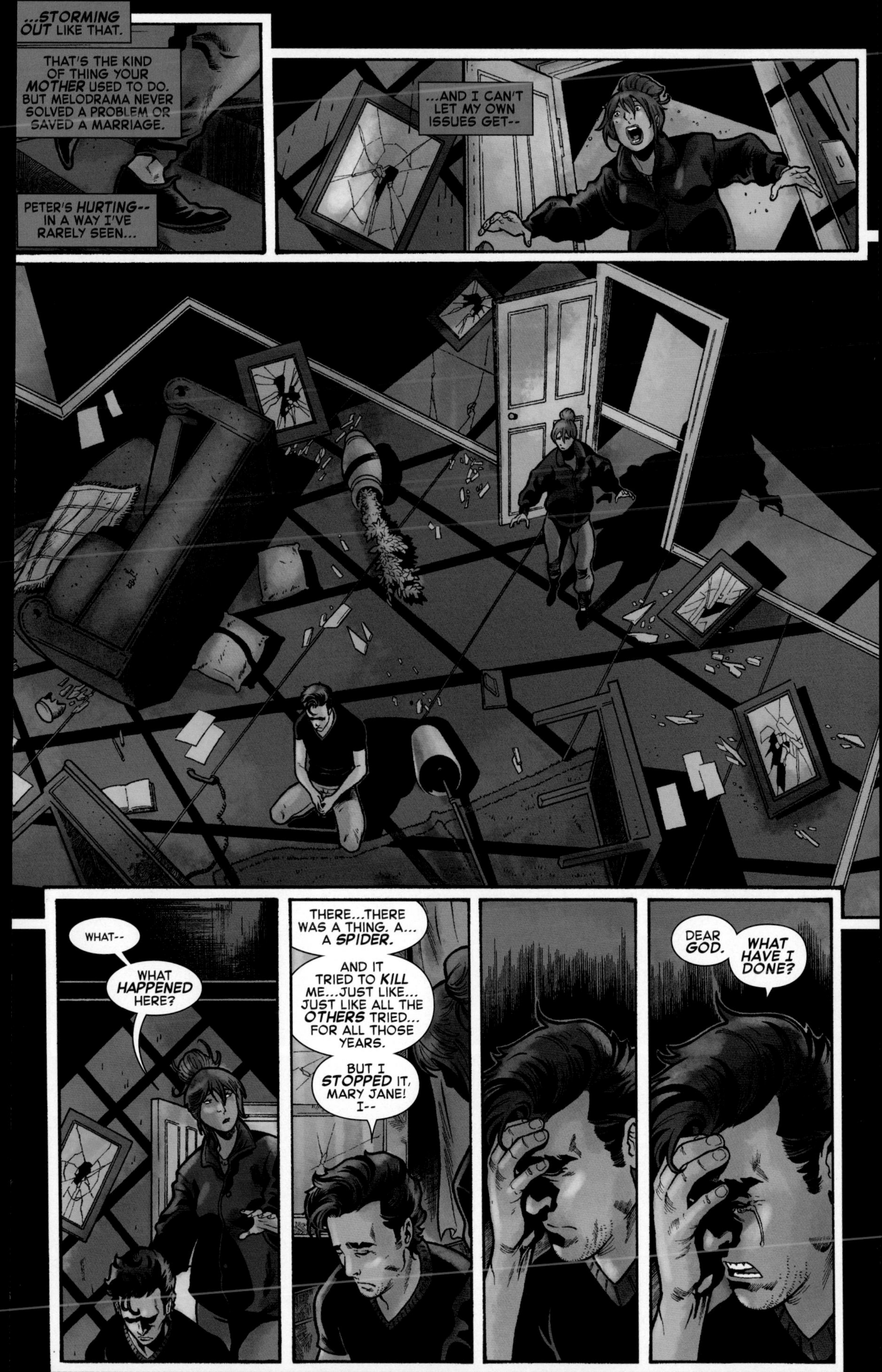

...STORMING OUT LIKE THAT.
THAT'S THE KIND OF THING YOUR MOTHER USED TO DO. BUT MELODRAMA NEVER SOLVED A PROBLEM OR SAVED A MARRIAGE.
PETER'S HURTING-- IN A WAY I'VE RARELY SEEN...
...AND I CAN'T LET MY OWN ISSUES GET--
WHAT--
WHAT HAPPENED HERE?
THERE...THERE WAS A THING. A... A SPIDER.
AND IT TRIED TO KILL ME...JUST LIKE... JUST LIKE ALL THE OTHERS TRIED... FOR ALL THOSE YEARS.
BUT I STOPPED IT, MARY JANE! I--
DEAR GOD.
WHAT HAVE I DONE?

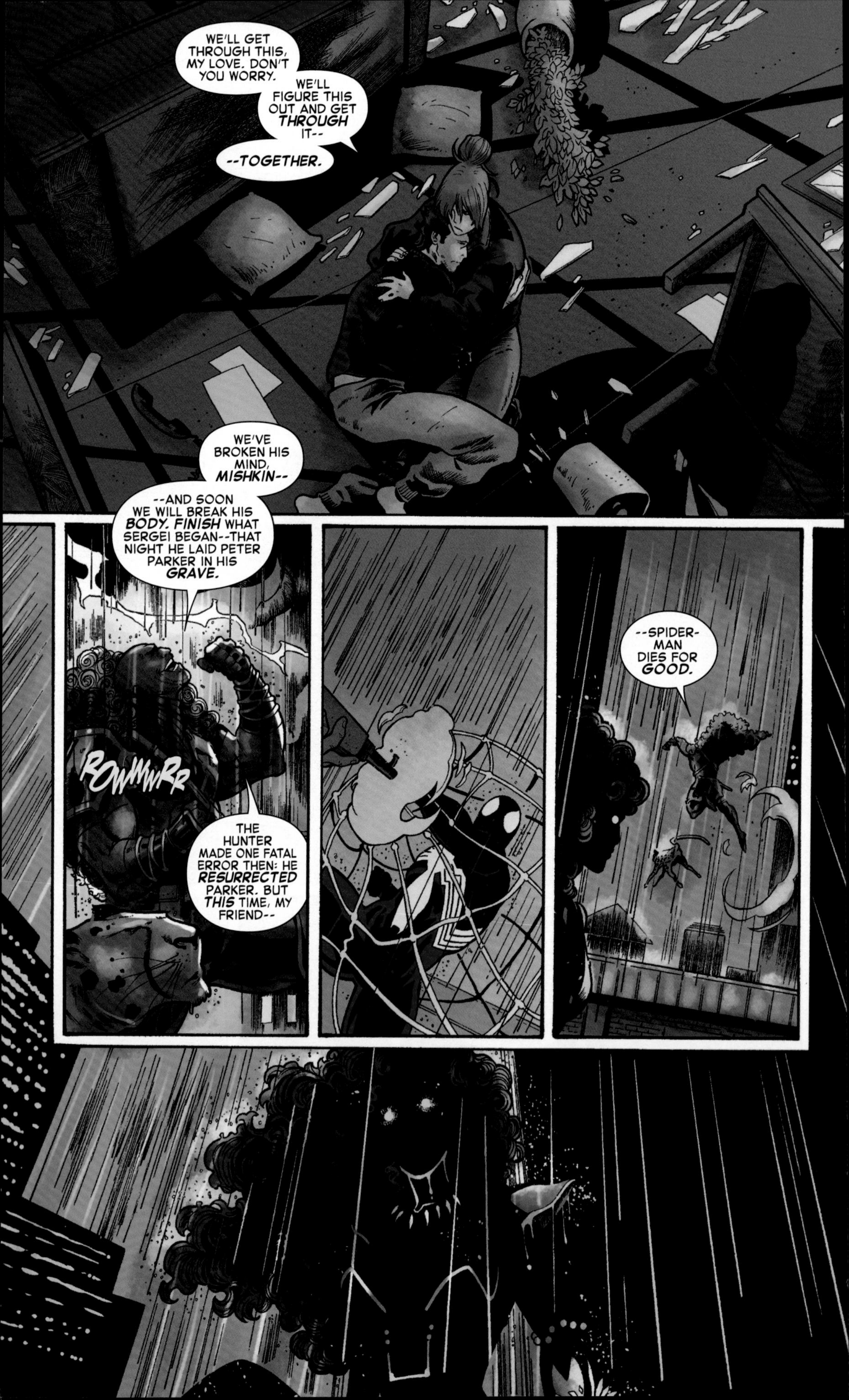
WE'LL GET THROUGH THIS, MY LOVE. DON'T YOU WORRY.
WE'LL FIGURE THIS OUT AND GET THROUGH IT--
--TOGETHER.
WE'VE BROKEN HIS MIND, MISHKIN--
--AND SOON WE WILL BREAK HIS BODY. FINISH WHAT SERGEI BEGAN--THAT NIGHT HE LAID PETER PARKER IN HIS GRAVE.
ROWWWRR
THE HUNTER MADE ONE FATAL ERROR THEN: HE RESURRECTED PARKER. BUT THIS TIME, MY FRIEND--
--SPIDER-MAN DIES FOR GOOD.

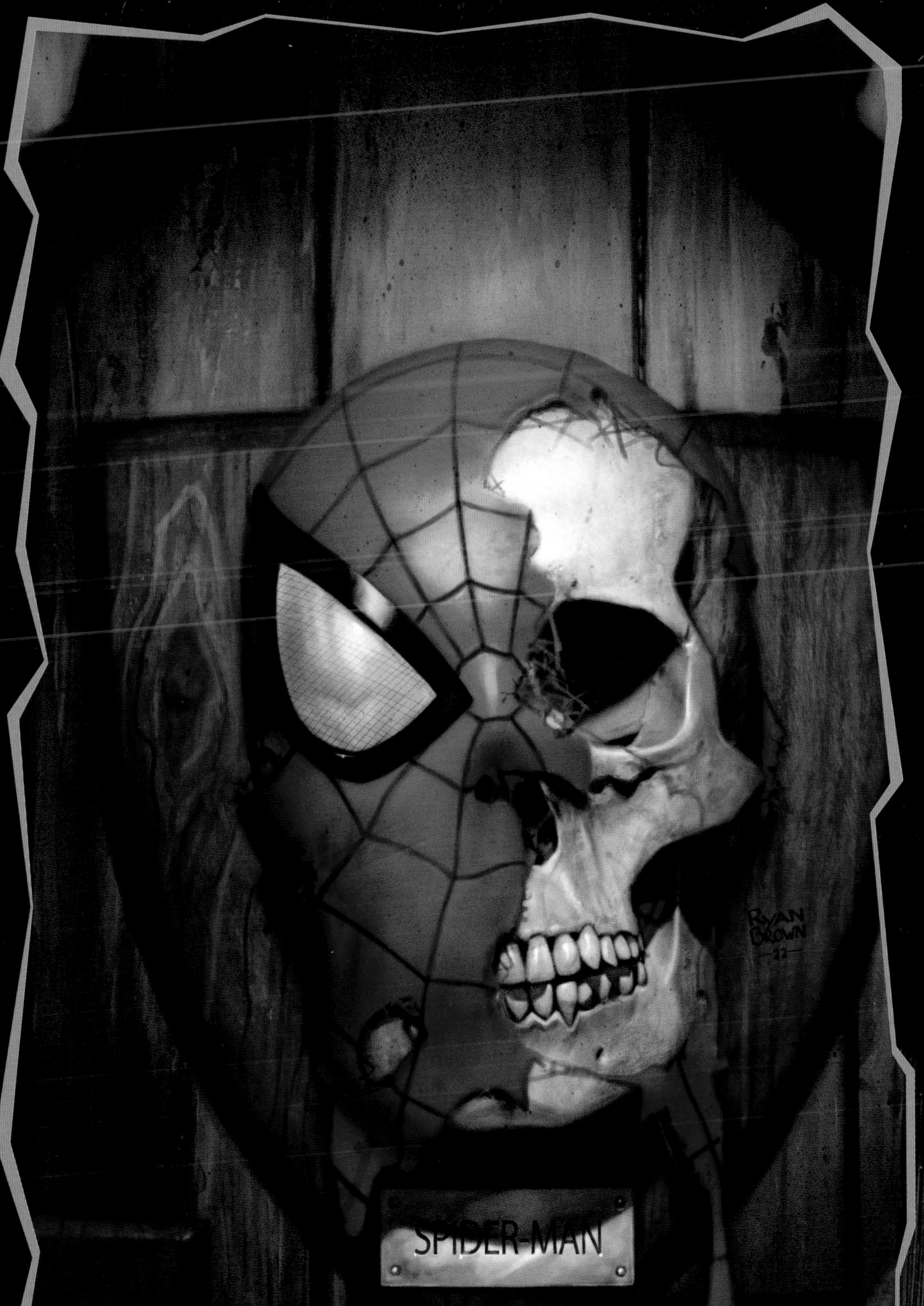
SPIDER-MAN
RYAN BROWN 22

Z

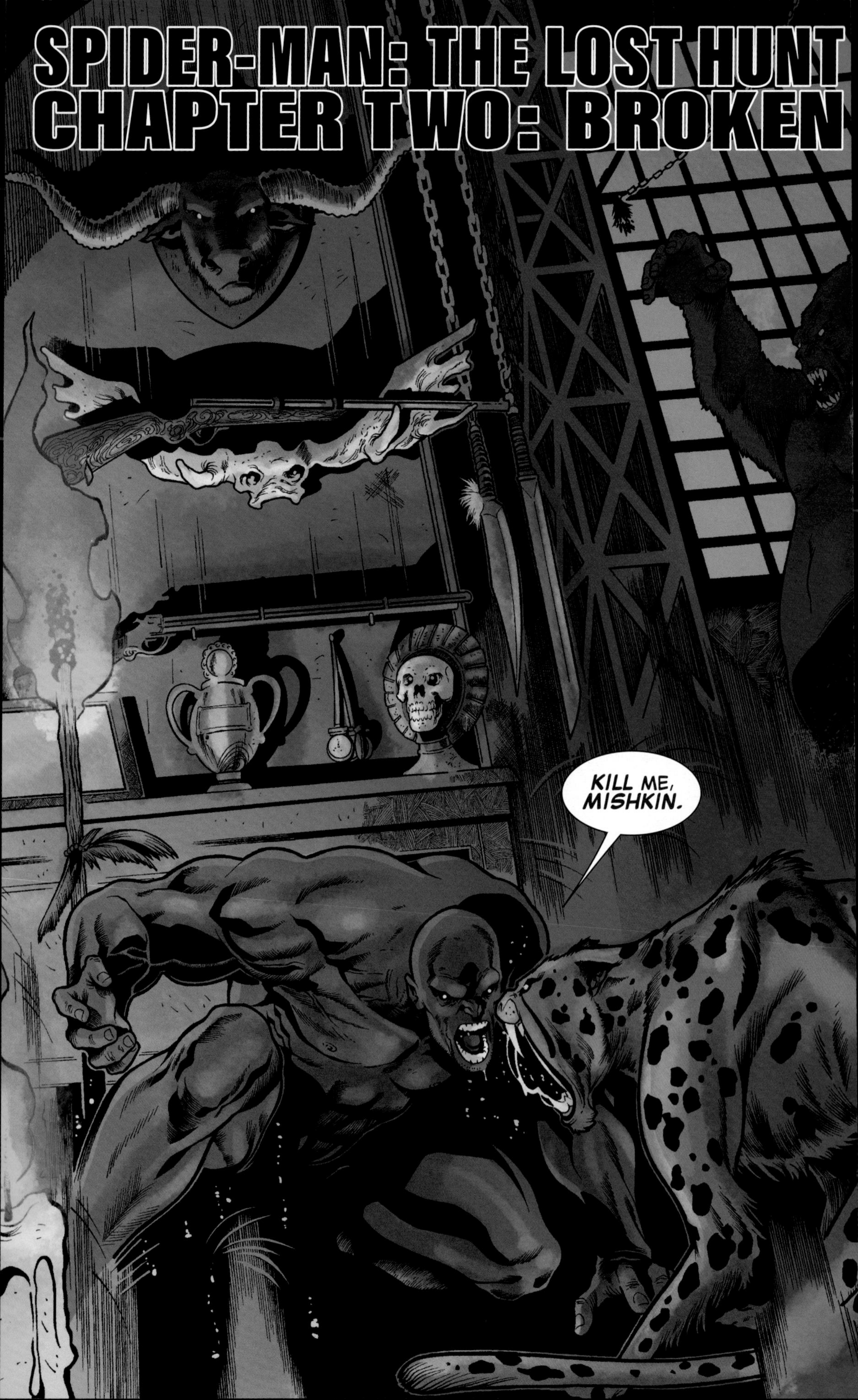
SPIDER-MAN: THE LOST HUNT
CHAPTER TWO: BROKEN
KILL ME, MISHKIN.

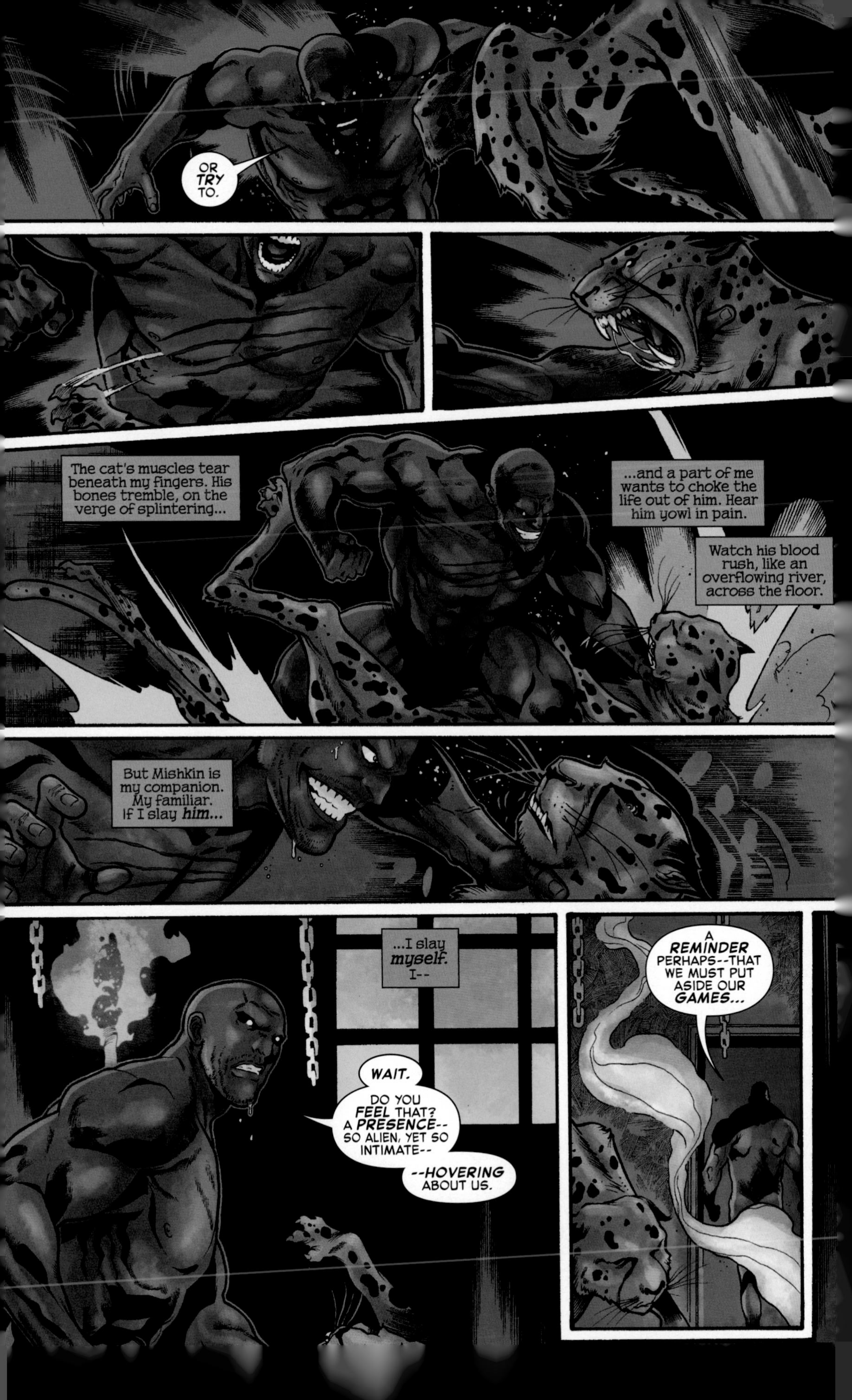
OR TRY TO.
The cat's muscles tear beneath my fingers. His bones tremble, on the verge of splintering...
...and a part of me wants to choke the life out of him. Hear him yowl in pain.
Watch his blood rush, like an overflowing river, across the floor.
But Mishkin is my companion. My familiar. If I slay him...
...I slay myself. I--
WAIT.
DO YOU FEEL THAT? A PRESENCE-- SO ALIEN, YET SO INTIMATE--
--HOVERING ABOUT US.
A REMINDER PERHAPS--THAT WE MUST PUT ASIDE OUR GAMES...

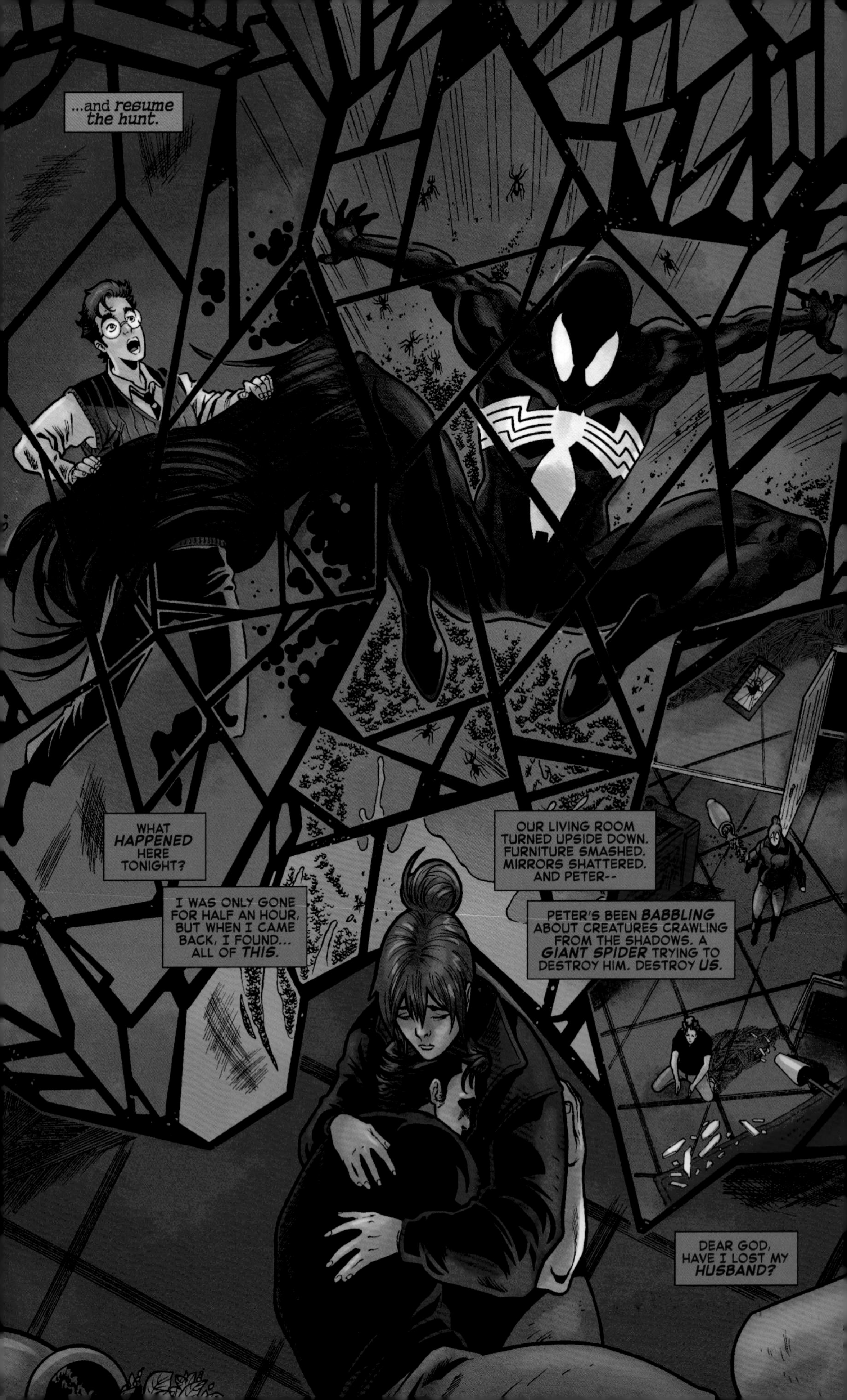
...and resume the hunt.
WHAT HAPPENED HERE TONIGHT?
I WAS ONLY GONE FOR HALF AN HOUR, BUT WHEN I CAME BACK, I FOUND... ALL OF THIS.
OUR LIVING ROOM TURNED UPSIDE DOWN. FURNITURE SMASHED. MIRRORS SHATTERED. AND PETER--
PETER'S BEEN BABBLING ABOUT CREATURES CRAWLING FROM THE SHADOWS. A GIANT SPIDER TRYING TO DESTROY HIM. DESTROY US.
DEAR GOD, HAVE I LOST MY HUSBAND?

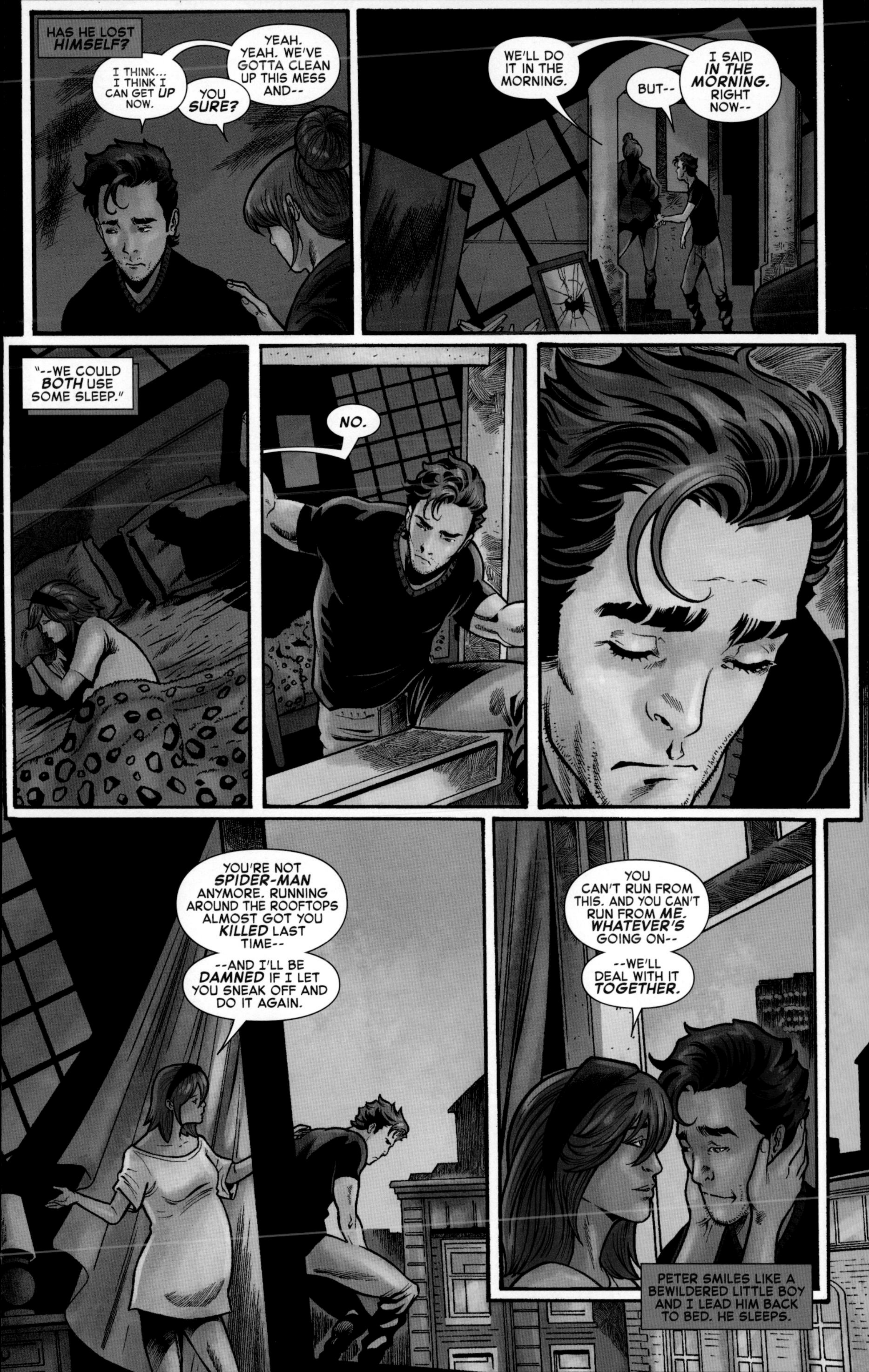
HAS HE LOST HIMSELF?
I THINK... I THINK I CAN GET UP NOW.
YOU SURE?
YEAH. YEAH. WE'VE GOTTA CLEAN UP THIS MESS AND--
WE'LL DO IT IN THE MORNING.
BUT--
I SAID IN THE MORNING. RIGHT NOW--
"--WE COULD BOTH USE SOME SLEEP."
NO.
YOU'RE NOT SPIDER-MAN ANYMORE. RUNNING AROUND THE ROOFTOPS ALMOST GOT YOU KILLED LAST TIME--
--AND I'LL BE DAMNED IF I LET YOU SNEAK OFF AND DO IT AGAIN.
YOU CAN'T RUN FROM THIS. AND YOU CAN'T RUN FROM ME. WHATEVER'S GOING ON--
--WE'LL DEAL WITH IT TOGETHER.
PETER SMILES LIKE A BEWILDERED LITTLE BOY AND I LEAD HIM BACK TO BED. HE SLEEPS.

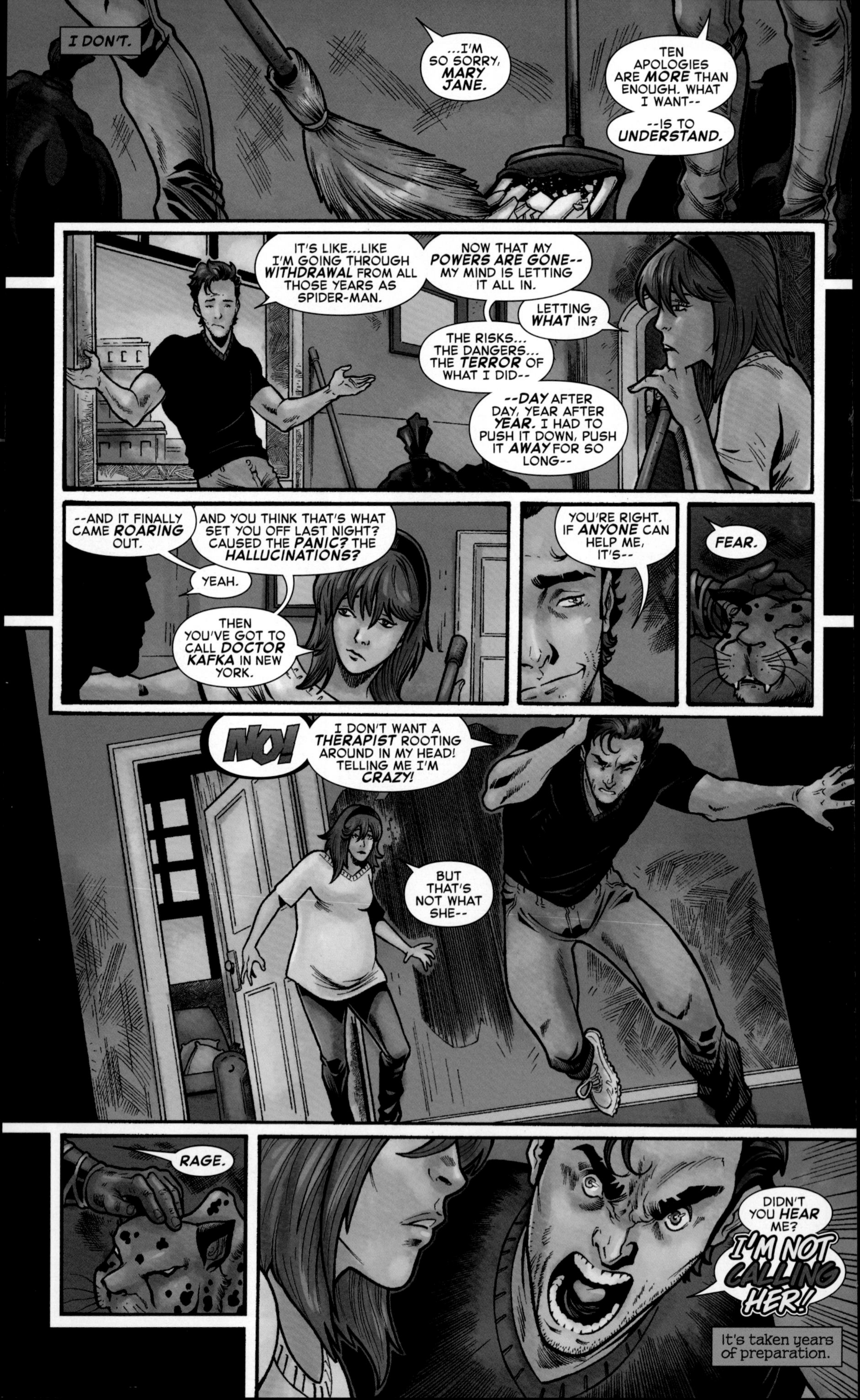
I DON'T.
...I'M SO SORRY, MARY JANE.
TEN APOLOGIES ARE MORE THAN ENOUGH. WHAT I WANT--
--IS TO UNDERSTAND.
IT'S LIKE...LIKE I'M GOING THROUGH WITHDRAWAL FROM ALL THOSE YEARS AS SPIDER-MAN.
NOW THAT MY POWERS ARE GONE-- MY MIND IS LETTING IT ALL IN.
LETTING WHAT IN?
THE RISKS... THE DANGERS... THE TERROR OF WHAT I DID--
--DAY AFTER DAY, YEAR AFTER YEAR. I HAD TO PUSH IT DOWN, PUSH IT AWAY FOR SO LONG--
--AND IT FINALLY CAME ROARING OUT.
AND YOU THINK THAT'S WHAT SET YOU OFF LAST NIGHT? CAUSED THE PANIC? THE HALLUCINATIONS?
YEAH.
THEN YOU'VE GOT TO CALL DOCTOR KAFKA IN NEW YORK.
YOU'RE RIGHT. IF ANYONE CAN HELP ME, IT'S--
FEAR.
NO!
I DON'T WANT A THERAPIST ROOTING AROUND IN MY HEAD! TELLING ME I'M CRAZY!
BUT THAT'S NOT WHAT SHE--
RAGE.
DIDN'T YOU HEAR ME?
I'M NOT CALLING HER!
It's taken years of preparation.

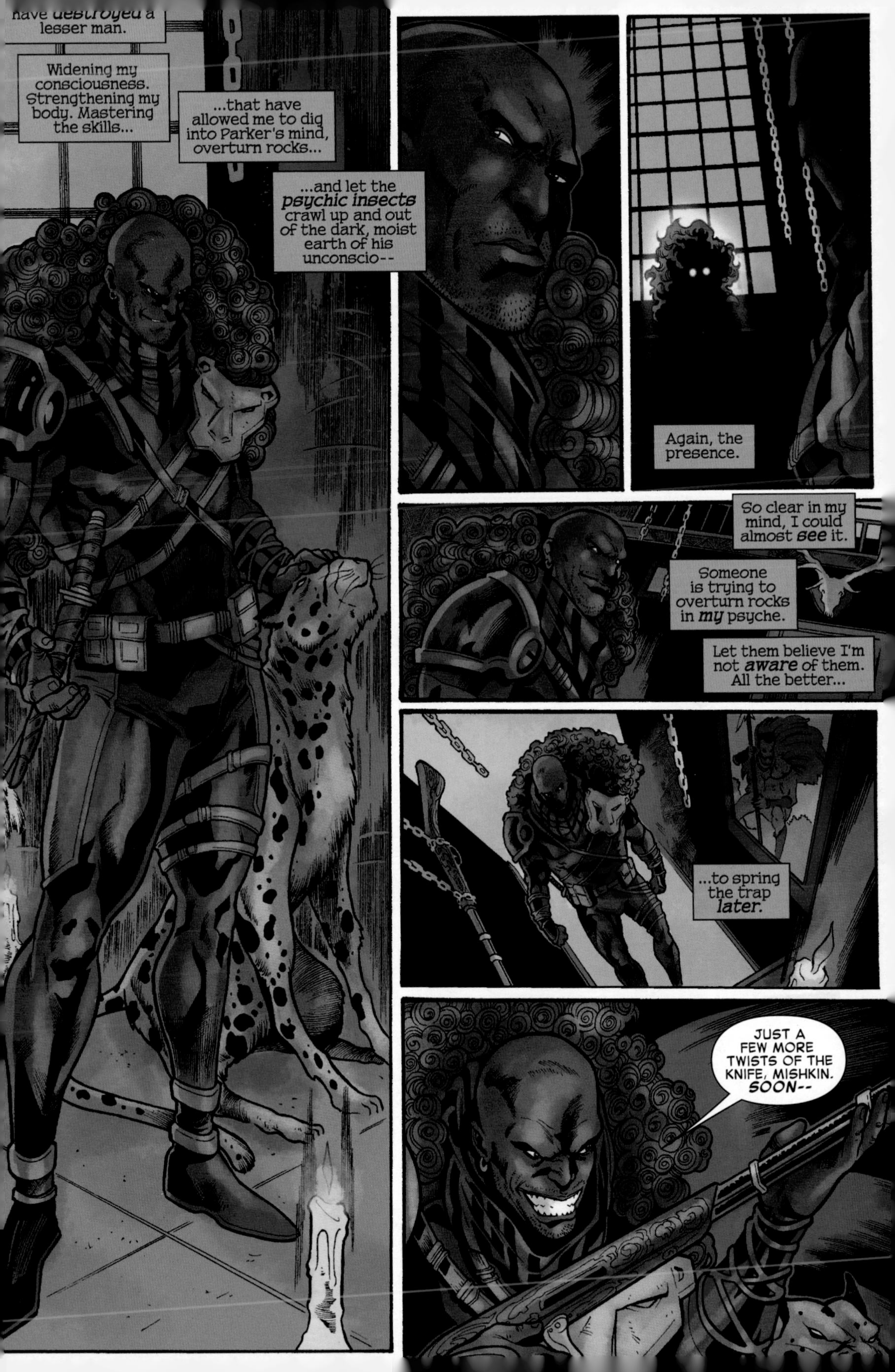
have destroyed a lesser man.
Widening my consciousness. Strengthening my body. Mastering the skills...
...that have allowed me to dig into Parker's mind, overturn rocks...
...and let the psychic insects crawl up and out of the dark, moist earth of his unconscio--
Again, the presence.
So clear in my mind, I could almost see it.
Someone is trying to overturn rocks in my psyche.
Let them believe I'm not aware of them. All the better...
...to spring the trap later.
JUST A FEW MORE TWISTS OF THE KNIFE, MISHKIN. SOON--

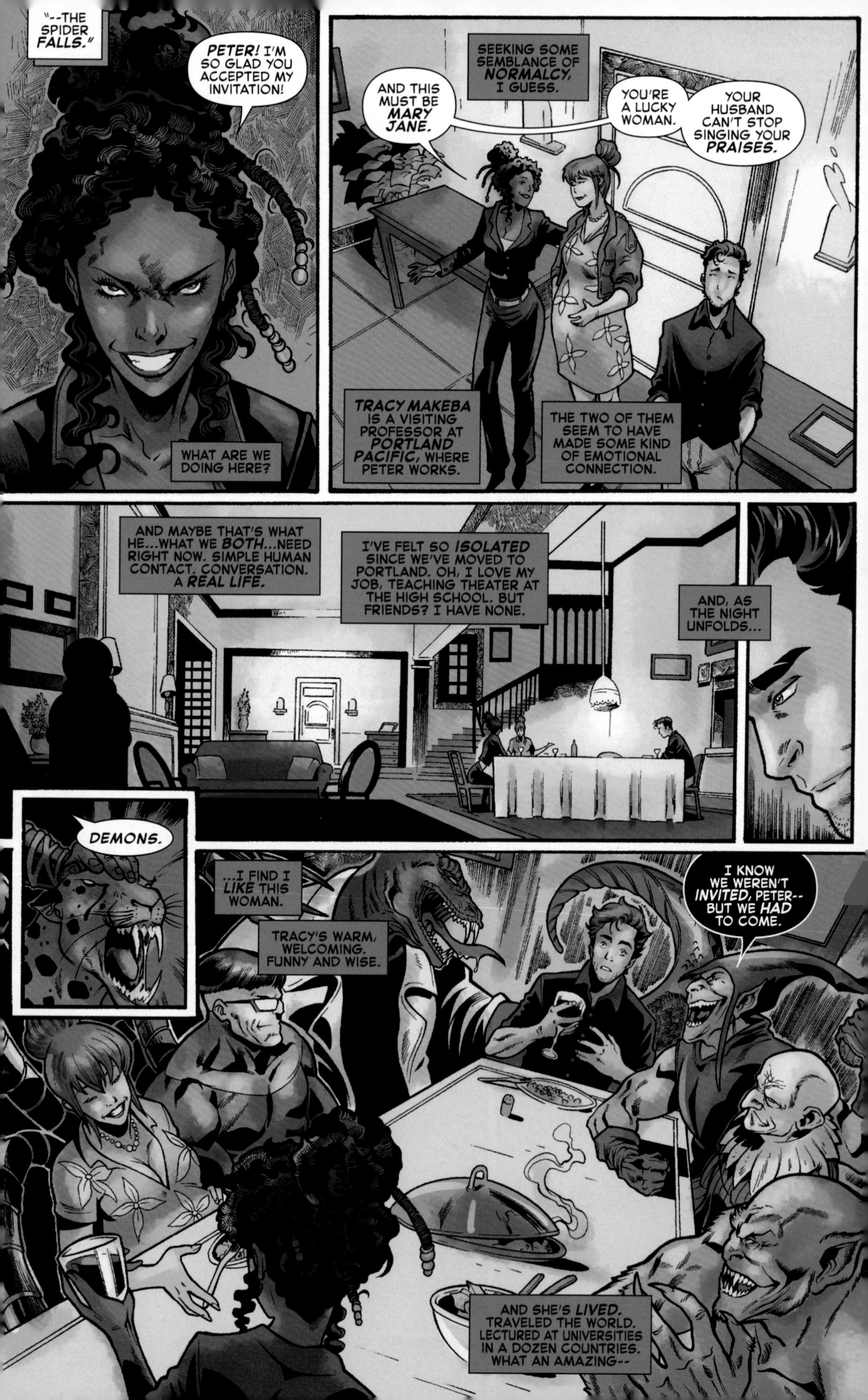
"--THE SPIDER FALLS."
PETER! I'M SO GLAD YOU ACCEPTED MY INVITATION!
WHAT ARE WE DOING HERE?
SEEKING SOME SEMBLANCE OF NORMALCY, I GUESS.
AND THIS MUST BE MARY JANE.
YOU'RE A LUCKY WOMAN.
YOUR HUSBAND CAN'T STOP SINGING YOUR PRAISES.
TRACY MAKEBA IS A VISITING PROFESSOR AT PORTLAND PACIFIC, WHERE PETER WORKS.
THE TWO OF THEM SEEM TO HAVE MADE SOME KIND OF EMOTIONAL CONNECTION.
AND MAYBE THAT'S WHAT HE...WHAT WE BOTH...NEED RIGHT NOW. SIMPLE HUMAN CONTACT. CONVERSATION. A REAL LIFE.
I'VE FELT SO ISOLATED SINCE WE'VE MOVED TO PORTLAND. OH, I LOVE MY JOB, TEACHING THEATER AT THE HIGH SCHOOL. BUT FRIENDS? I HAVE NONE.
AND, AS THE NIGHT UNFOLDS...
DEMONS.
...I FIND I LIKE THIS WOMAN.
TRACY'S WARM, WELCOMING. FUNNY AND WISE.
I KNOW WE WEREN'T INVITED, PETER-- BUT WE HAD TO COME.
AND SHE'S LIVED. TRAVELED THE WORLD. LECTURED AT UNIVERSITIES IN A DOZEN COUNTRIES. WHAT AN AMAZING--

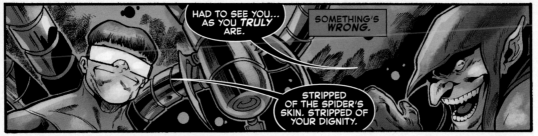

HAD TO SEE YOU... AS YOU *TRULY* ARE.

SOMETHING'S *WRONG*.

STRIPPED OF THE SPIDER'S SKIN. STRIPPED OF YOUR DIGNITY.

A WEAK, INEFFECTUAL... *NOTHING*.

I CAN SEE IT IN HIS FACE.

A *SSSPINELESS*, NEUROTIC *COWARD*.

AND *THESE* TWO! WHAT *DELICIOUSSSS MEALS* THEY'D MAKE!

WHAT A PLEASURE TO SSSSUCK THE *TASTY FLESH* FROM THEIR *BONESSS*!

E PANIC HIS EYES.

STOP IT.

SWEETIE-- --YOU *OKAY*...?

HIS HANDS ARE *TREMBLING*.

MAKEBA NOTICES TOO...

GO AHEAD, VERMIN! *INDULGE* YOURSELF!

YUMMMM.

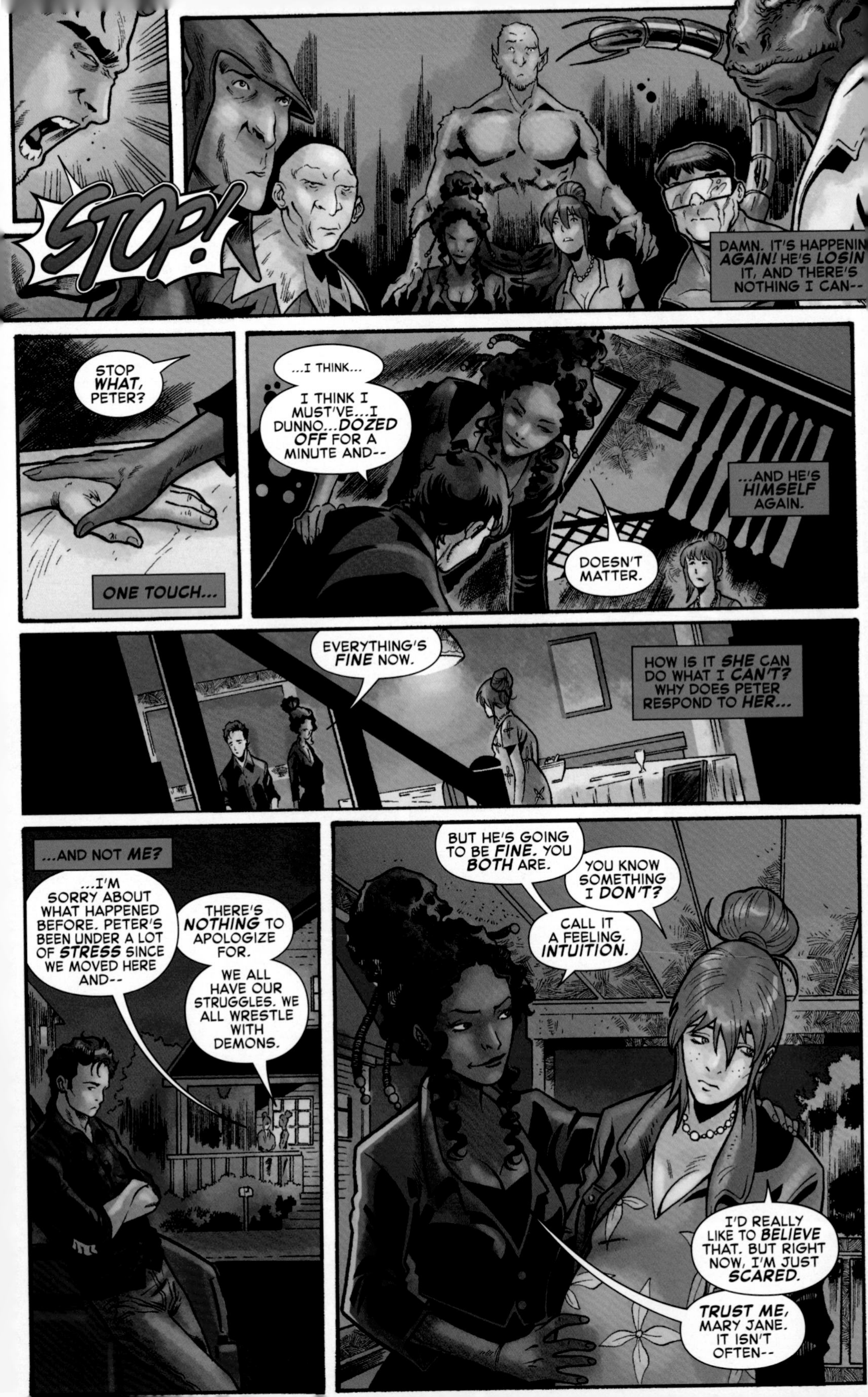
STOP!
DAMN. IT'S HAPPENIN AGAIN! HE'S LOSIN IT, AND THERE'S NOTHING I CAN--
STOP WHAT, PETER?
ONE TOUCH...
...I THINK...
I THINK I MUST'VE...I DUNNO...DOZED OFF FOR A MINUTE AND--
DOESN'T MATTER.
...AND HE'S HIMSELF AGAIN.
EVERYTHING'S FINE NOW.
HOW IS IT SHE CAN DO WHAT I CAN'T? WHY DOES PETER RESPOND TO HER...
...AND NOT ME?
...I'M SORRY ABOUT WHAT HAPPENED BEFORE. PETER'S BEEN UNDER A LOT OF STRESS SINCE WE MOVED HERE AND--
THERE'S NOTHING TO APOLOGIZE FOR.
WE ALL HAVE OUR STRUGGLES. WE ALL WRESTLE WITH DEMONS.
BUT HE'S GOING TO BE FINE. YOU BOTH ARE.
YOU KNOW SOMETHING I DON'T?
CALL IT A FEELING. INTUITION.
I'D REALLY LIKE TO BELIEVE THAT. BUT RIGHT NOW, I'M JUST SCARED.
TRUST ME, MARY JANE. IT ISN'T OFTEN--

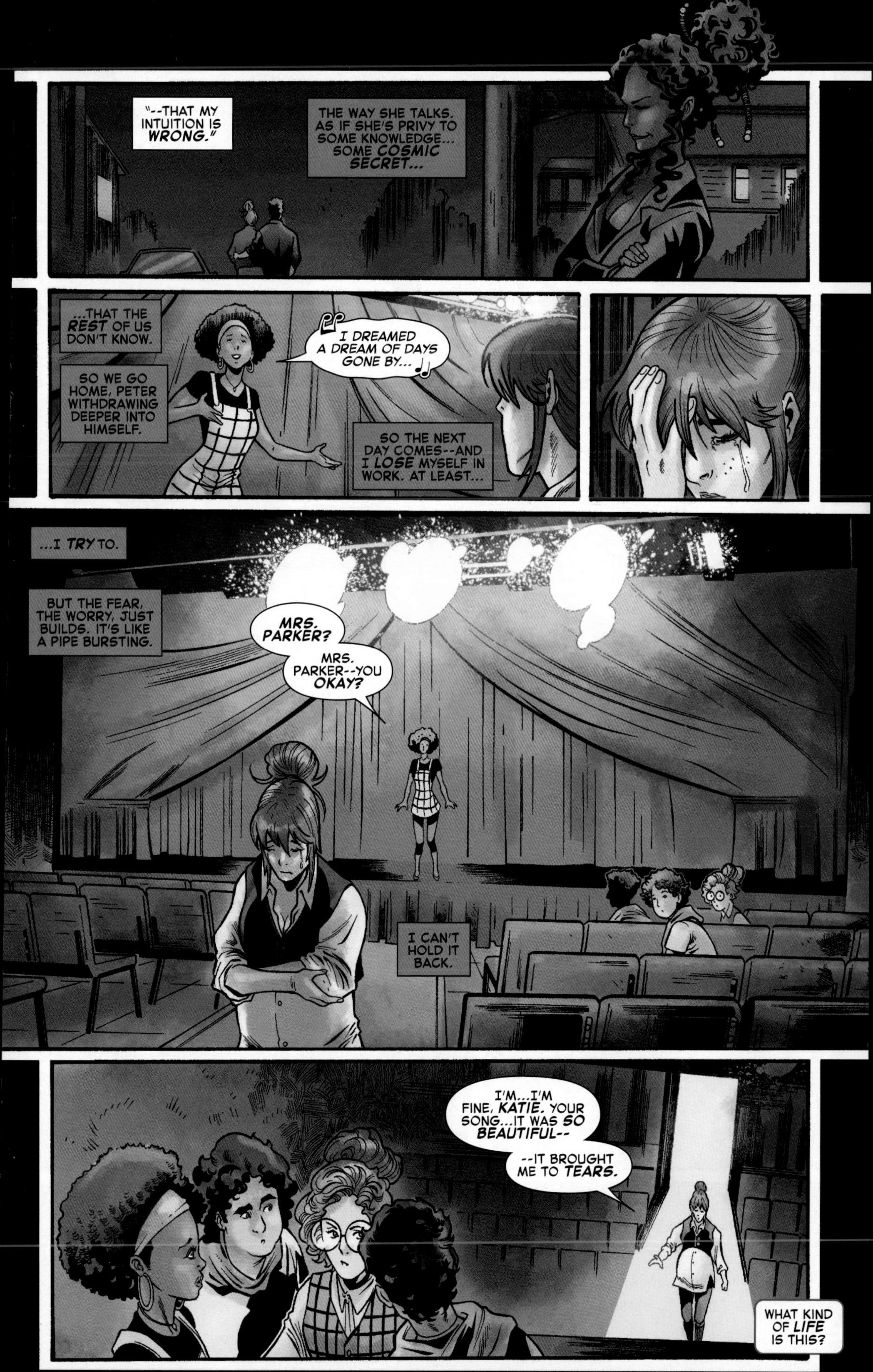
"--THAT MY INTUITION IS WRONG."
THE WAY SHE TALKS. AS IF SHE'S PRIVY TO SOME KNOWLEDGE... SOME COSMIC SECRET...
...THAT THE REST OF US DON'T KNOW.
SO WE GO HOME, PETER WITHDRAWING DEEPER INTO HIMSELF.
I DREAMED A DREAM OF DAYS GONE BY...
SO THE NEXT DAY COMES--AND I LOSE MYSELF IN WORK. AT LEAST...
...I TRY TO.
BUT THE FEAR, THE WORRY, JUST BUILDS. IT'S LIKE A PIPE BURSTING.
MRS. PARKER?
MRS. PARKER--YOU OKAY?
I CAN'T HOLD IT BACK.
I'M...I'M FINE, KATIE. YOUR SONG...IT WAS SO BEAUTIFUL--
--IT BROUGHT ME TO TEARS.
WHAT KIND OF LIFE IS THIS?

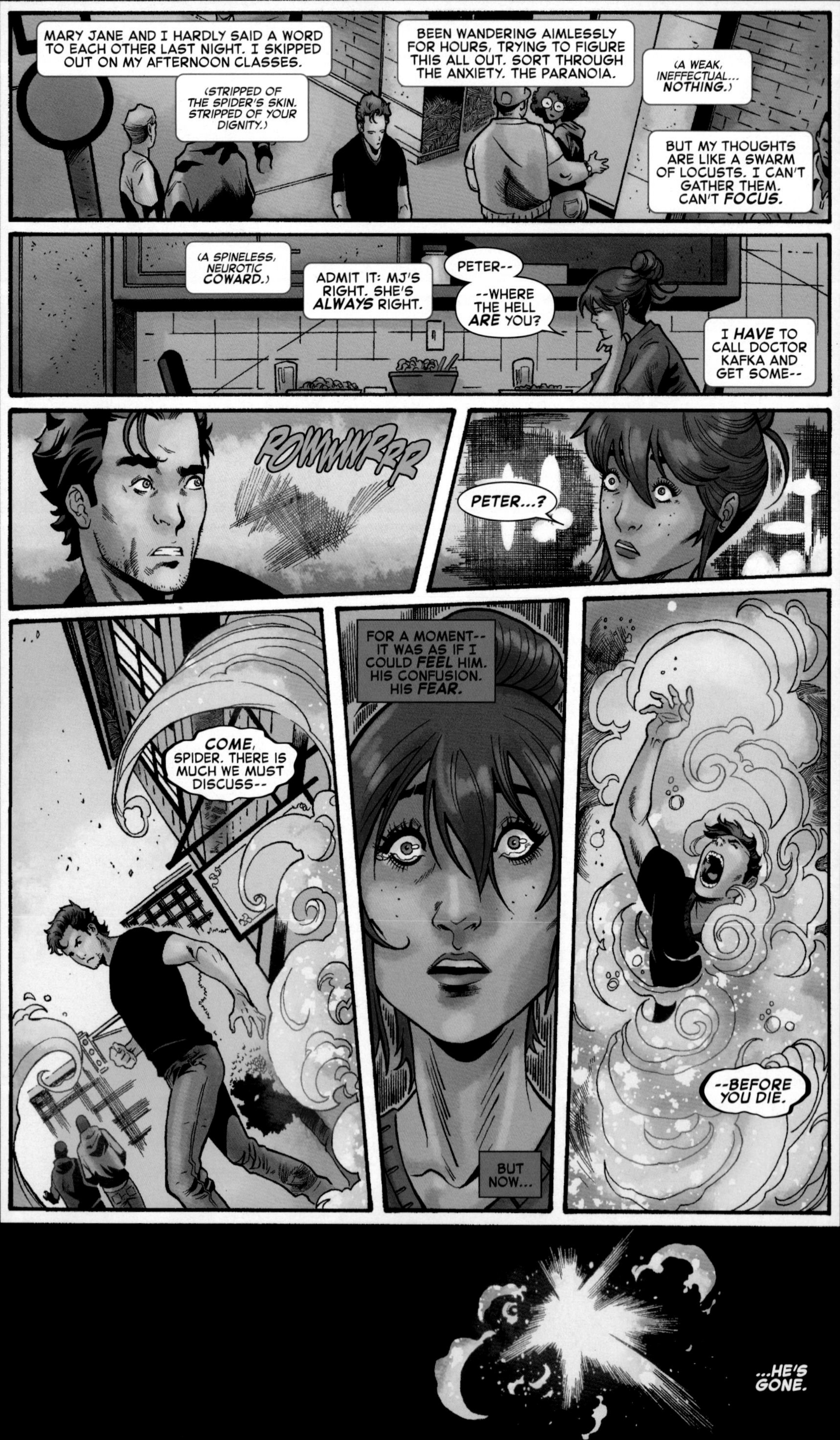

MARY JANE AND I HARDLY SAID A WORD TO EACH OTHER LAST NIGHT. I SKIPPED OUT ON MY AFTERNOON CLASSES.
(STRIPPED OF THE SPIDER'S SKIN. STRIPPED OF YOUR DIGNITY.)
BEEN WANDERING AIMLESSLY FOR HOURS, TRYING TO FIGURE THIS ALL OUT. SORT THROUGH THE ANXIETY. THE PARANOIA.
(A WEAK, INEFFECTUAL... NOTHING.)
BUT MY THOUGHTS ARE LIKE A SWARM OF LOCUSTS. I CAN'T GATHER THEM. CAN'T FOCUS.
(A SPINELESS, NEUROTIC COWARD.)
ADMIT IT: MJ'S RIGHT. SHE'S ALWAYS RIGHT.
PETER--
--WHERE THE HELL ARE YOU?
I HAVE TO CALL DOCTOR KAFKA AND GET SOME--
ROWWWRRR
PETER...?
COME, SPIDER. THERE IS MUCH WE MUST DISCUSS--
FOR A MOMENT-- IT WAS AS IF I COULD FEEL HIM. HIS CONFUSION. HIS FEAR.
BUT NOW...
--BEFORE YOU DIE.
...HE'S GONE.

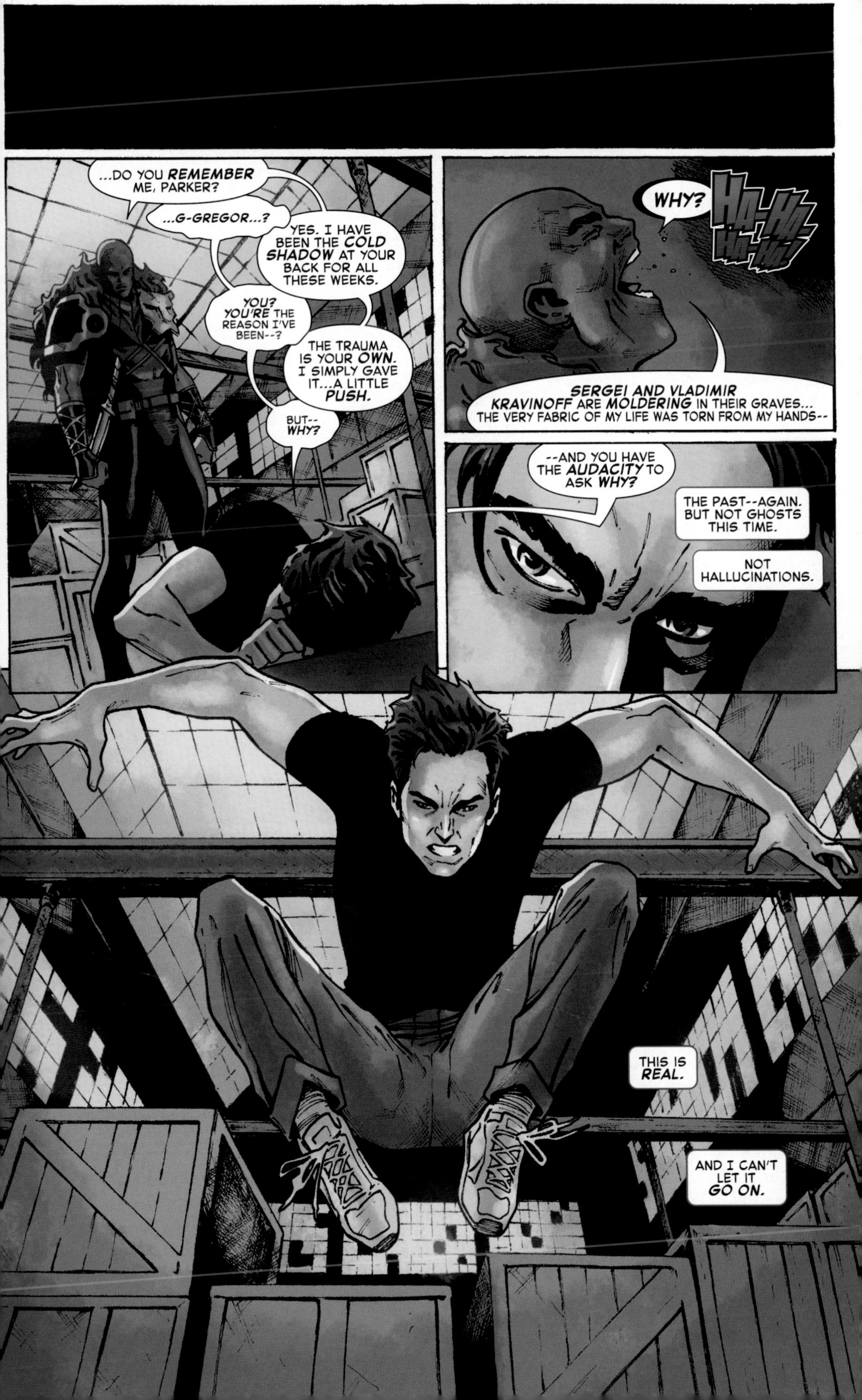
...DO YOU REMEMBER ME, PARKER?
...G-GREGOR...?
YES. I HAVE BEEN THE COLD SHADOW AT YOUR BACK FOR ALL THESE WEEKS.
YOU? YOU'RE THE REASON I'VE BEEN--?
THE TRAUMA IS YOUR OWN. I SIMPLY GAVE IT...A LITTLE PUSH.
BUT-- WHY?
WHY?
HA-HA HA-HA!
SERGEI AND VLADIMIR KRAVINOFF ARE MOLDERING IN THEIR GRAVES... THE VERY FABRIC OF MY LIFE WAS TORN FROM MY HANDS--
--AND YOU HAVE THE AUDACITY TO ASK WHY?
THE PAST--AGAIN. BUT NOT GHOSTS THIS TIME.
NOT HALLUCINATIONS.
THIS IS REAL.
AND I CAN'T LET IT GO ON.

I WON'T LET IT GO ON!

SKRAAAAAK!

I MAY NOT HAVE MY POWERS ANYMORE, BUT I'VE TAKEN ON DOZENS OF LUNATICS LIKE GREGOR...

BOOM!

...AND I HAVE SKILLS... REFLEXES...

...HONED BY YEARS OF BATTLE.

YOU TRIED TO SHATTER MY MIND...DESTROY MY LIFE--

--BECAUSE YOU WERE SEEKING REVENGE? REVENGE FOR WHAT?

RRRRRRRR

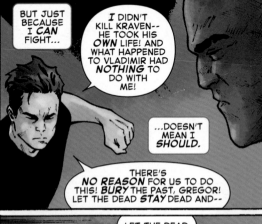

BUT JUST BECAUSE I CAN FIGHT...

I DIDN'T KILL KRAVEN-- HE TOOK HIS OWN LIFE! AND WHAT HAPPENED TO VLADIMIR HAD NOTHING TO DO WITH ME!

...DOESN'T MEAN I SHOULD.

THERE'S NO REASON FOR US TO DO THIS! BURY THE PAST, GREGOR! LET THE DEAD STAY DEAD AND--

LET THE DEAD STAY DEAD?

TELL ME--

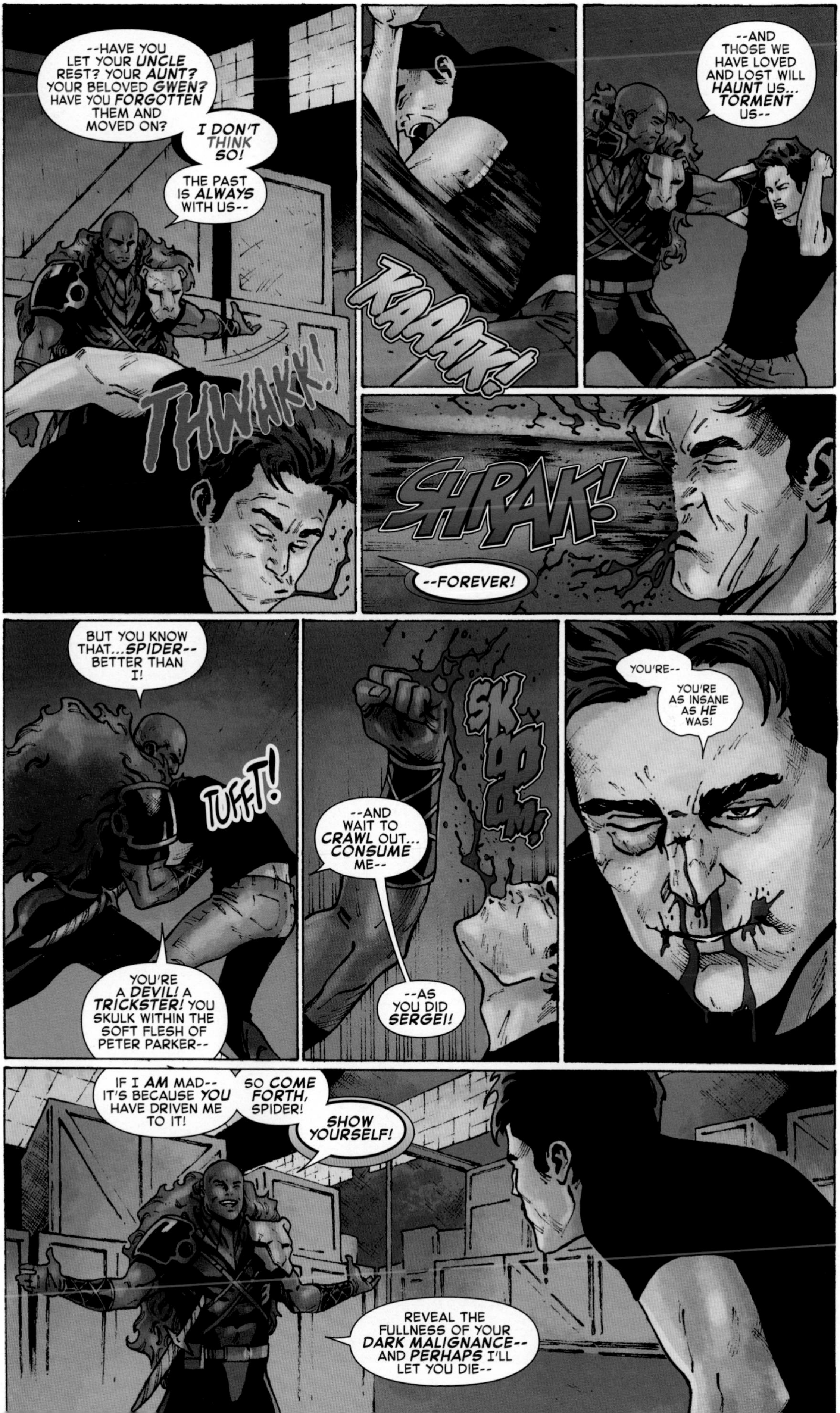
--HAVE YOU LET YOUR UNCLE REST? YOUR AUNT? YOUR BELOVED GWEN? HAVE YOU FORGOTTEN THEM AND MOVED ON?
I DON'T THINK SO!
THE PAST IS ALWAYS WITH US--
THWAKK!
KRAAAK!
--AND THOSE WE HAVE LOVED AND LOST WILL HAUNT US... TORMENT US--
SHRAKK!
--FOREVER!
BUT YOU KNOW THAT...SPIDER-- BETTER THAN I!
TUFFT!
YOU'RE A DEVIL! A TRICKSTER! YOU SKULK WITHIN THE SOFT FLESH OF PETER PARKER--
--AND WAIT TO CRAWL OUT... CONSUME ME--
SKROOM!
--AS YOU DID SERGEI!
YOU'RE--
YOU'RE AS INSANE AS HE WAS!
IF I AM MAD-- IT'S BECAUSE YOU HAVE DRIVEN ME TO IT!
SO COME FORTH, SPIDER!
SHOW YOURSELF!
REVEAL THE FULLNESS OF YOUR DARK MALIGNANCE-- AND PERHAPS I'LL LET YOU DIE--

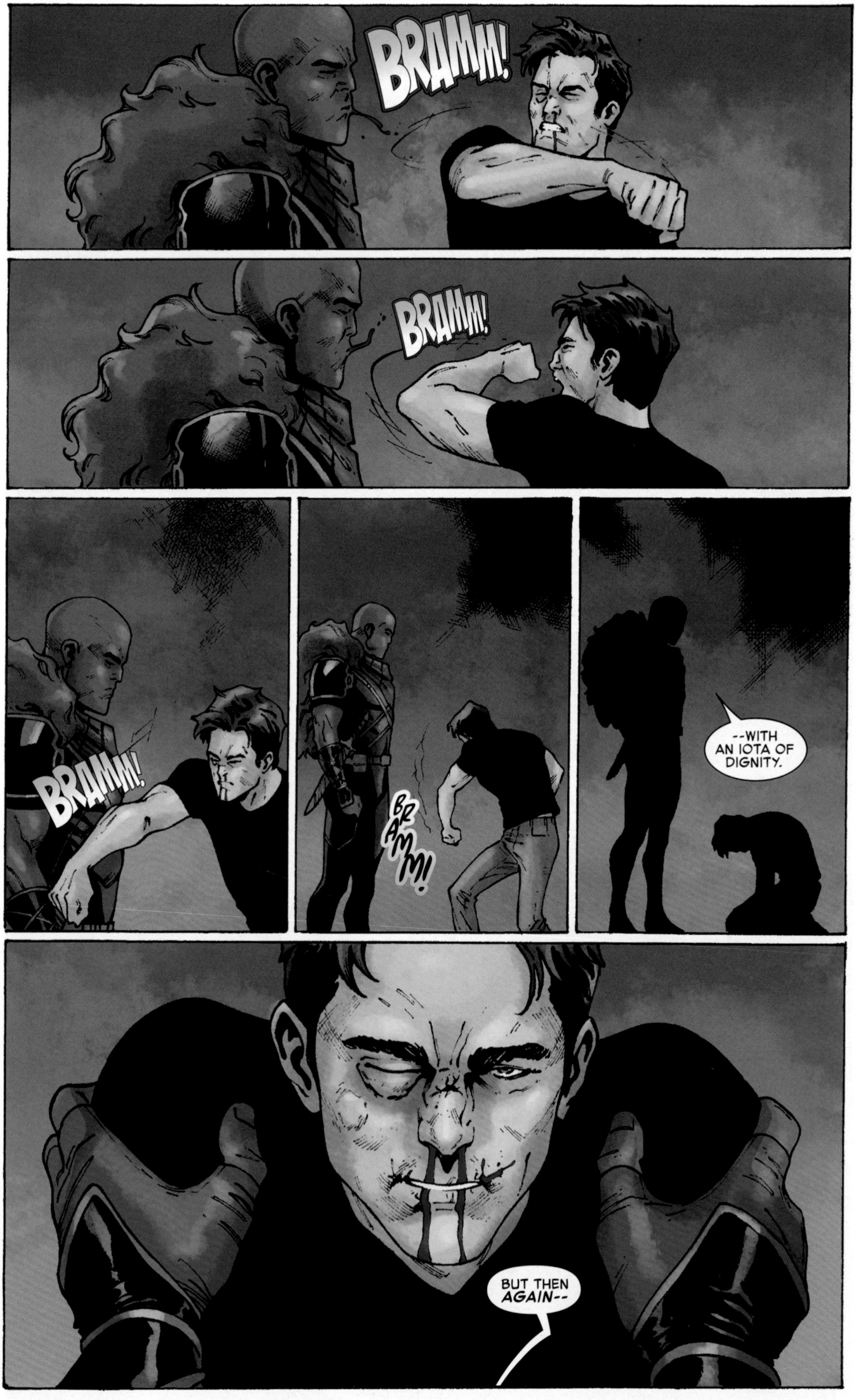
BRAMM!
BRAMM!
BRAMM!
BRAMM!
--WITH AN IOTA OF DIGNITY.
BUT THEN AGAIN--

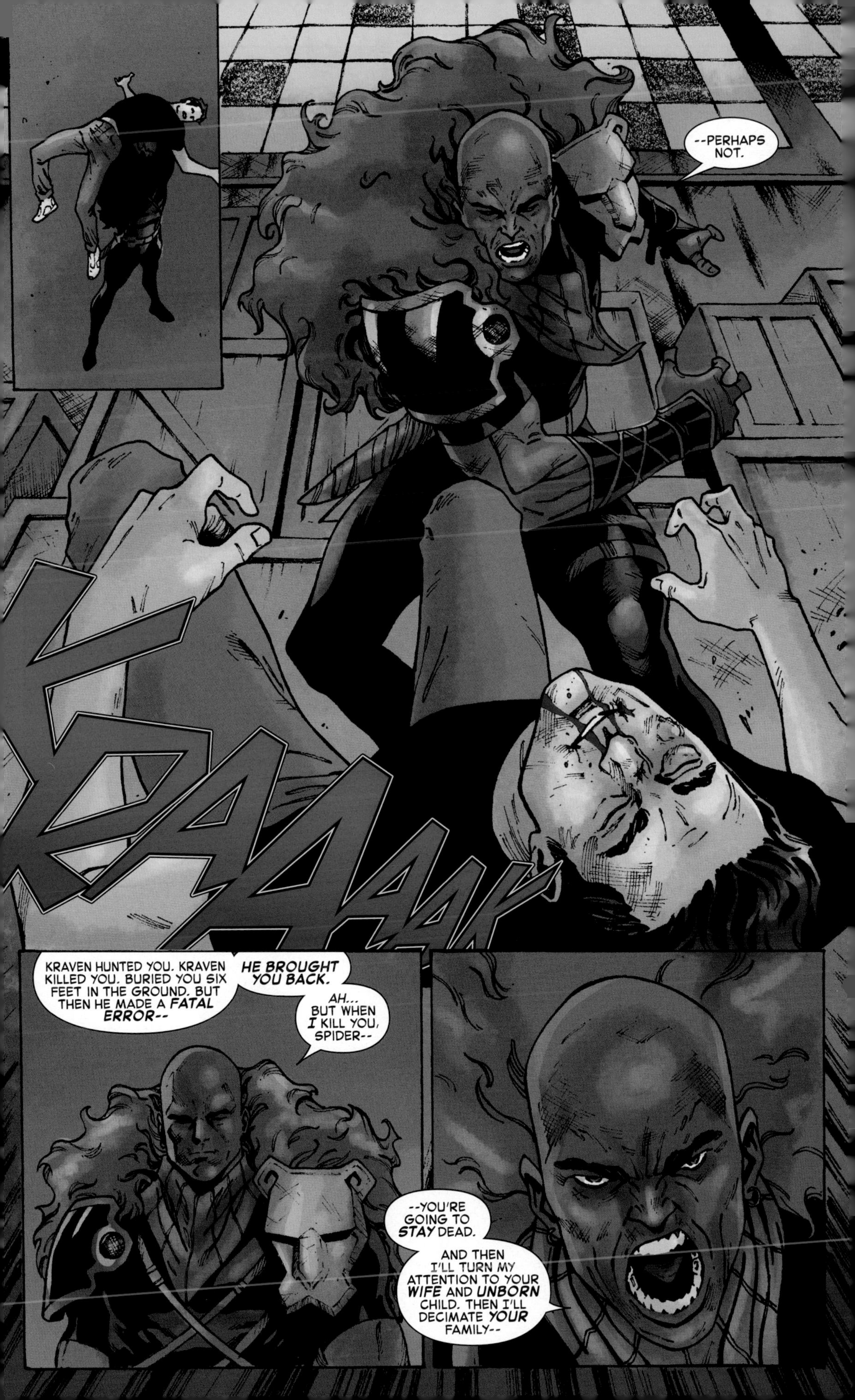
--PERHAPS NOT.
KKAAAK
KRAVEN HUNTED YOU. KRAVEN KILLED YOU. BURIED YOU SIX FEET IN THE GROUND. BUT THEN HE MADE A FATAL ERROR--
HE BROUGHT YOU BACK.
AH... BUT WHEN I KILL YOU, SPIDER--
--YOU'RE GOING TO STAY DEAD.
AND THEN I'LL TURN MY ATTENTION TO YOUR WIFE AND UNBORN CHILD. THEN I'LL DECIMATE YOUR FAMILY--

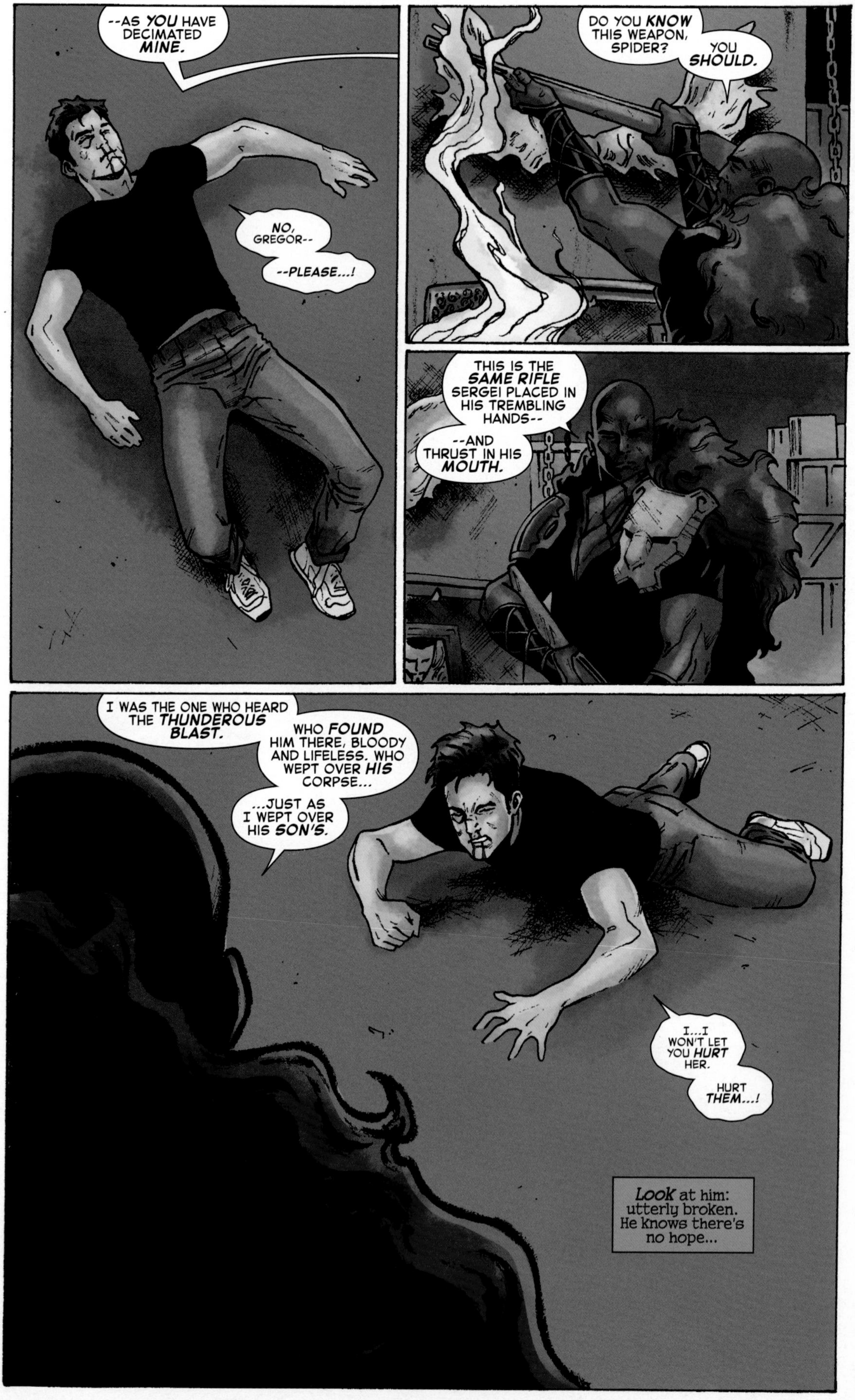
--AS YOU HAVE DECIMATED MINE.
NO, GREGOR--
--PLEASE...!
DO YOU KNOW THIS WEAPON, SPIDER?
YOU SHOULD.
THIS IS THE SAME RIFLE SERGEI PLACED IN HIS TREMBLING HANDS--
--AND THRUST IN HIS MOUTH.
I WAS THE ONE WHO HEARD THE THUNDEROUS BLAST.
WHO FOUND HIM THERE, BLOODY AND LIFELESS. WHO WEPT OVER HIS CORPSE...
...JUST AS I WEPT OVER HIS SON'S.
I...I WON'T LET YOU HURT HER.
HURT THEM...!
Look at him: utterly broken. He knows there's no hope...

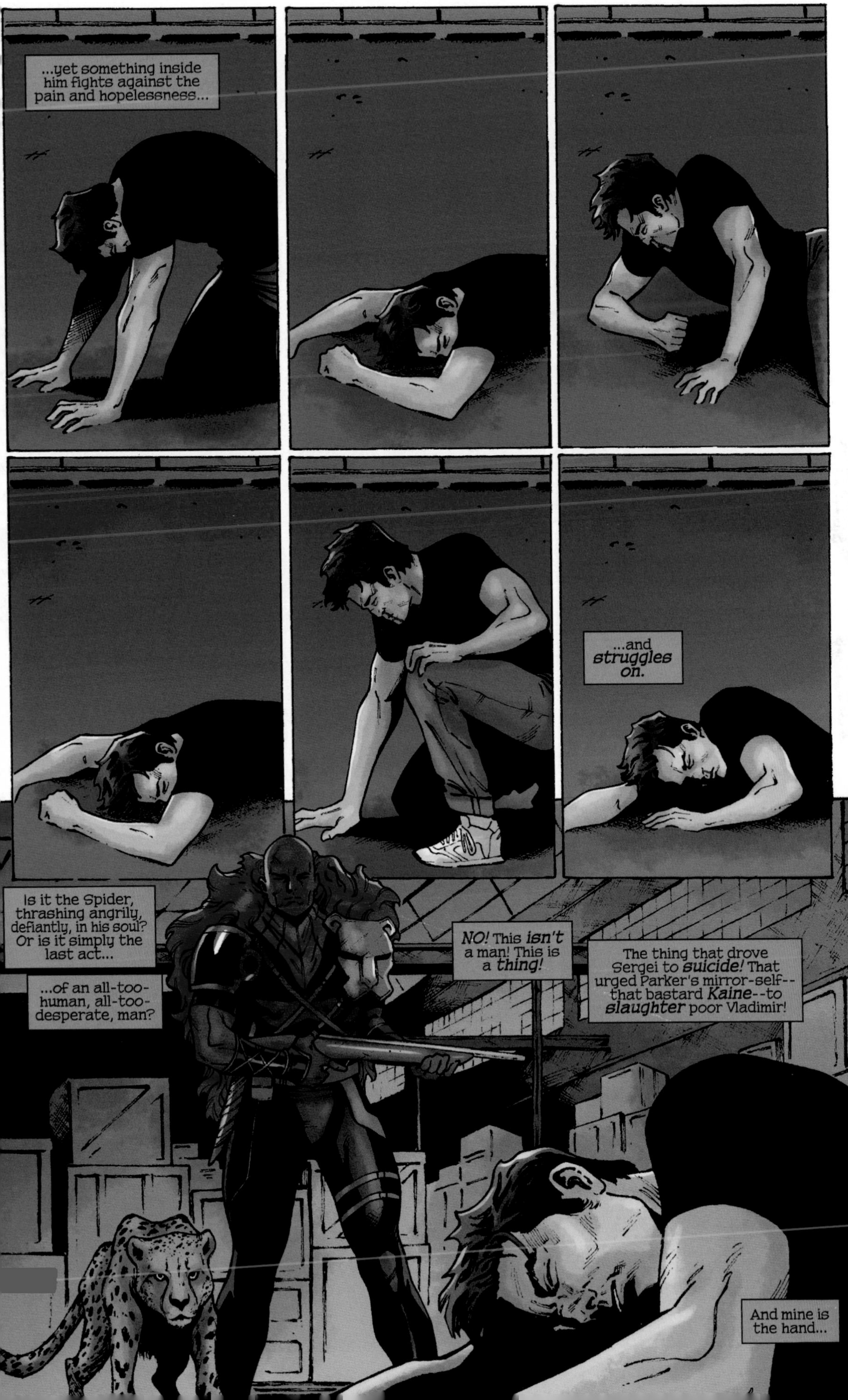
...yet something inside him fights against the pain and hopelessness...
...and struggles on.
Is it the Spider, thrashing angrily, defiantly, in his soul? Or is it simply the last act...
...of an all-too-human, all-too-desperate, man?
NO! This isn't a man! This is a thing!
The thing that drove Sergei to suicide! That urged Parker's mirror-self--that bastard Kaine--to slaughter poor Vladimir!
And mine is the hand...

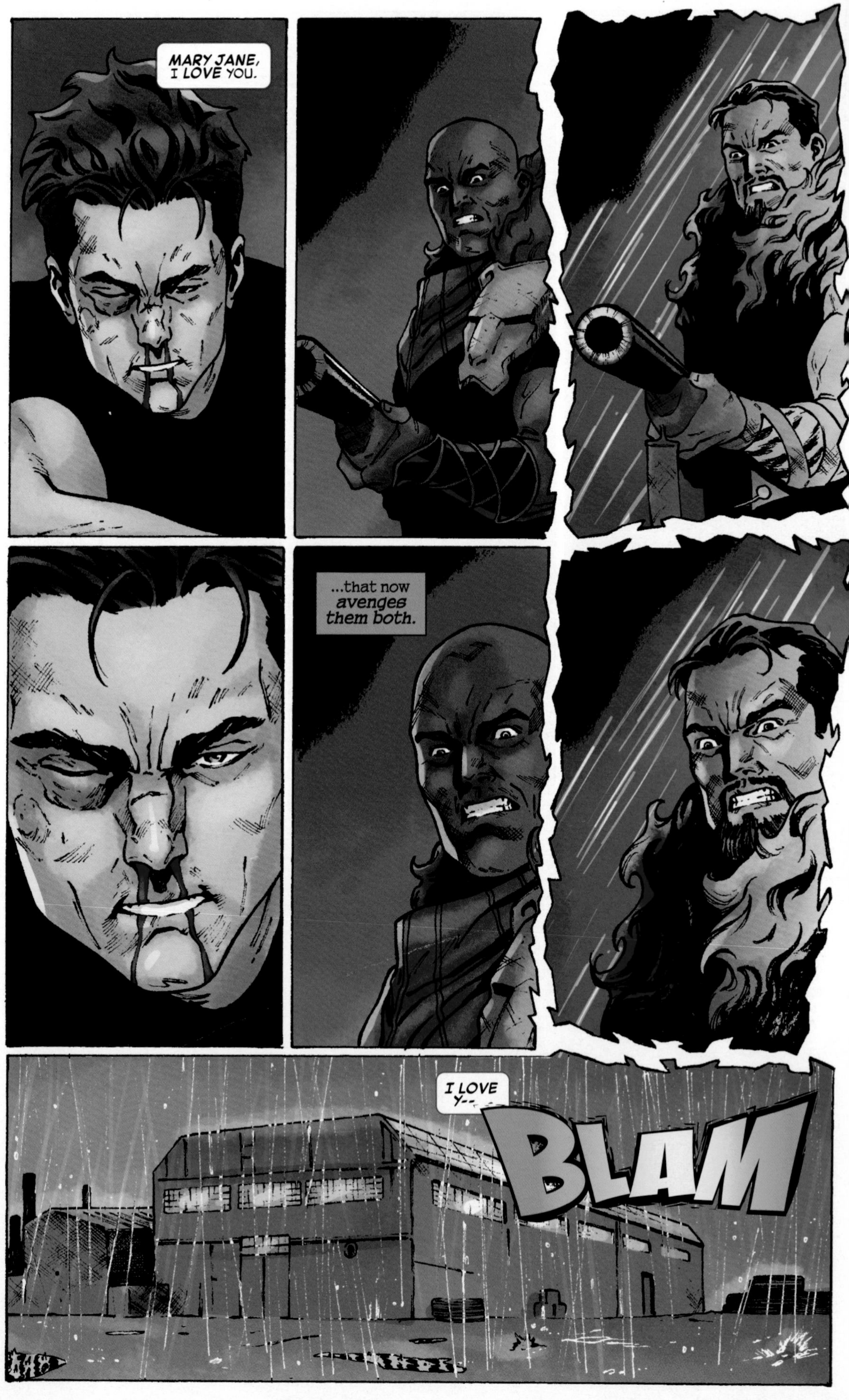
MARY JANE, I LOVE YOU.
...that now avenges them both.
I LOVE Y--
BLAM

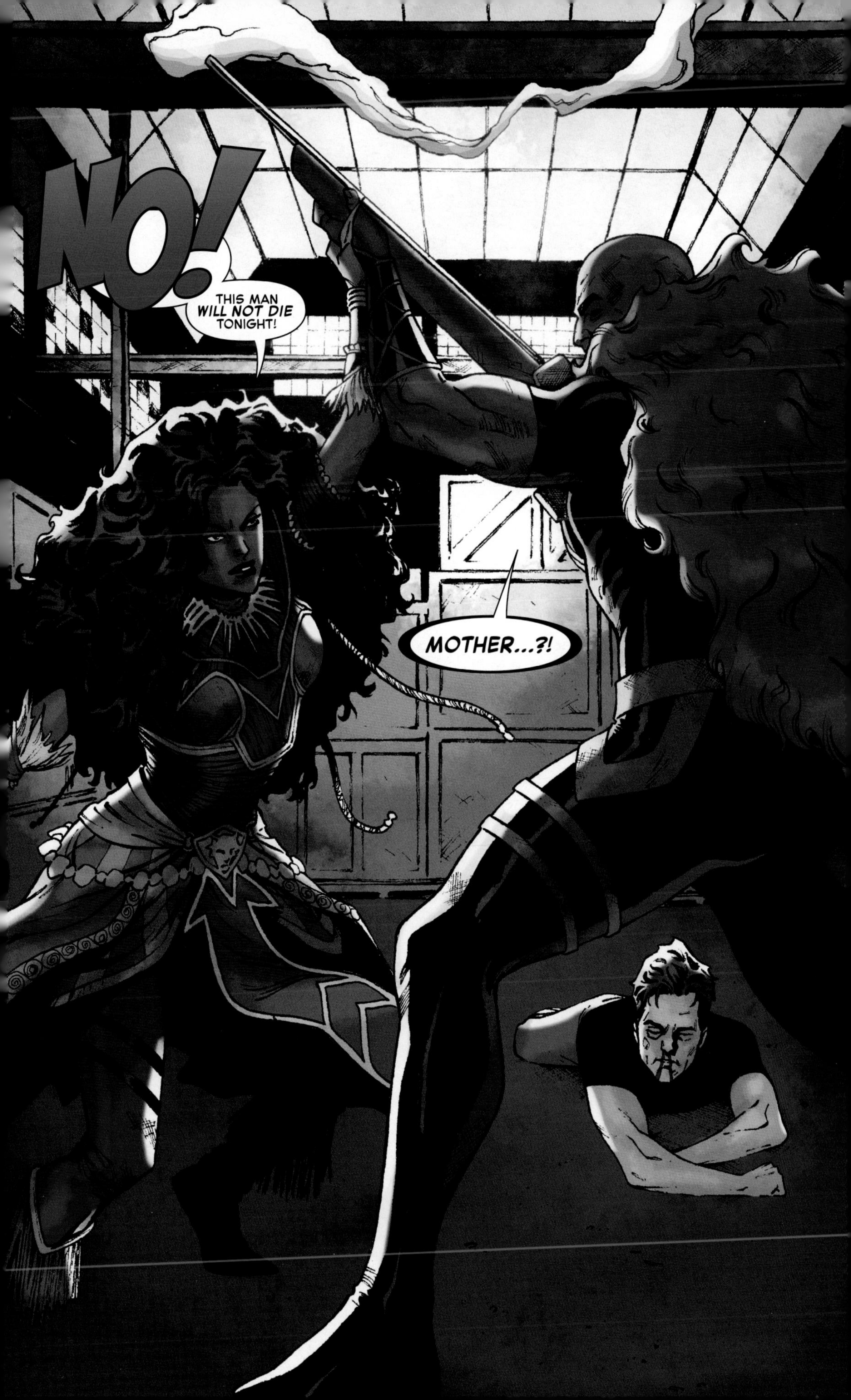
NO!
THIS MAN WILL NOT DIE TONIGHT!
MOTHER...?!

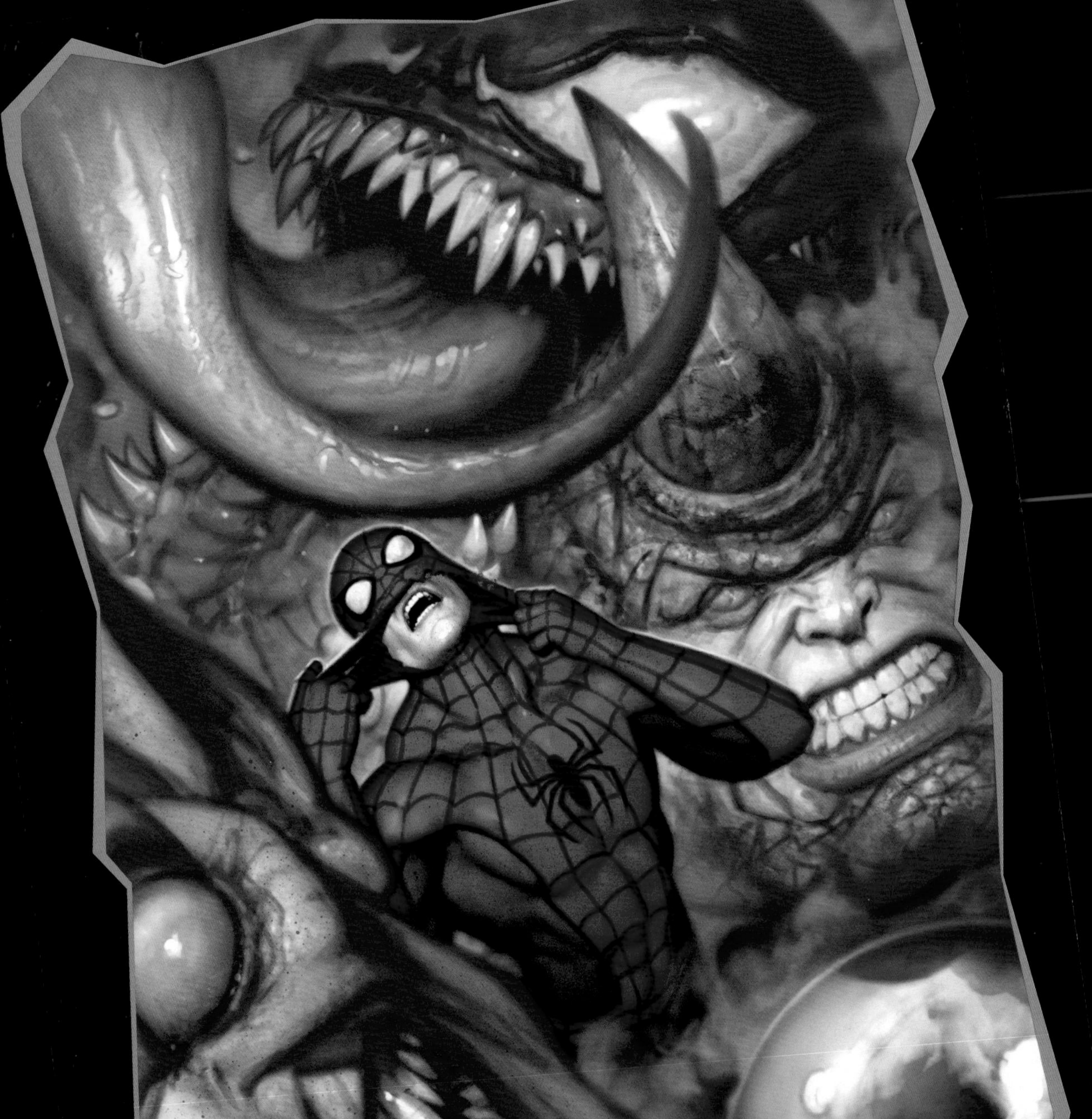
RYAN
BROWN
22

3

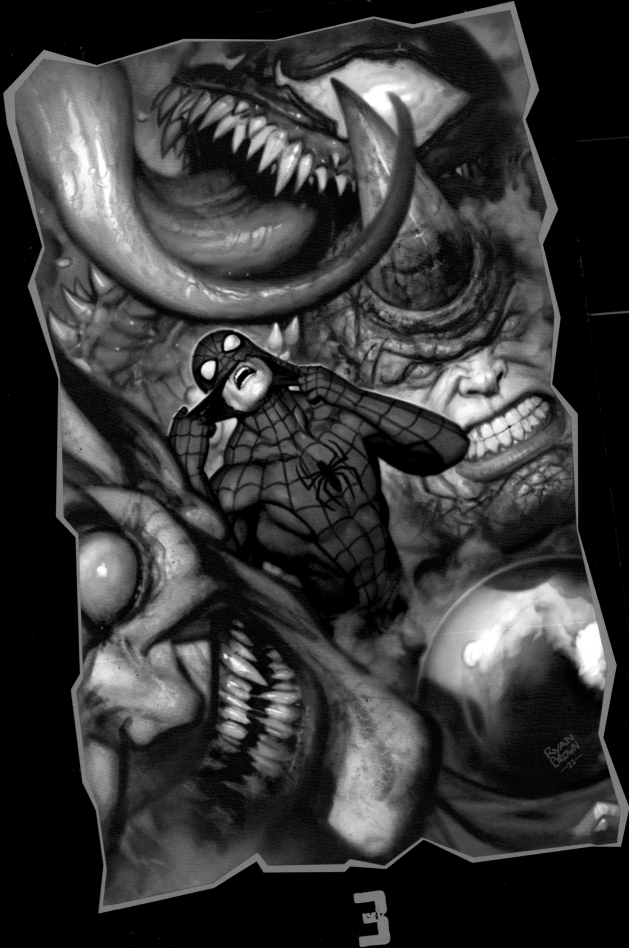

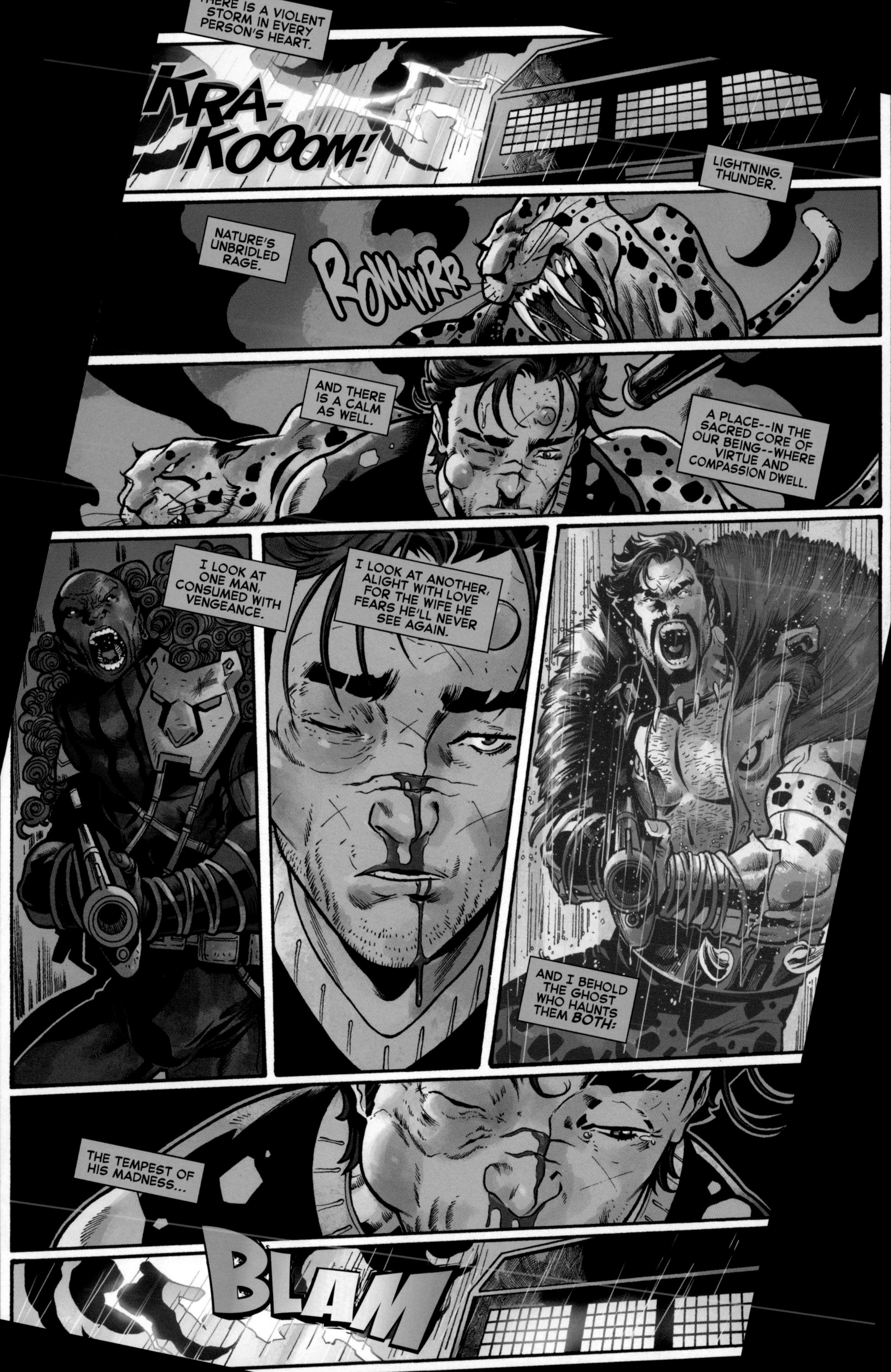
THERE IS A VIOLENT STORM IN EVERY PERSON'S HEART.
KRA-KOOOOM!
LIGHTNING. THUNDER.
NATURE'S UNBRIDLED RAGE.
RQWWRR
AND THERE IS A CALM AS WELL.
A PLACE--IN THE SACRED CORE OF OUR BEING--WHERE VIRTUE AND COMPASSION DWELL.
I LOOK AT ONE MAN, CONSUMED WITH VENGEANCE.
I LOOK AT ANOTHER, ALIGHT WITH LOVE FOR THE WIFE HE FEARS HE'LL NEVER SEE AGAIN.
AND I BEHOLD THE GHOST WHO HAUNTS THEM *BOTH*:
THE TEMPEST OF HIS MADNESS...
BLAM

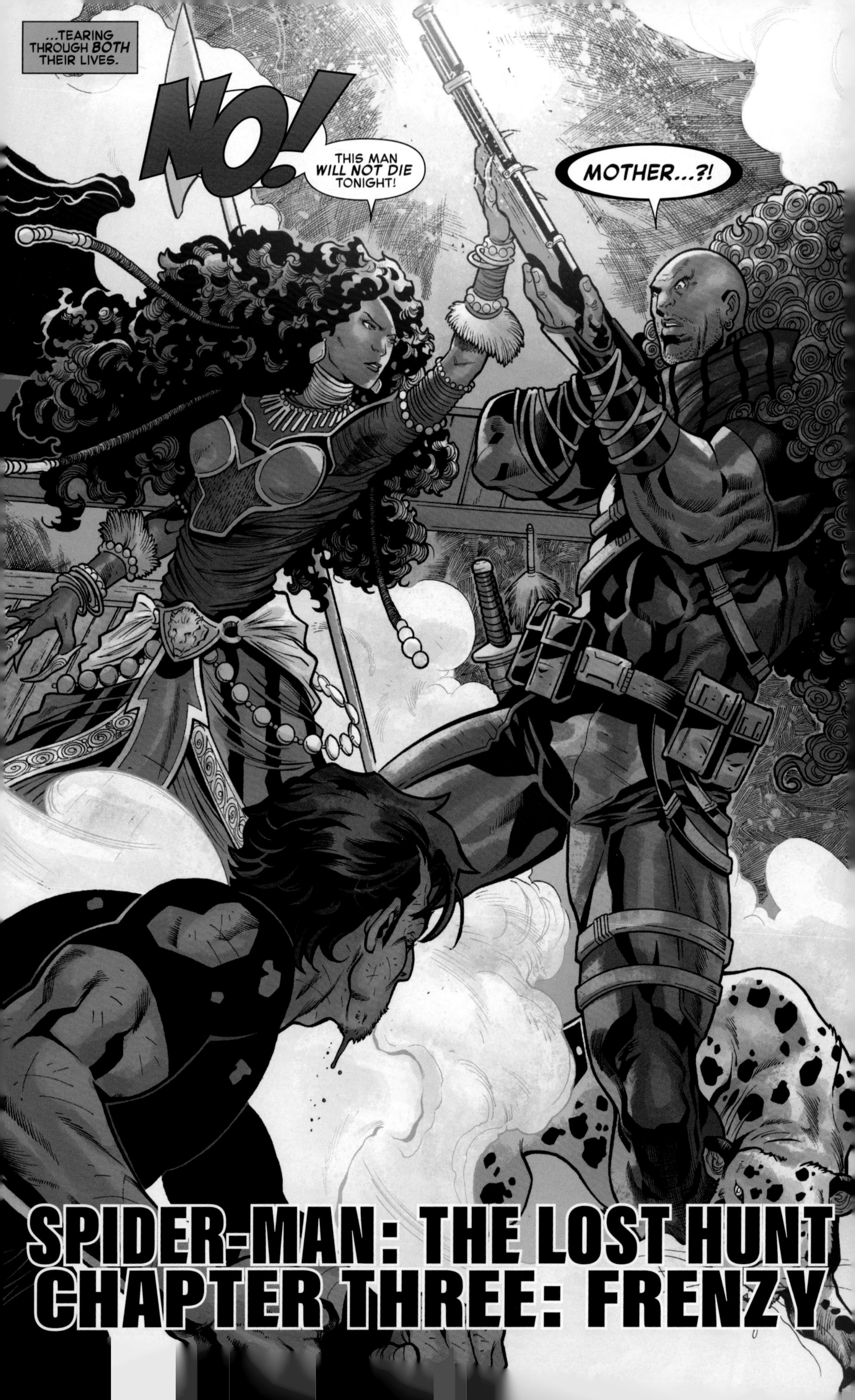
...TEARING THROUGH BOTH THEIR LIVES.
NO!
THIS MAN WILL NOT DIE TONIGHT!
MOTHER...?!
SPIDER-MAN: THE LOST HUNT
CHAPTER THREE: FRENZY

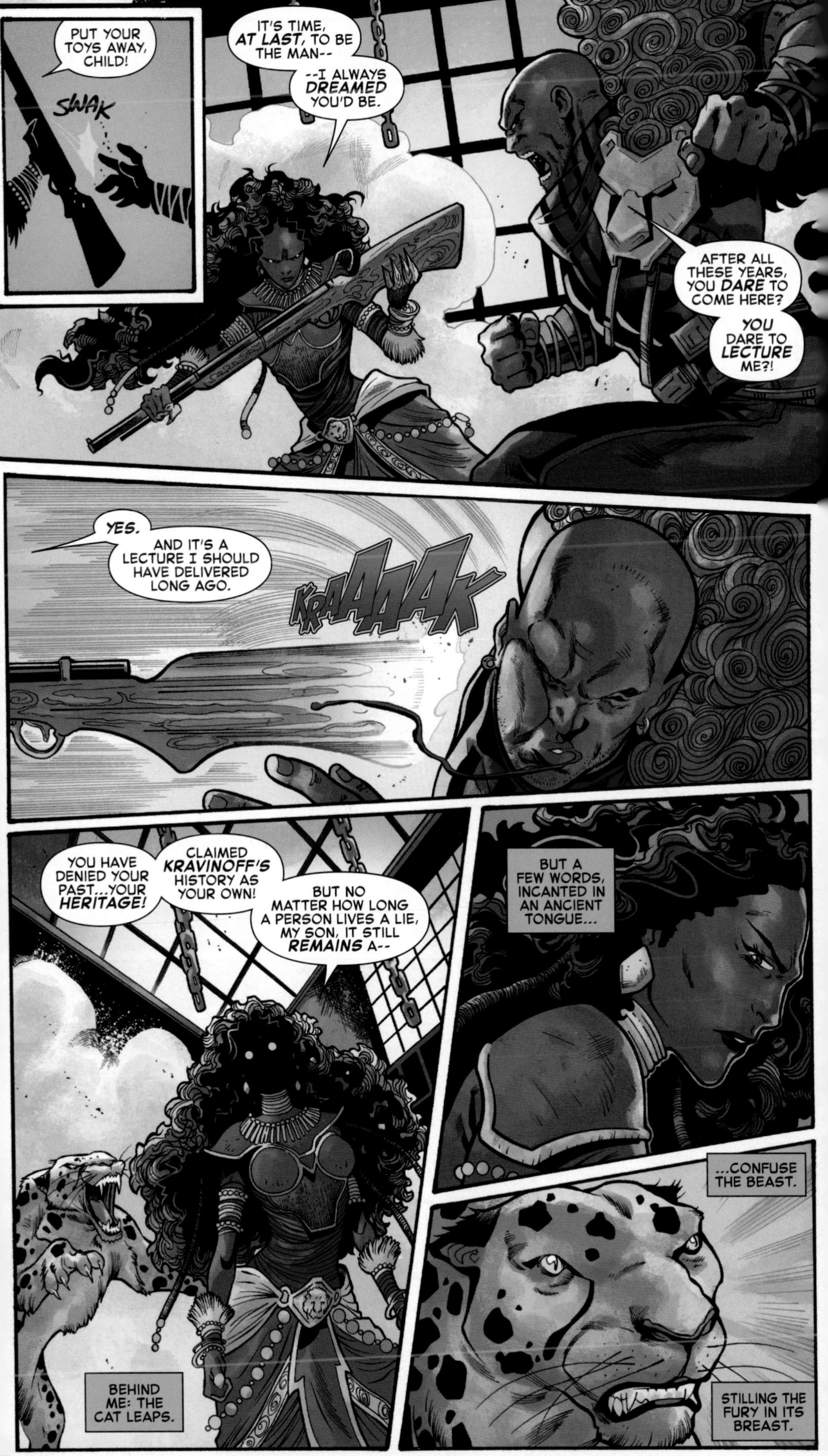
PUT YOUR TOYS AWAY, CHILD!
SWAK
IT'S TIME, AT LAST, TO BE THE MAN--
--I ALWAYS DREAMED YOU'D BE.
AFTER ALL THESE YEARS, YOU DARE TO COME HERE?
YOU DARE TO LECTURE ME?!
YES.
AND IT'S A LECTURE I SHOULD HAVE DELIVERED LONG AGO.
KRAAAAK
YOU HAVE DENIED YOUR PAST...YOUR HERITAGE!
CLAIMED KRAVINOFF'S HISTORY AS YOUR OWN!
BUT NO MATTER HOW LONG A PERSON LIVES A LIE, MY SON, IT STILL REMAINS A--
BEHIND ME: THE CAT LEAPS.
BUT A FEW WORDS, INCANTED IN AN ANCIENT TONGUE...
...CONFUSE THE BEAST.
STILLING THE FURY IN ITS BREAST.

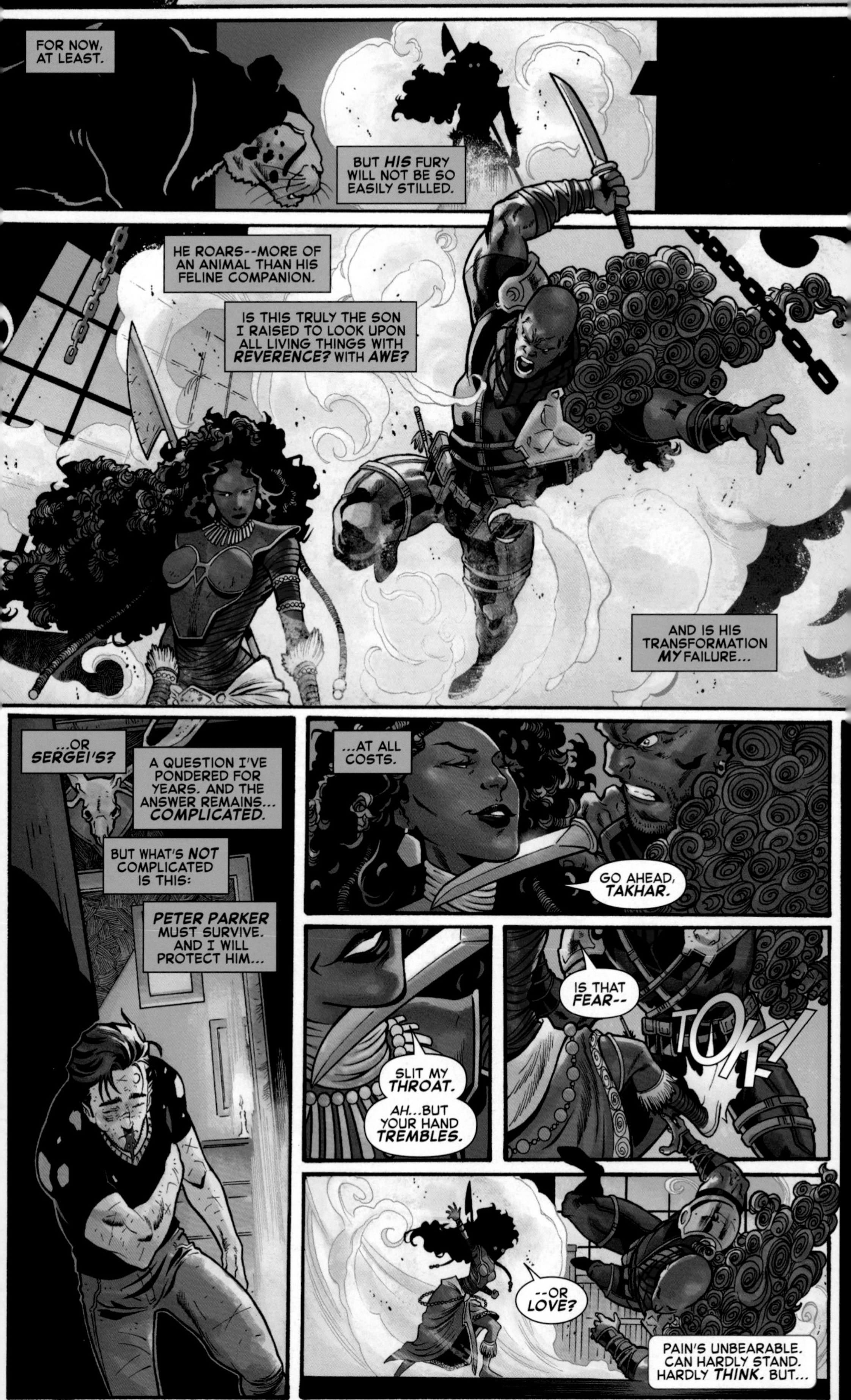
FOR NOW, AT LEAST.
BUT HIS FURY WILL NOT BE SO EASILY STILLED.
HE ROARS--MORE OF AN ANIMAL THAN HIS FELINE COMPANION.
IS THIS TRULY THE SON I RAISED TO LOOK UPON ALL LIVING THINGS WITH REVERENCE? WITH AWE?
AND IS HIS TRANSFORMATION MY FAILURE...
...OR SERGEI'S?
A QUESTION I'VE PONDERED FOR YEARS. AND THE ANSWER REMAINS... COMPLICATED.
BUT WHAT'S NOT COMPLICATED IS THIS:
PETER PARKER MUST SURVIVE. AND I WILL PROTECT HIM...
...AT ALL COSTS.
GO AHEAD, TAKHAR.
SLIT MY THROAT.
AH...BUT YOUR HAND TREMBLES.
IS THAT FEAR--
TOK!
--OR LOVE?
PAIN'S UNBEARABLE. CAN HARDLY STAND. HARDLY THINK. BUT...

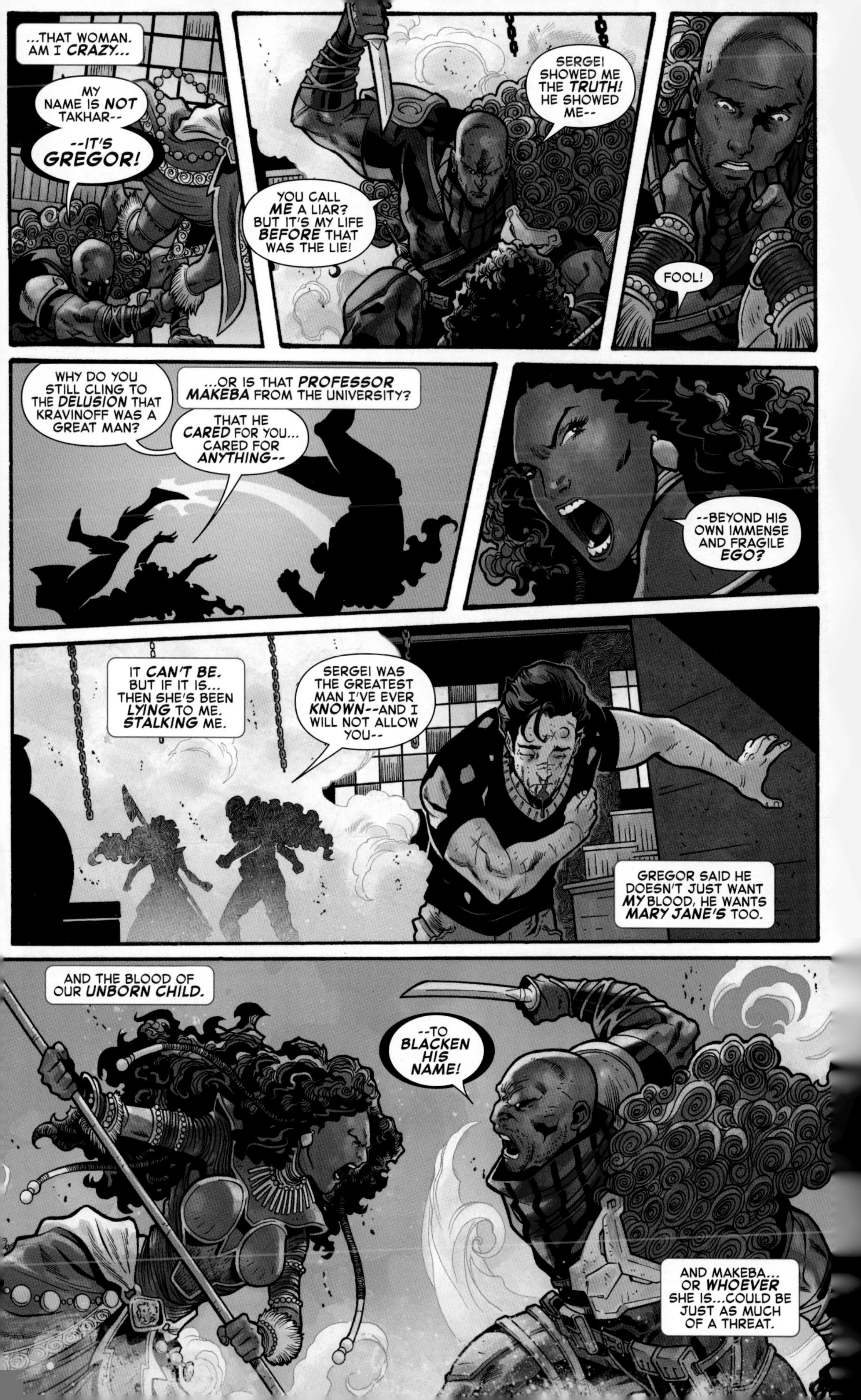

...THAT WOMAN. AM I CRAZY...
MY NAME IS NOT TAKHAR--
--IT'S GREGOR!
YOU CALL ME A LIAR? BUT IT'S MY LIFE BEFORE THAT WAS THE LIE!
SERGEI SHOWED ME THE TRUTH! HE SHOWED ME--
FOOL!
WHY DO YOU STILL CLING TO THE DELUSION THAT KRAVINOFF WAS A GREAT MAN?
...OR IS THAT PROFESSOR MAKEBA FROM THE UNIVERSITY?
THAT HE CARED FOR YOU... CARED FOR ANYTHING--
--BEYOND HIS OWN IMMENSE AND FRAGILE EGO?
IT CAN'T BE. BUT IF IT IS... THEN SHE'S BEEN LYING TO ME. STALKING ME.
SERGEI WAS THE GREATEST MAN I'VE EVER KNOWN--AND I WILL NOT ALLOW YOU--
GREGOR SAID HE DOESN'T JUST WANT MY BLOOD, HE WANTS MARY JANE'S TOO.
AND THE BLOOD OF OUR UNBORN CHILD.
--TO BLACKEN HIS NAME!
AND MAKEBA... OR WHOEVER SHE IS...COULD BE JUST AS MUCH OF A THREAT.

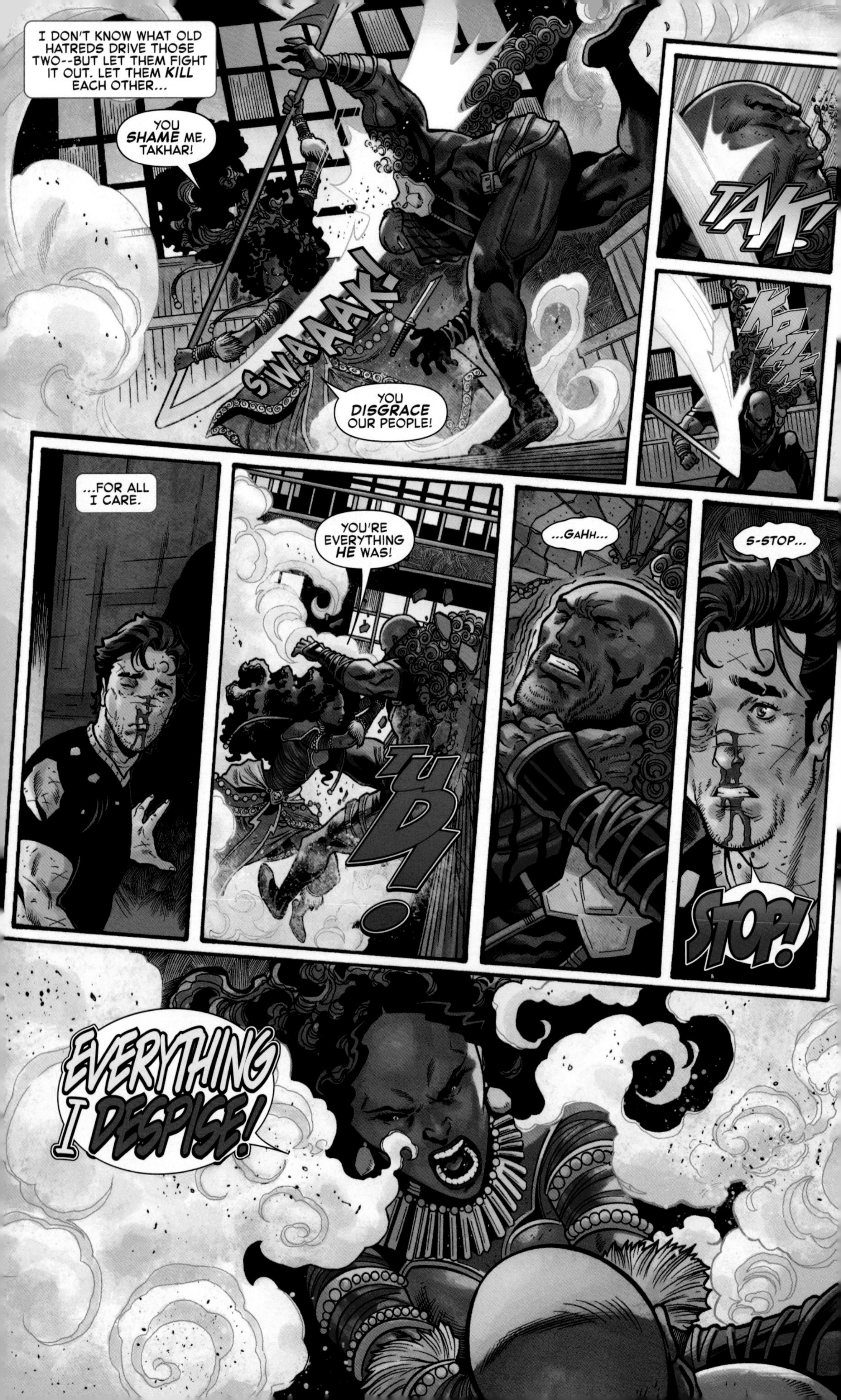
I DON'T KNOW WHAT OLD HATREDS DRIVE THOSE TWO--BUT LET THEM FIGHT IT OUT. LET THEM KILL EACH OTHER...
YOU SHAME ME, TAKHAR!
SWAAAK!
YOU DISGRACE OUR PEOPLE!
TAK!
...FOR ALL I CARE.
YOU'RE EVERYTHING HE WAS!
THUD!
...GAHH...
S-STOP...
STOP!
EVERYTHING I DESPISE!

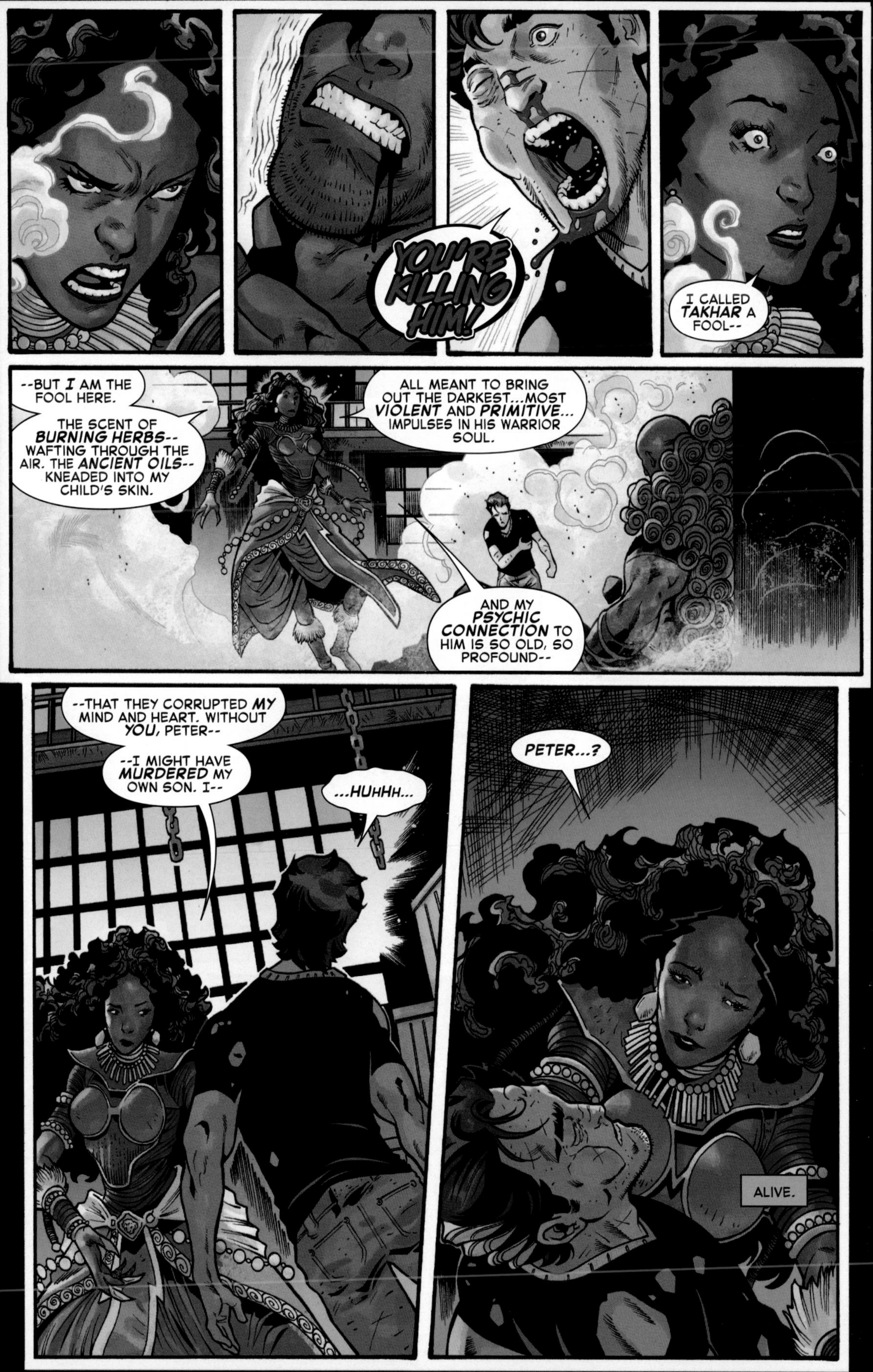
YOU'RE KILLING HIM!
I CALLED TAKHAR A FOOL--
--BUT I AM THE FOOL HERE.
THE SCENT OF BURNING HERBS-- WAFTING THROUGH THE AIR. THE ANCIENT OILS-- KNEADED INTO MY CHILD'S SKIN.
ALL MEANT TO BRING OUT THE DARKEST...MOST VIOLENT AND PRIMITIVE... IMPULSES IN HIS WARRIOR SOUL.
AND MY PSYCHIC CONNECTION TO HIM IS SO OLD, SO PROFOUND--
--THAT THEY CORRUPTED MY MIND AND HEART. WITHOUT YOU, PETER--
--I MIGHT HAVE MURDERED MY OWN SON. I--
...HUHHH...
PETER...?
ALIVE.

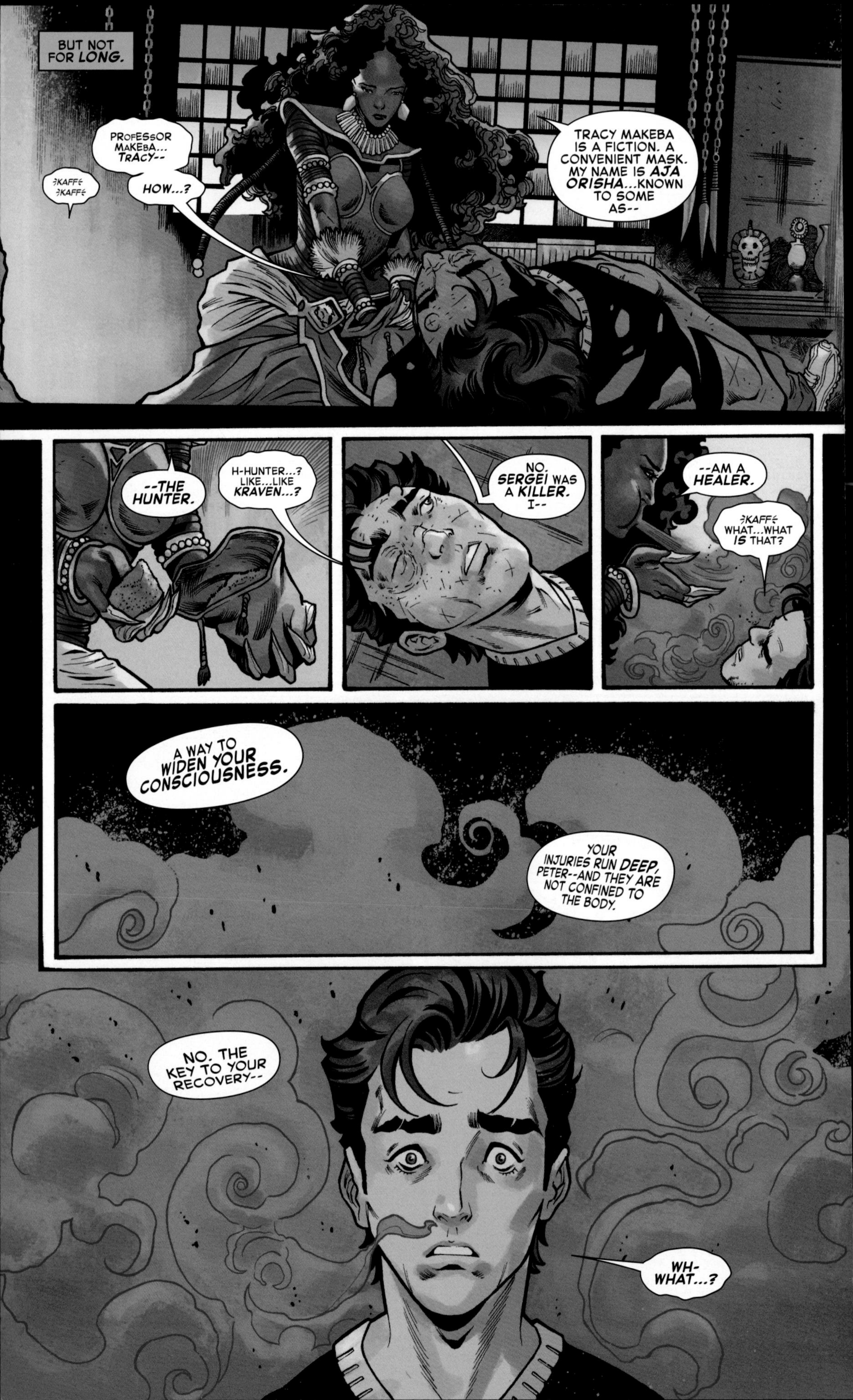
BUT NOT FOR LONG.
PROFESSOR MAKEBA... TRACY--
HOW...?
≱KAFF≰ ≱KAFF≰
TRACY MAKEBA IS A FICTION. A CONVENIENT MASK. MY NAME IS AJA ORISHA...KNOWN TO SOME AS--
--THE HUNTER.
H-HUNTER...? LIKE...LIKE KRAVEN...?
NO. SERGEI WAS A KILLER. I--
--AM A HEALER.
≱KAFF≰ WHAT...WHAT IS THAT?
A WAY TO WIDEN YOUR CONSCIOUSNESS.
YOUR INJURIES RUN DEEP, PETER--AND THEY ARE NOT CONFINED TO THE BODY.
NO. THE KEY TO YOUR RECOVERY--
WH-WHAT...?

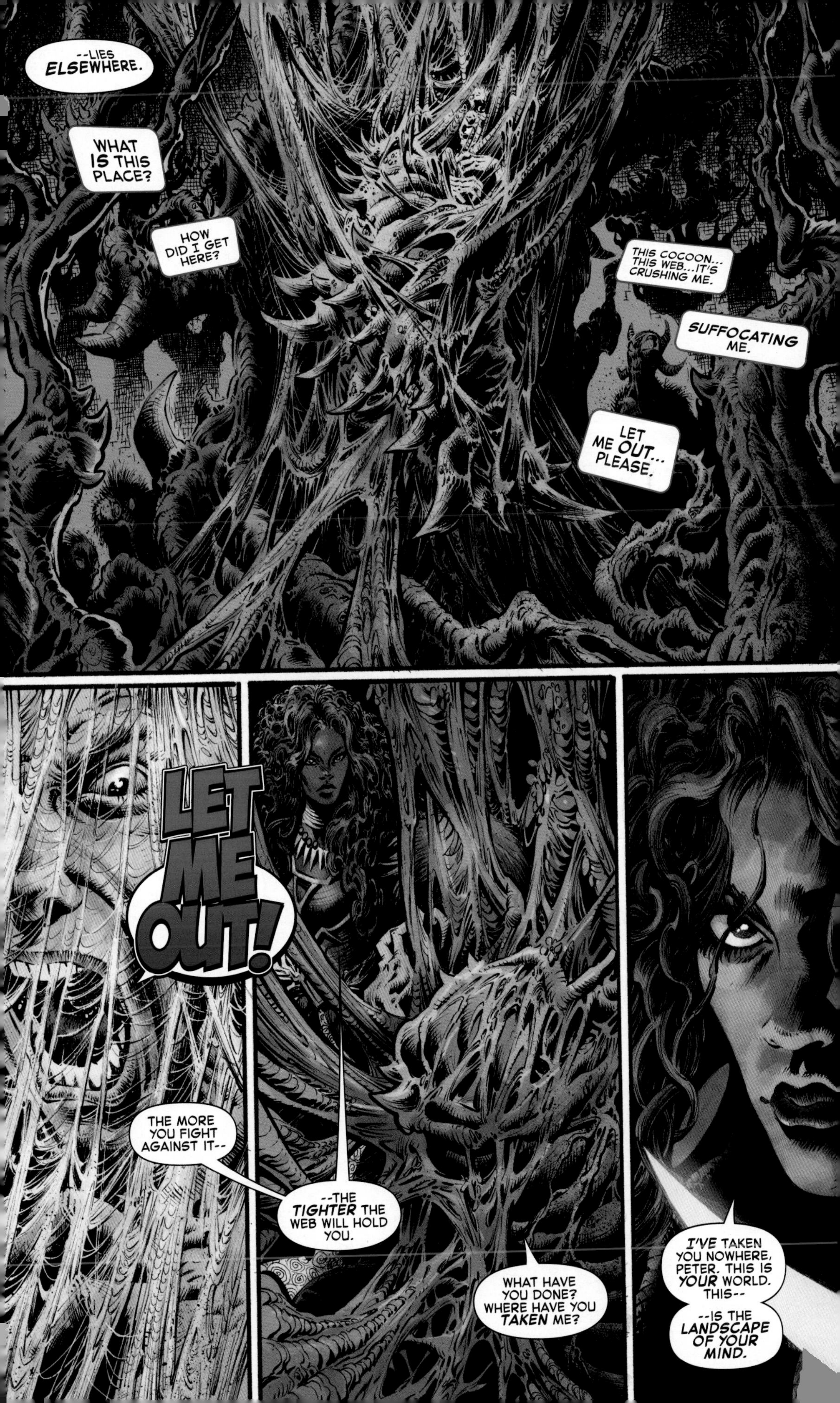

--LIES ELSEWHERE.
WHAT IS THIS PLACE?
HOW DID I GET HERE?
THIS COCOON... THIS WEB...IT'S CRUSHING ME.
SUFFOCATING ME.
LET ME OUT... PLEASE.
LET ME OUT!
THE MORE YOU FIGHT AGAINST IT--
--THE TIGHTER THE WEB WILL HOLD YOU.
WHAT HAVE YOU DONE? WHERE HAVE YOU TAKEN ME?
I'VE TAKEN YOU NOWHERE, PETER. THIS IS YOUR WORLD. THIS--
--IS THE LANDSCAPE OF YOUR MIND.

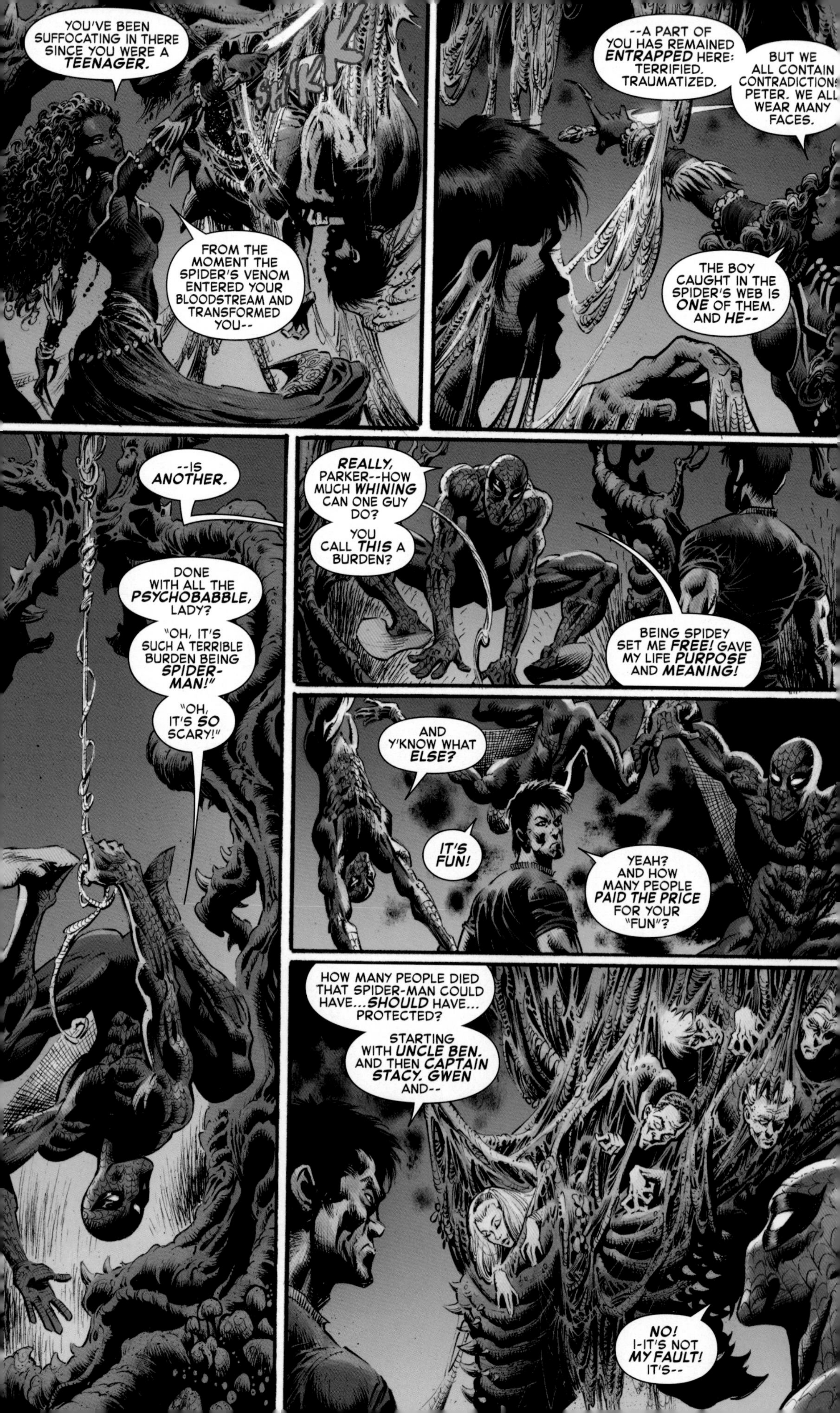
YOU'VE BEEN SUFFOCATING IN THERE SINCE YOU WERE A TEENAGER.
SHKK
FROM THE MOMENT THE SPIDER'S VENOM ENTERED YOUR BLOODSTREAM AND TRANSFORMED YOU--
--A PART OF YOU HAS REMAINED ENTRAPPED HERE: TERRIFIED. TRAUMATIZED.
BUT WE ALL CONTAIN CONTRADICTIONS, PETER. WE ALL WEAR MANY FACES.
THE BOY CAUGHT IN THE SPIDER'S WEB IS ONE OF THEM. AND HE--
--IS ANOTHER.
DONE WITH ALL THE PSYCHOBABBLE, LADY?
"OH, IT'S SUCH A TERRIBLE BURDEN BEING SPIDER-MAN!"
"OH, IT'S SO SCARY!"
REALLY, PARKER--HOW MUCH WHINING CAN ONE GUY DO?
YOU CALL THIS A BURDEN?
BEING SPIDEY SET ME FREE! GAVE MY LIFE PURPOSE AND MEANING!
AND Y'KNOW WHAT ELSE?
IT'S FUN!
YEAH? AND HOW MANY PEOPLE PAID THE PRICE FOR YOUR "FUN"?
HOW MANY PEOPLE DIED THAT SPIDER-MAN COULD HAVE...SHOULD HAVE... PROTECTED?
STARTING WITH UNCLE BEN. AND THEN CAPTAIN STACY. GWEN AND--
NO! I-IT'S NOT MY FAULT! IT'S--

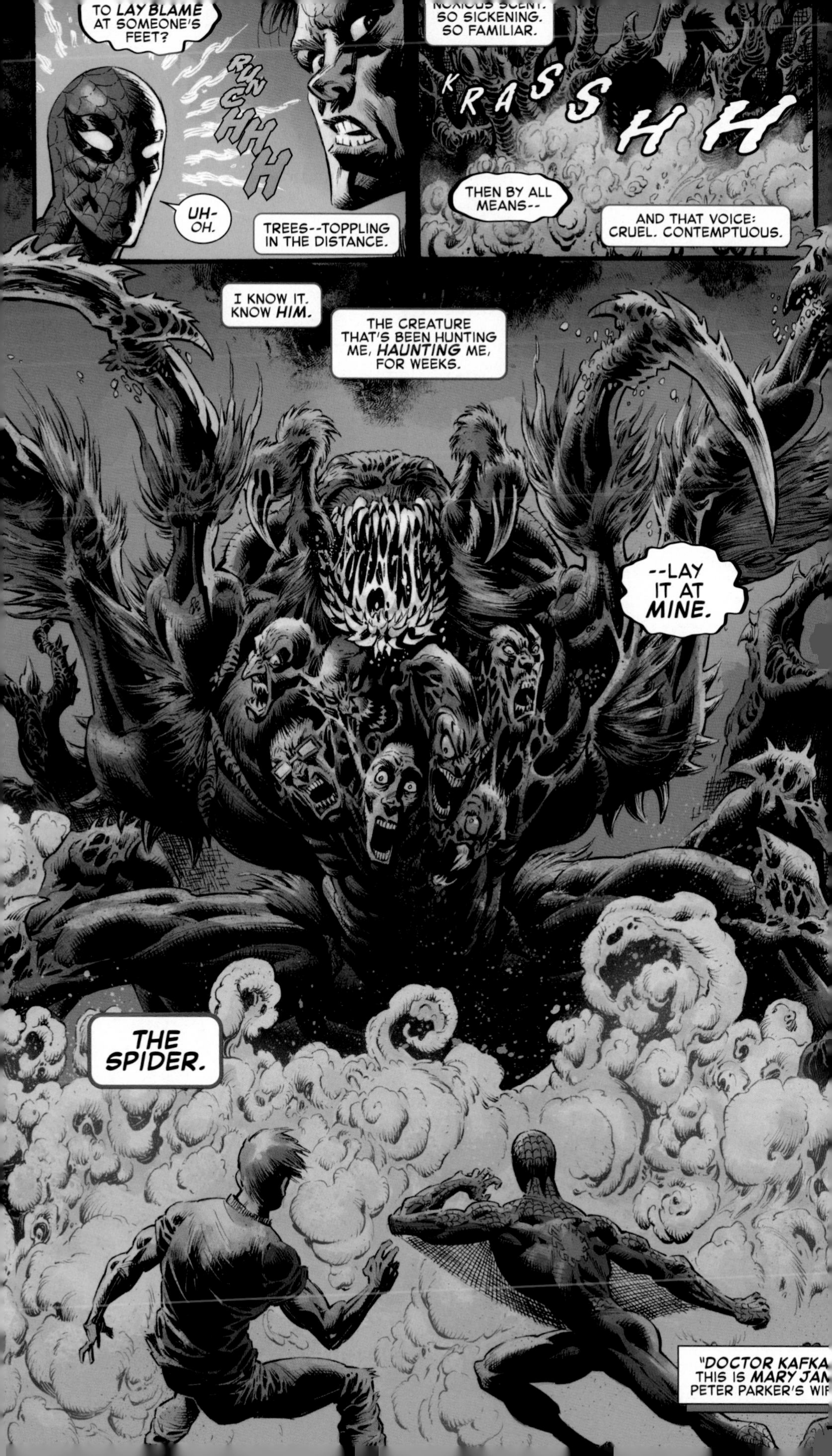

TO LAY BLAME AT SOMEONE'S FEET?
RUNCHHHH
UH-OH.
TREES--TOPPLING IN THE DISTANCE.
SO SICKENING. SO FAMILIAR.
KRASSHH
THEN BY ALL MEANS--
AND THAT VOICE: CRUEL. CONTEMPTUOUS.
I KNOW IT. KNOW HIM.
THE CREATURE THAT'S BEEN HUNTING ME, HAUNTING ME, FOR WEEKS.
--LAY IT AT MINE.
THE SPIDER.
"DOCTOR KAFKA THIS IS MARY JAN PETER PARKER'S WIF

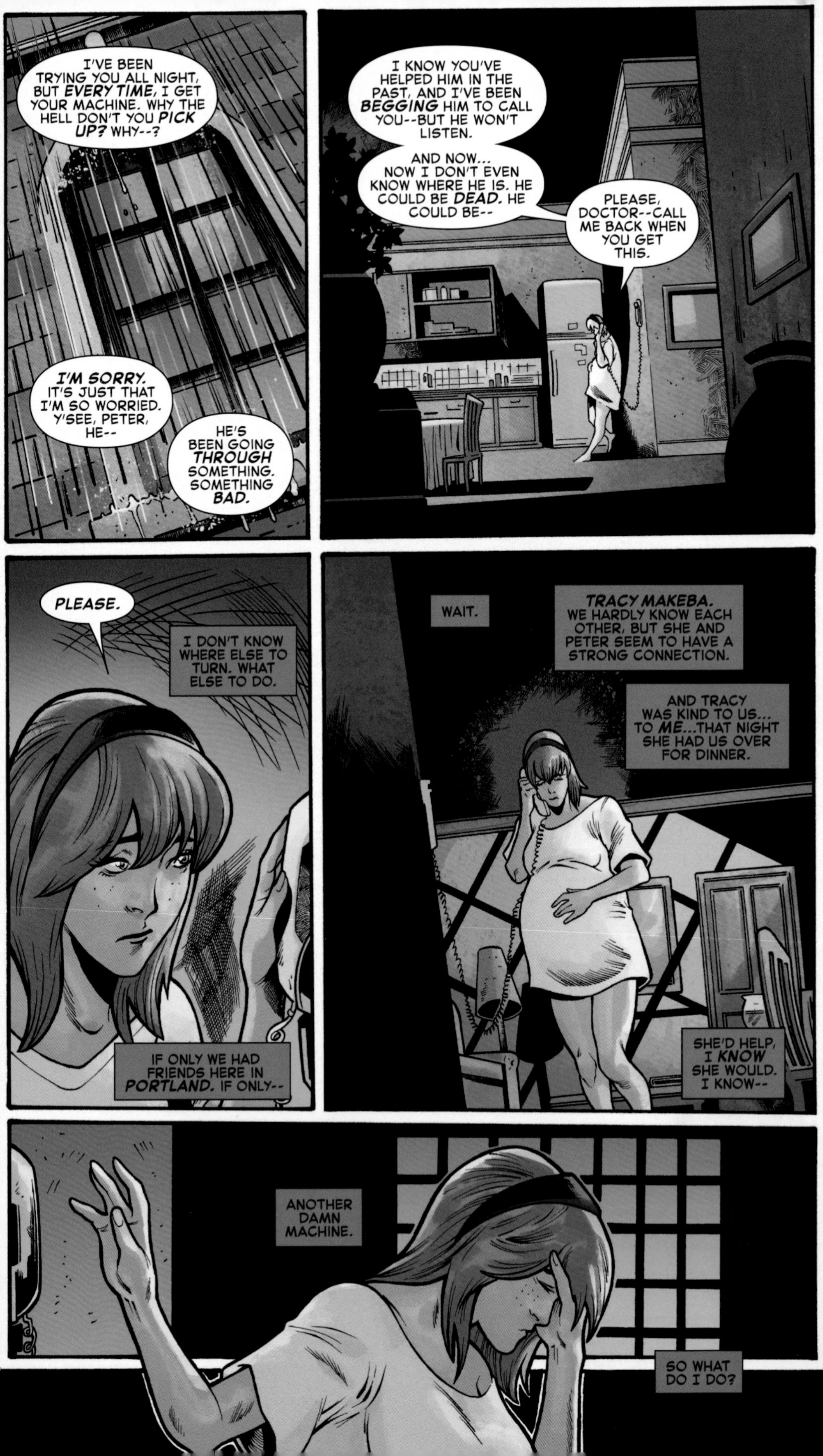
I'VE BEEN TRYING YOU ALL NIGHT, BUT *EVERY TIME,* I GET YOUR MACHINE. WHY THE HELL DON'T YOU *PICK UP?* WHY--?
I'M SORRY. IT'S JUST THAT I'M SO WORRIED. Y'SEE, PETER, HE--
HE'S BEEN GOING *THROUGH* SOMETHING. SOMETHING *BAD.*
I KNOW YOU'VE HELPED HIM IN THE PAST, AND I'VE BEEN *BEGGING* HIM TO CALL YOU--BUT HE WON'T LISTEN.
AND NOW... NOW I DON'T EVEN KNOW WHERE HE IS. HE COULD BE *DEAD.* HE COULD BE--
PLEASE, DOCTOR--CALL ME BACK WHEN YOU GET THIS.
PLEASE.
I DON'T KNOW WHERE ELSE TO TURN. WHAT ELSE TO DO.
IF ONLY WE HAD FRIENDS HERE IN *PORTLAND.* IF ONLY--
WAIT.
TRACY MAKEBA. WE HARDLY KNOW EACH OTHER, BUT SHE AND PETER SEEM TO HAVE A STRONG CONNECTION.
AND TRACY WAS KIND TO US... TO *ME*...THAT NIGHT SHE HAD US OVER FOR DINNER.
SHE'D HELP, I *KNOW* SHE WOULD. I KNOW--
ANOTHER DAMN MACHINE.
SO WHAT DO I DO?

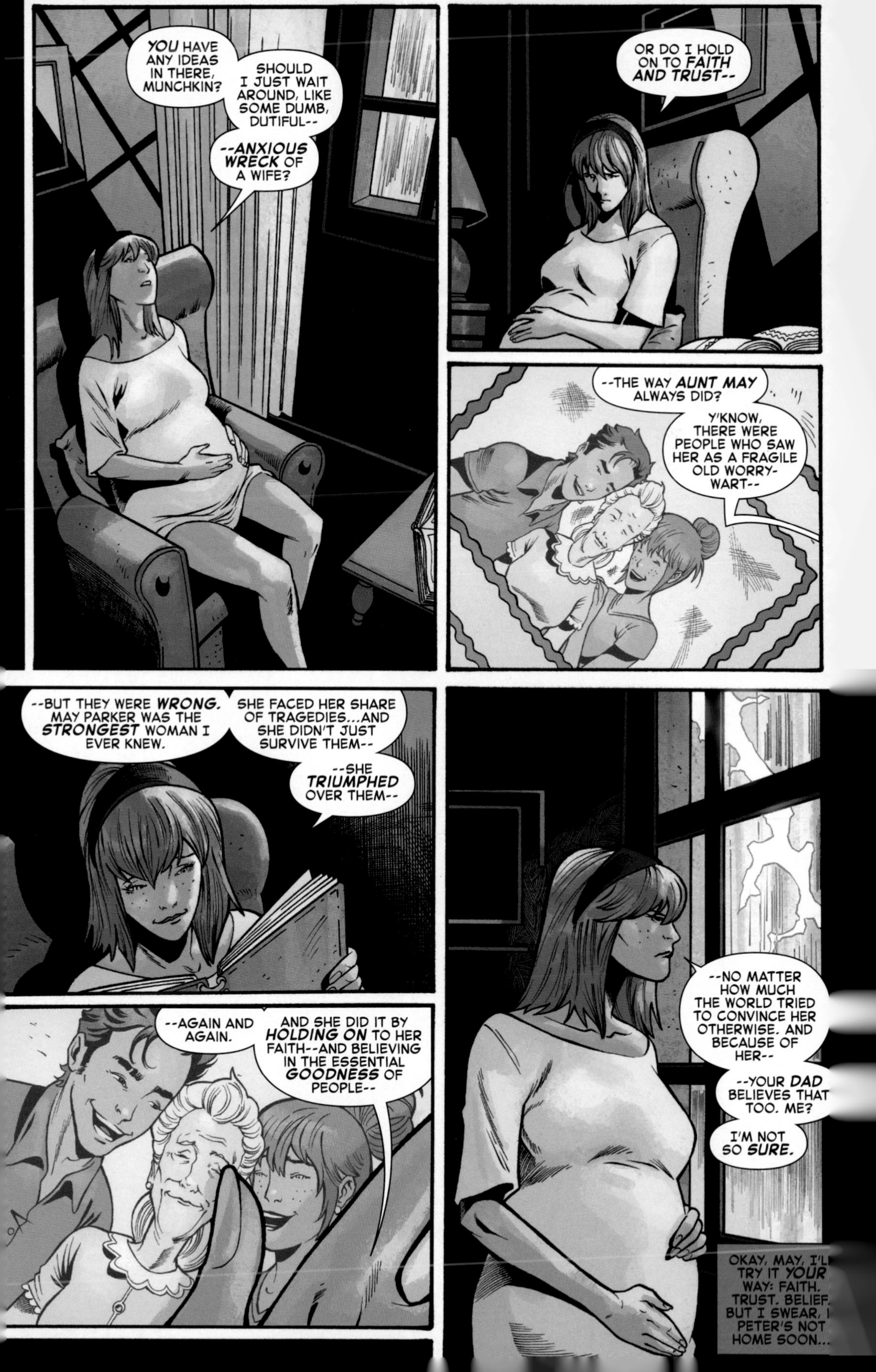

YOU HAVE ANY IDEAS IN THERE, MUNCHKIN?
SHOULD I JUST WAIT AROUND, LIKE SOME DUMB, DUTIFUL--
--ANXIOUS WRECK OF A WIFE?
OR DO I HOLD ON TO FAITH AND TRUST--
--THE WAY AUNT MAY ALWAYS DID?
Y'KNOW, THERE WERE PEOPLE WHO SAW HER AS A FRAGILE OLD WORRY-WART--
--BUT THEY WERE WRONG. MAY PARKER WAS THE STRONGEST WOMAN I EVER KNEW.
SHE FACED HER SHARE OF TRAGEDIES...AND SHE DIDN'T JUST SURVIVE THEM--
--SHE TRIUMPHED OVER THEM--
--AGAIN AND AGAIN.
AND SHE DID IT BY HOLDING ON TO HER FAITH--AND BELIEVING IN THE ESSENTIAL GOODNESS OF PEOPLE--
--NO MATTER HOW MUCH THE WORLD TRIED TO CONVINCE HER OTHERWISE. AND BECAUSE OF HER--
--YOUR DAD BELIEVES THAT TOO. ME?
I'M NOT SO SURE.
OKAY, MAY, I'L TRY IT YOUR WAY: FAITH. TRUST. BELIEF. BUT I SWEAR, I PETER'S NOT HOME SOON...

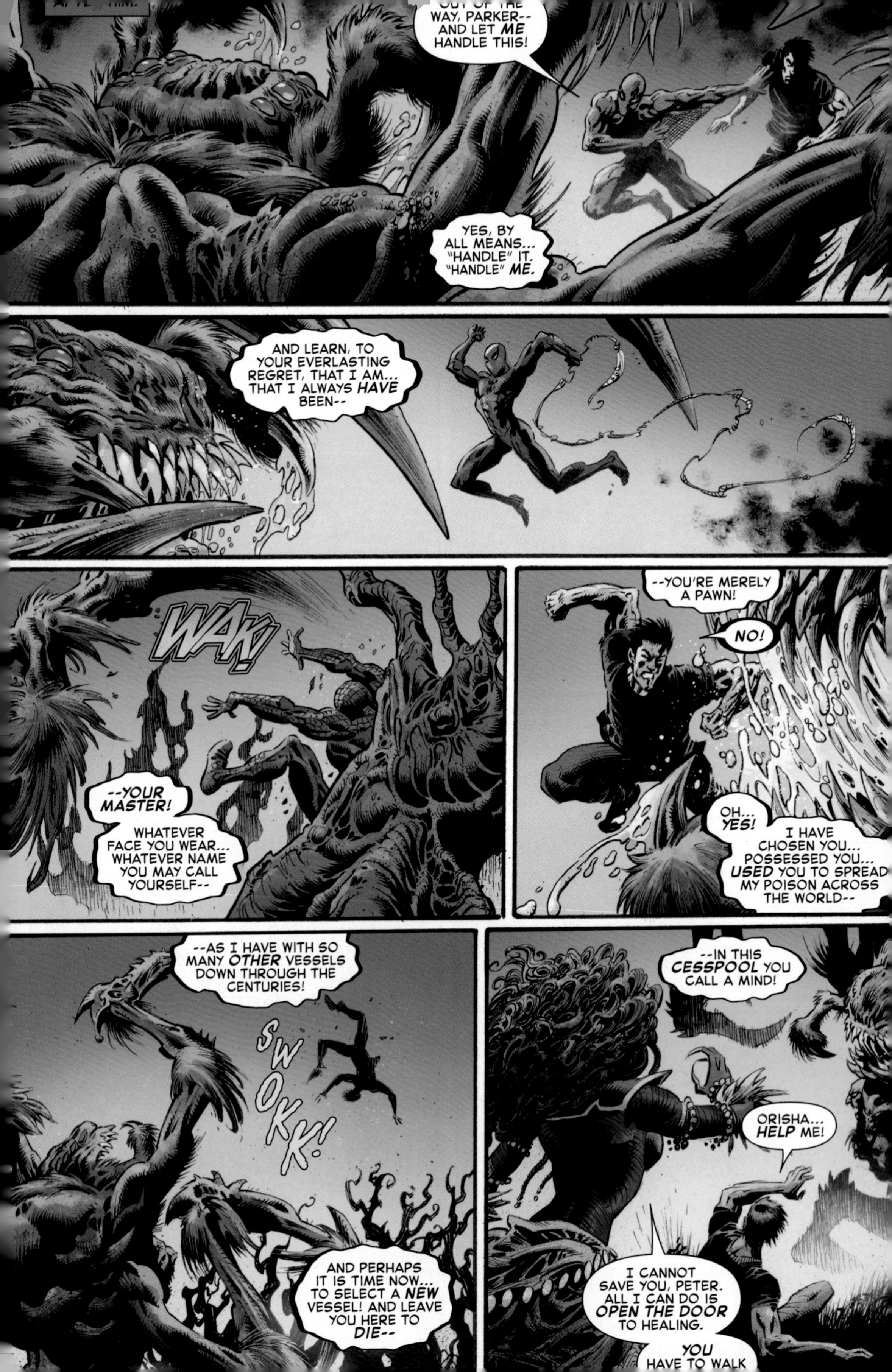

WAY, PARKER-- AND LET ME HANDLE THIS!
YES, BY ALL MEANS... "HANDLE" IT. "HANDLE" ME.
AND LEARN, TO YOUR EVERLASTING REGRET, THAT I AM... THAT I ALWAYS HAVE BEEN--
WAK!
--YOUR MASTER!
WHATEVER FACE YOU WEAR... WHATEVER NAME YOU MAY CALL YOURSELF--
--YOU'RE MERELY A PAWN!
NO!
OH... YES!
I HAVE CHOSEN YOU... POSSESSED YOU... USED YOU TO SPREAD MY POISON ACROSS THE WORLD--
--AS I HAVE WITH SO MANY OTHER VESSELS DOWN THROUGH THE CENTURIES!
SWOKK!
AND PERHAPS IT IS TIME NOW... TO SELECT A NEW VESSEL! AND LEAVE YOU HERE TO DIE--
--IN THIS CESSPOOL YOU CALL A MIND!
ORISHA... HELP ME!
I CANNOT SAVE YOU, PETER. ALL I CAN DO IS OPEN THE DOOR TO HEALING.
YOU HAVE TO WALK

--ON YOUR **OWN.**

I FEEL THE SPIDER'S CONSCIOUSNESS PULSING, *WRITHING,* ALL AROUND ME. DRAGGING ME DOWN.

DEVOURING ME.

I LOOK TO THE OTHER ONE...THE OTHER *ME*...FOR SALVATION...

...BUT HE'S *DYING.*

AND I'M *ALONE.*

BUT...BUT HAVEN'T I *ALWAYS* BEEN ALONE?

SPIDER-MAN ISN'T SOME SEPARATE ENTITY. SOMETHING THAT EXISTS *OUTSIDE* MYSELF.

FOR BETTER OR WORSE...MASK *ON* OR MASK *OFF*...

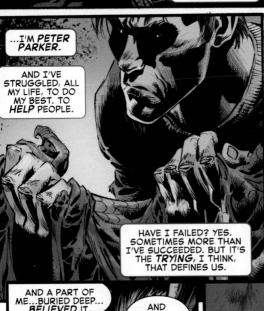

...I'M PETER PARKER.

AND I'VE STRUGGLED, ALL MY LIFE, TO DO MY BEST. TO *HELP* PEOPLE.

HAVE I FAILED? YES. SOMETIMES MORE THAN I'VE SUCCEEDED. BUT IT'S THE *TRYING,* I THINK, THAT DEFINES US.

THAT MAKES US *HUMAN.*

THERE...THERE *IS* NO SPIDER. NO ANCIENT, EVIL ENTITY.

INDEED. THAT WAS *KRAVEN'S* DELUSION. KRAVEN'S *MADNESS.*

HE COULDN'T EXPLAIN THE TERRIBLE TRAGEDIES HE'D KNOWN IN HIS LIFE, SO HIS TROUBLED MIND CREATED A MONSTER--

--AND *PROJECTED* IT ONTO YOU.

AND A PART OF ME...BURIED DEEP... *BELIEVED* IT.

MADE IT A SYMBOL OF ALL THE TRAGEDIES IN MY *OWN* LIFE.

AND GREGOR *MAGNIFIED* THAT BELIEF. USED IT AGAINST YOU.

I AM THE SPIDER! I WILL CONSUME YOU! I WILL--

YOU'LL DO NOTHING.

BECAUSE *YOU'RE* NOT REAL.

GONE. *FOREVER,* I HOPE.

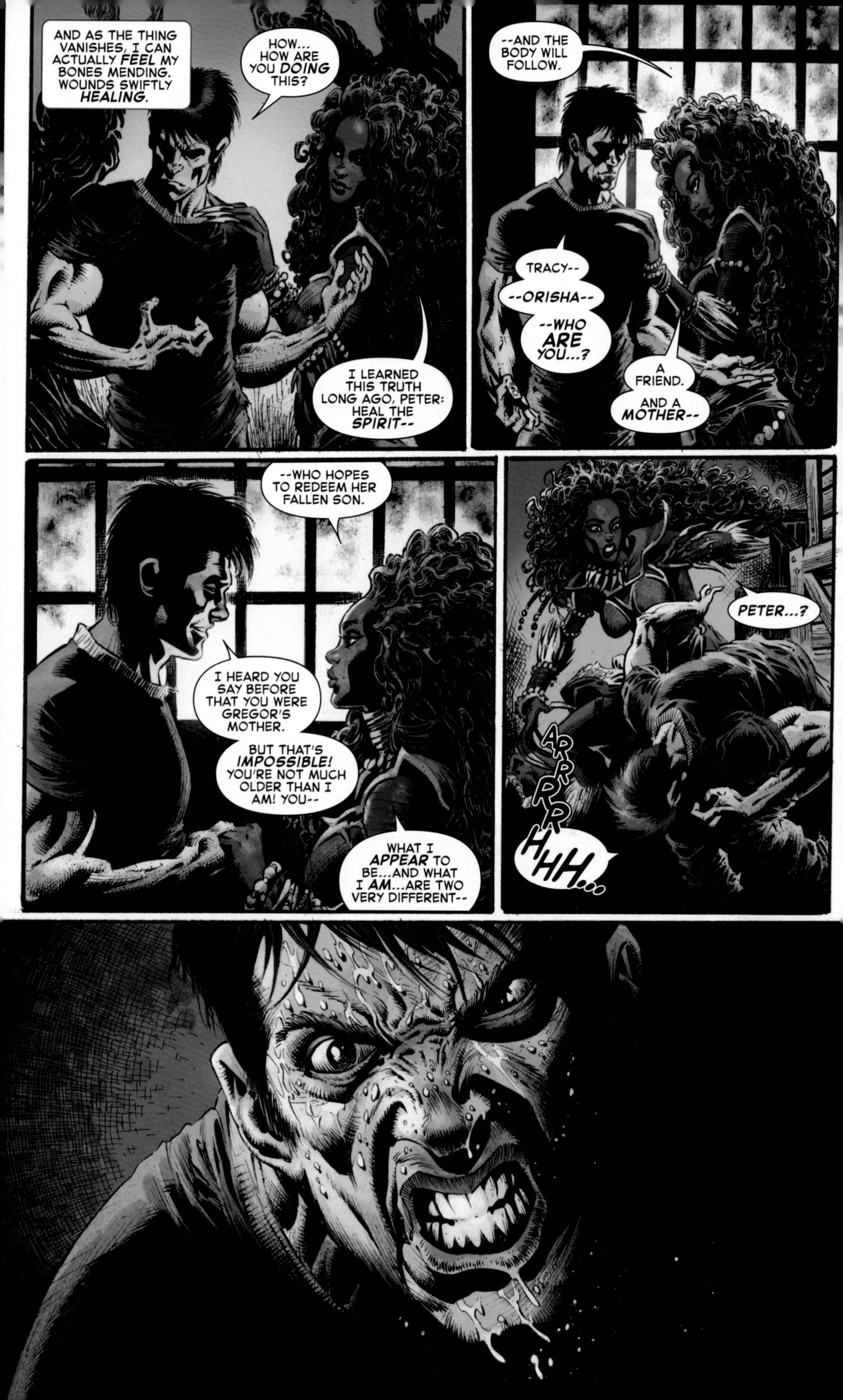
AND AS THE THING VANISHES, I CAN ACTUALLY FEEL MY BONES MENDING. WOUNDS SWIFTLY HEALING.
HOW... HOW ARE YOU DOING THIS?
I LEARNED THIS TRUTH LONG AGO, PETER: HEAL THE SPIRIT--
--AND THE BODY WILL FOLLOW.
TRACY--
--ORISHA--
--WHO ARE YOU...?
A FRIEND.
AND A MOTHER--
--WHO HOPES TO REDEEM HER FALLEN SON.
I HEARD YOU SAY BEFORE THAT YOU WERE GREGOR'S MOTHER.
BUT THAT'S IMPOSSIBLE! YOU'RE NOT MUCH OLDER THAN I AM! YOU--
WHAT I APPEAR TO BE...AND WHAT I AM...ARE TWO VERY DIFFERENT--
PETER...?
ARRRRHHH...

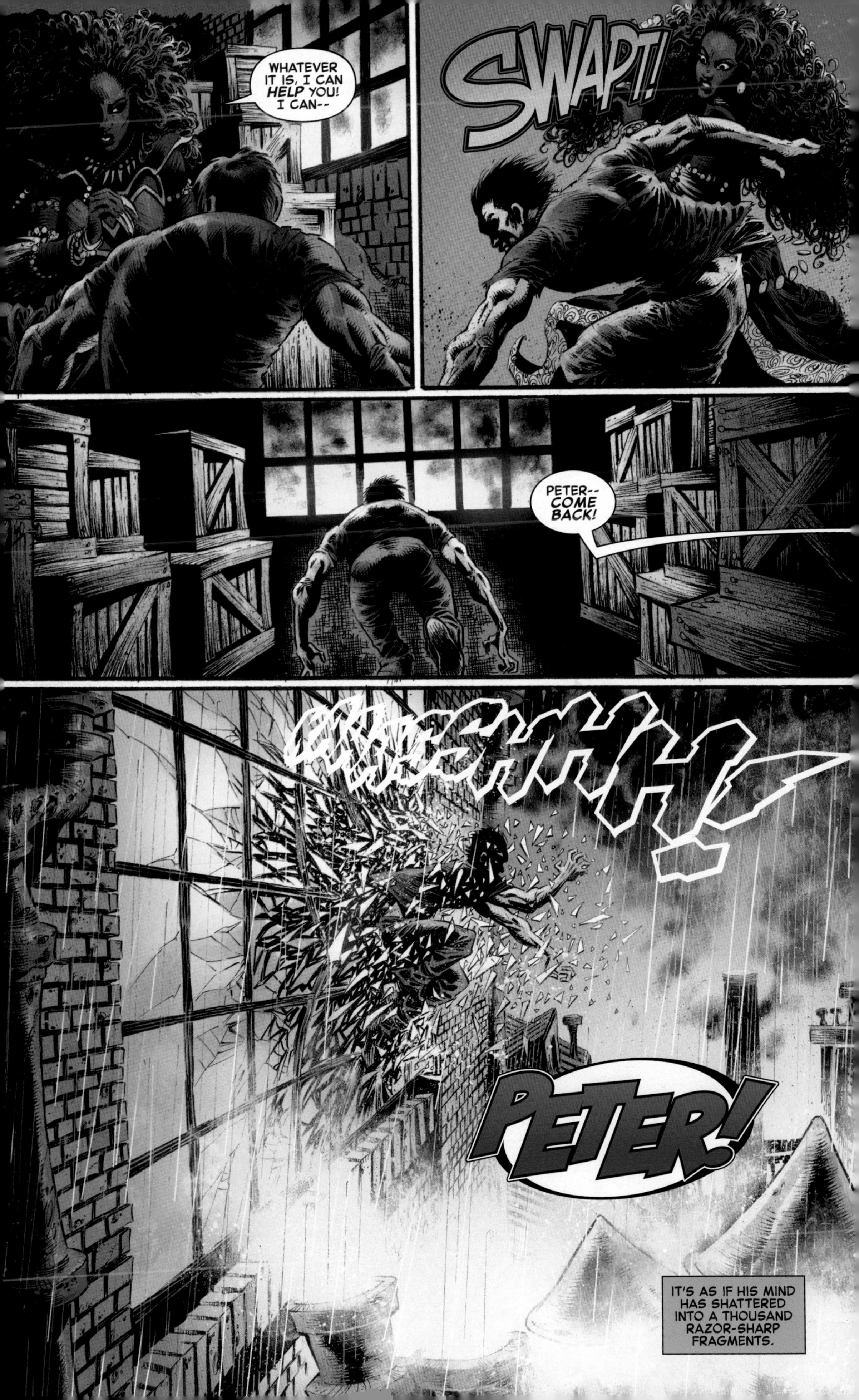
WHATEVER IT IS, I CAN HELP YOU! I CAN--
SWAPT!
PETER-- COME BACK!
PETER!
IT'S AS IF HIS MIND HAS SHATTERED INTO A THOUSAND RAZOR-SHARP FRAGMENTS.

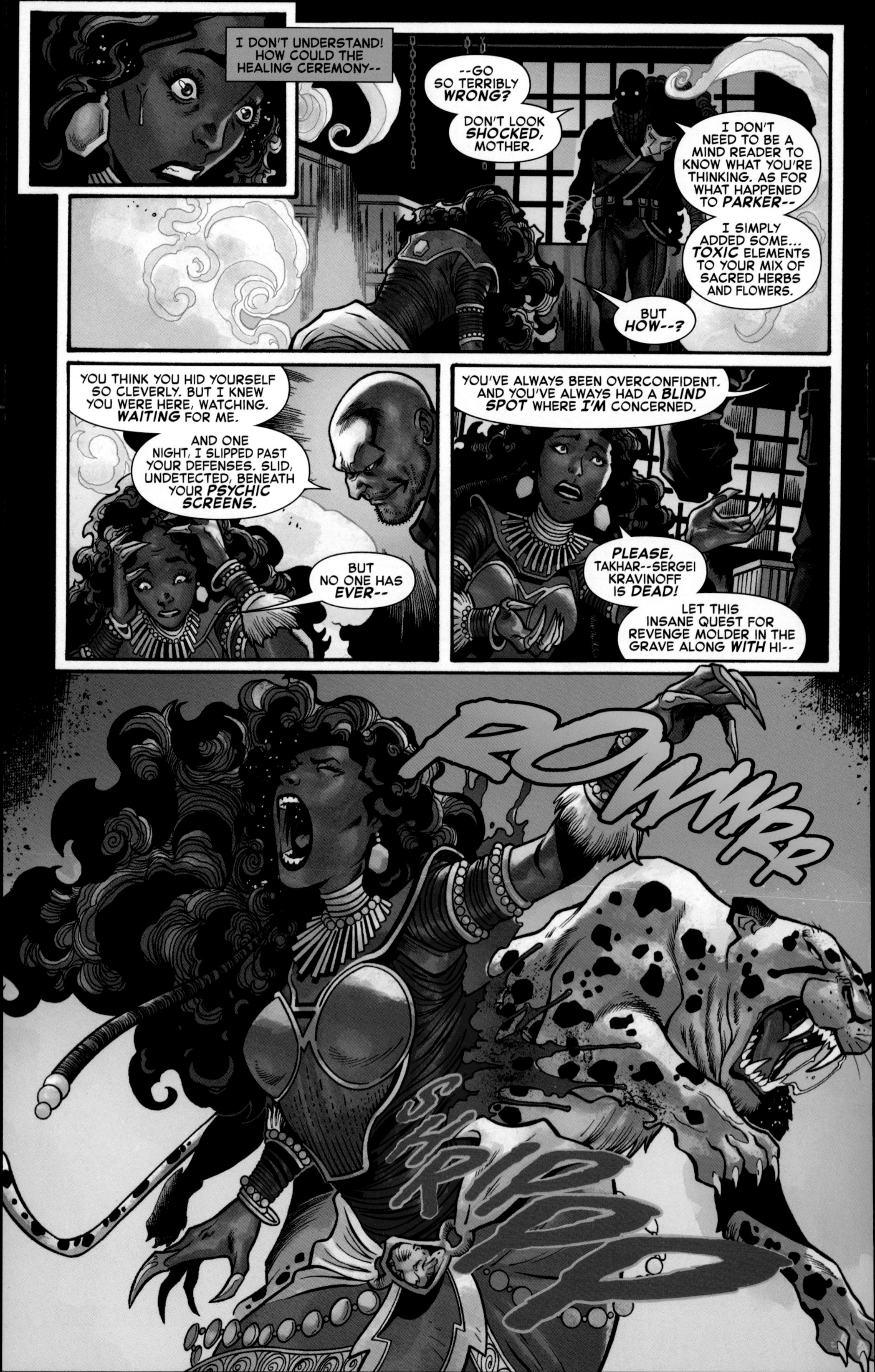
I DON'T UNDERSTAND! HOW COULD THE HEALING CEREMONY--
--GO SO TERRIBLY WRONG?
DON'T LOOK SHOCKED, MOTHER.
I DON'T NEED TO BE A MIND READER TO KNOW WHAT YOU'RE THINKING. AS FOR WHAT HAPPENED TO PARKER--
I SIMPLY ADDED SOME... TOXIC ELEMENTS TO YOUR MIX OF SACRED HERBS AND FLOWERS.
BUT HOW--?
YOU THINK YOU HID YOURSELF SO CLEVERLY. BUT I KNEW YOU WERE HERE, WATCHING. WAITING FOR ME.
AND ONE NIGHT, I SLIPPED PAST YOUR DEFENSES. SLID, UNDETECTED, BENEATH YOUR PSYCHIC SCREENS.
BUT NO ONE HAS EVER--
YOU'VE ALWAYS BEEN OVERCONFIDENT. AND YOU'VE ALWAYS HAD A BLIND SPOT WHERE I'M CONCERNED.
PLEASE, TAKHAR--SERGEI KRAVINOFF IS DEAD!
LET THIS INSANE QUEST FOR REVENGE MOLDER IN THE GRAVE ALONG WITH HI--
ROWWRR
SHRIPP

GOODBYE, MOTHER. I GO NOW TO *FINISH* THE WORK YOU INTERRUPTED. THE HUNT--

--ENDS TONIGHT.

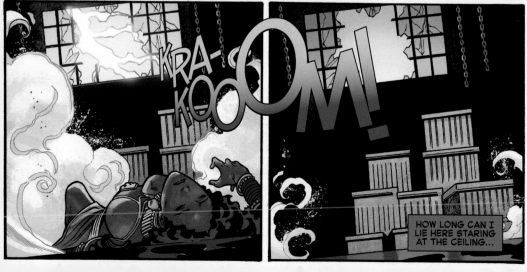

KRA-KOOOOM!

HOW LONG CAN I LIE HERE STARING AT THE CEILING...

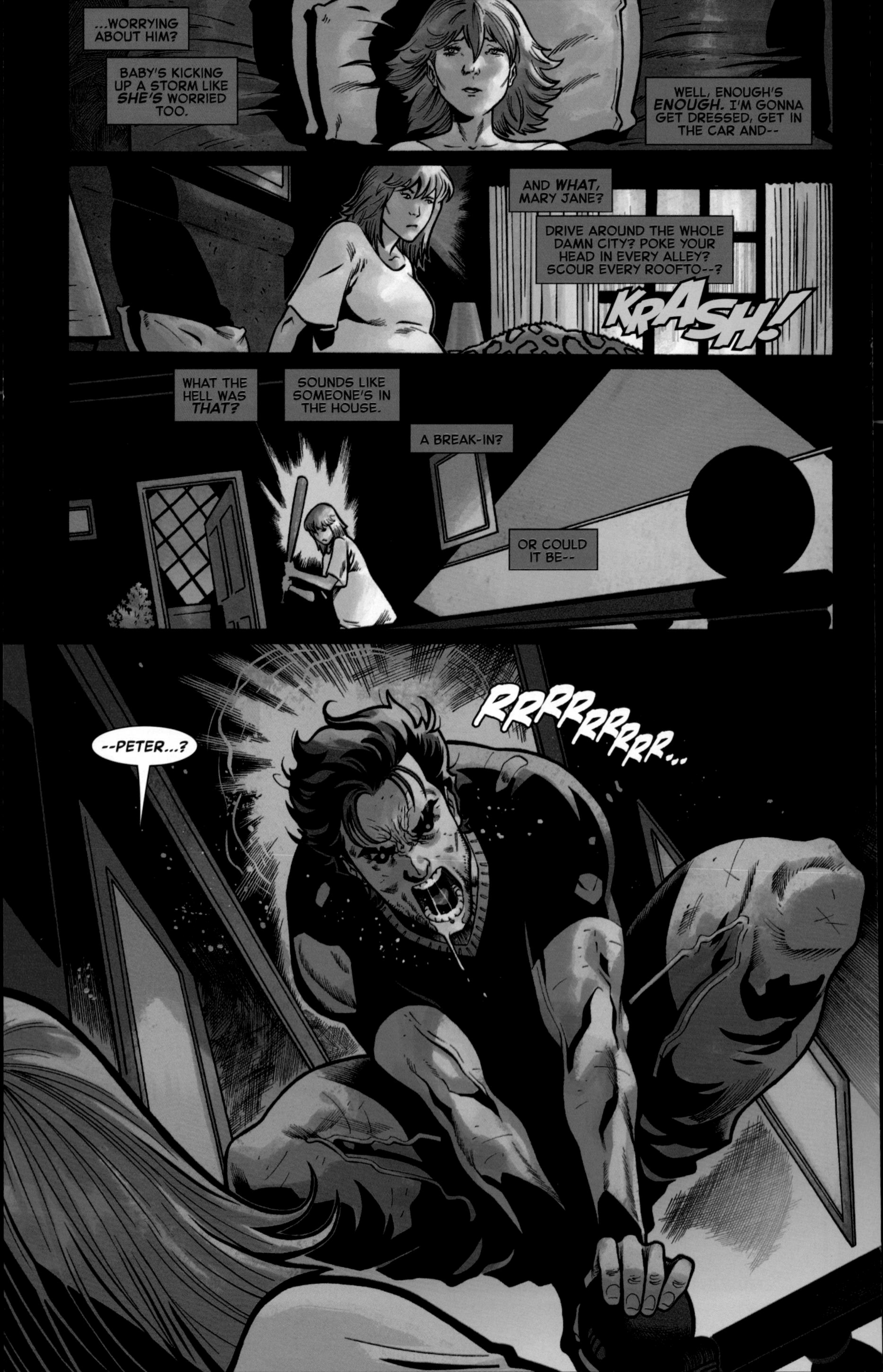
...WORRYING ABOUT HIM?
BABY'S KICKING UP A STORM LIKE SHE'S WORRIED TOO.
WELL, ENOUGH'S ENOUGH. I'M GONNA GET DRESSED, GET IN THE CAR AND--
AND WHAT, MARY JANE?
DRIVE AROUND THE WHOLE DAMN CITY? POKE YOUR HEAD IN EVERY ALLEY? SCOUR EVERY ROOFTO--?
KRASH!
WHAT THE HELL WAS THAT?
SOUNDS LIKE SOMEONE'S IN THE HOUSE.
A BREAK-IN?
OR COULD IT BE--
--PETER...?
RRRRRRRRRR...

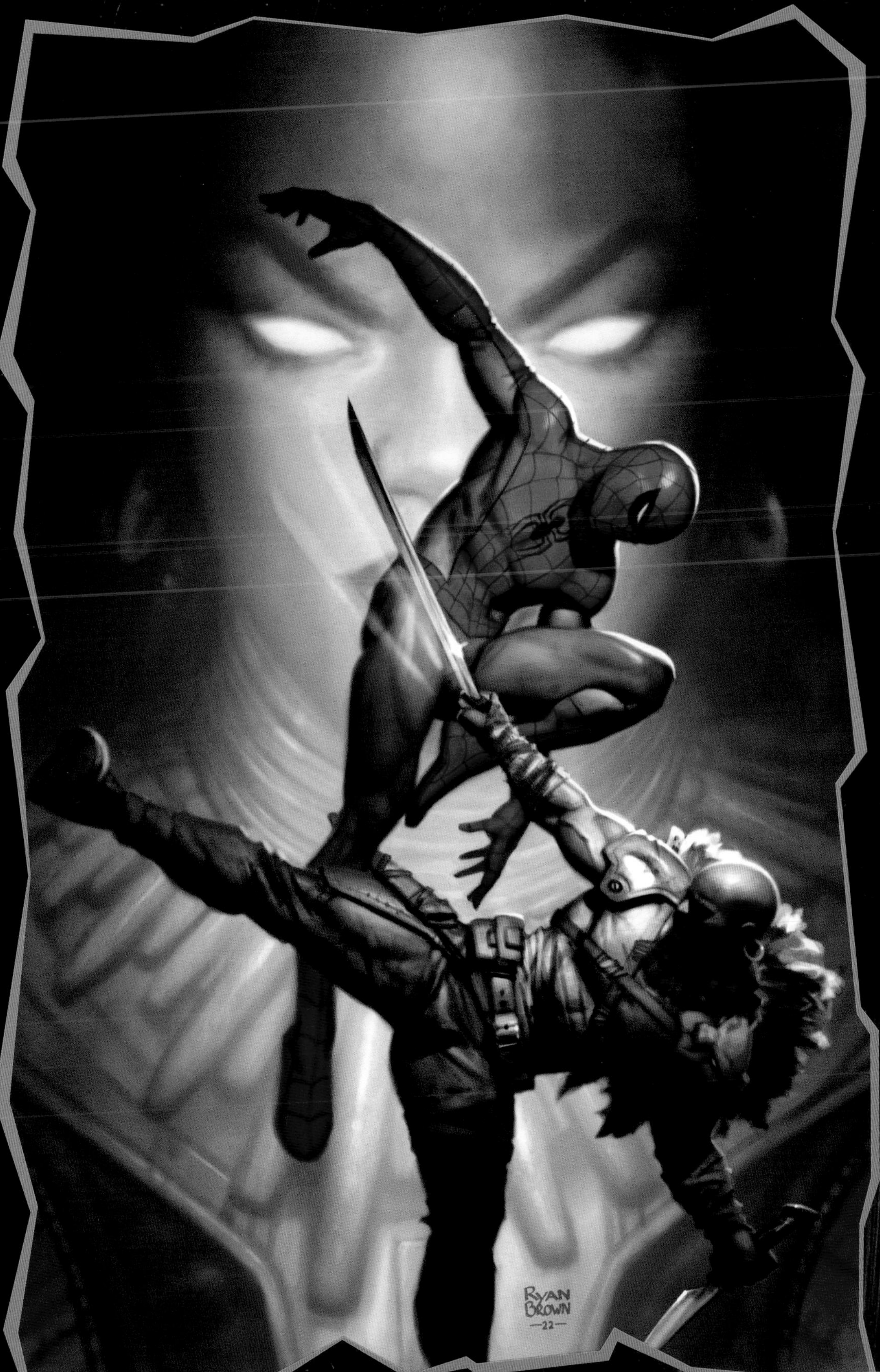
RYAN
BROWN
-22-

4

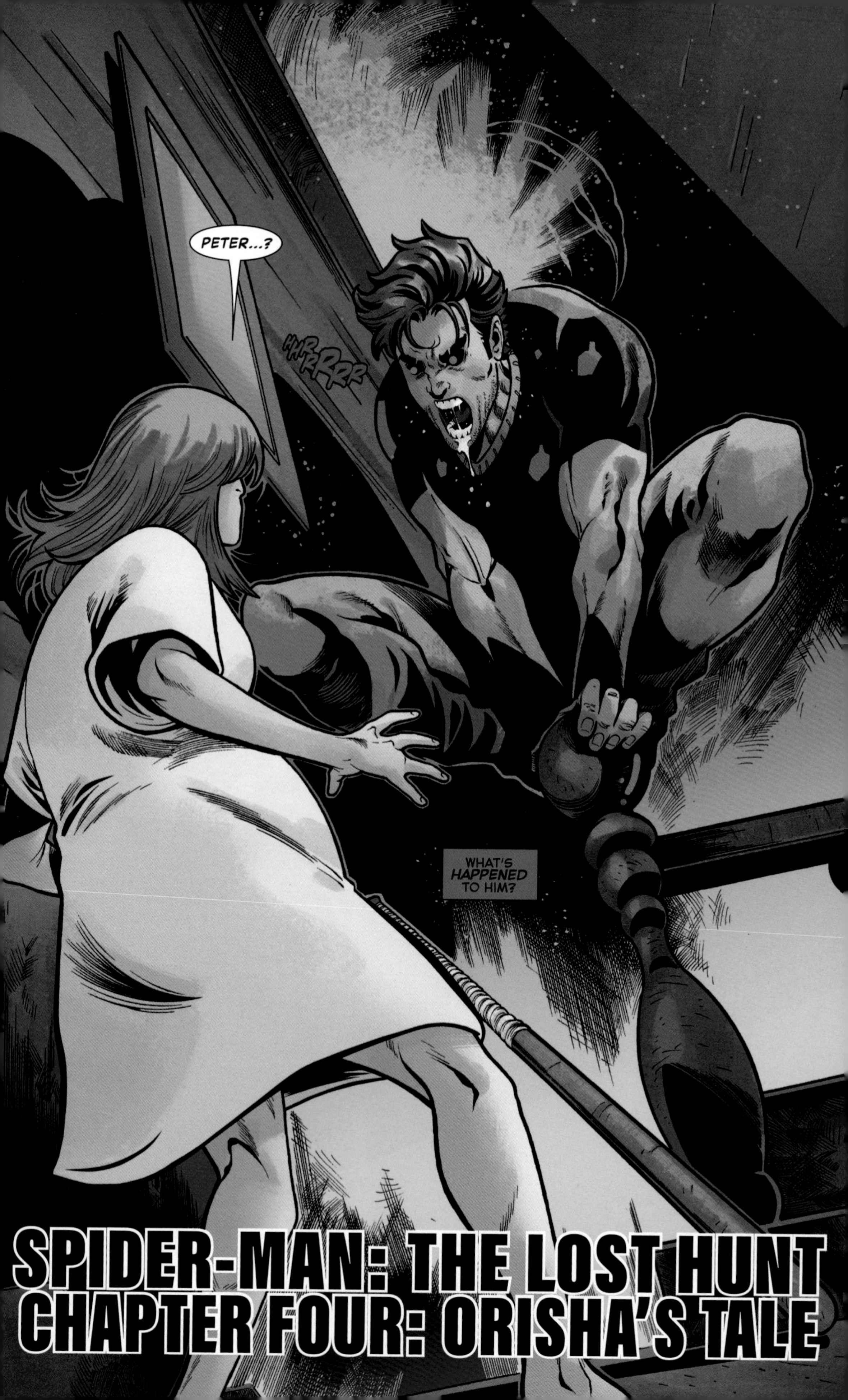
PETER...?
HHRRRRR
WHAT'S HAPPENED TO HIM?
SPIDER-MAN: THE LOST HUNT
CHAPTER FOUR: ORISHA'S TALE

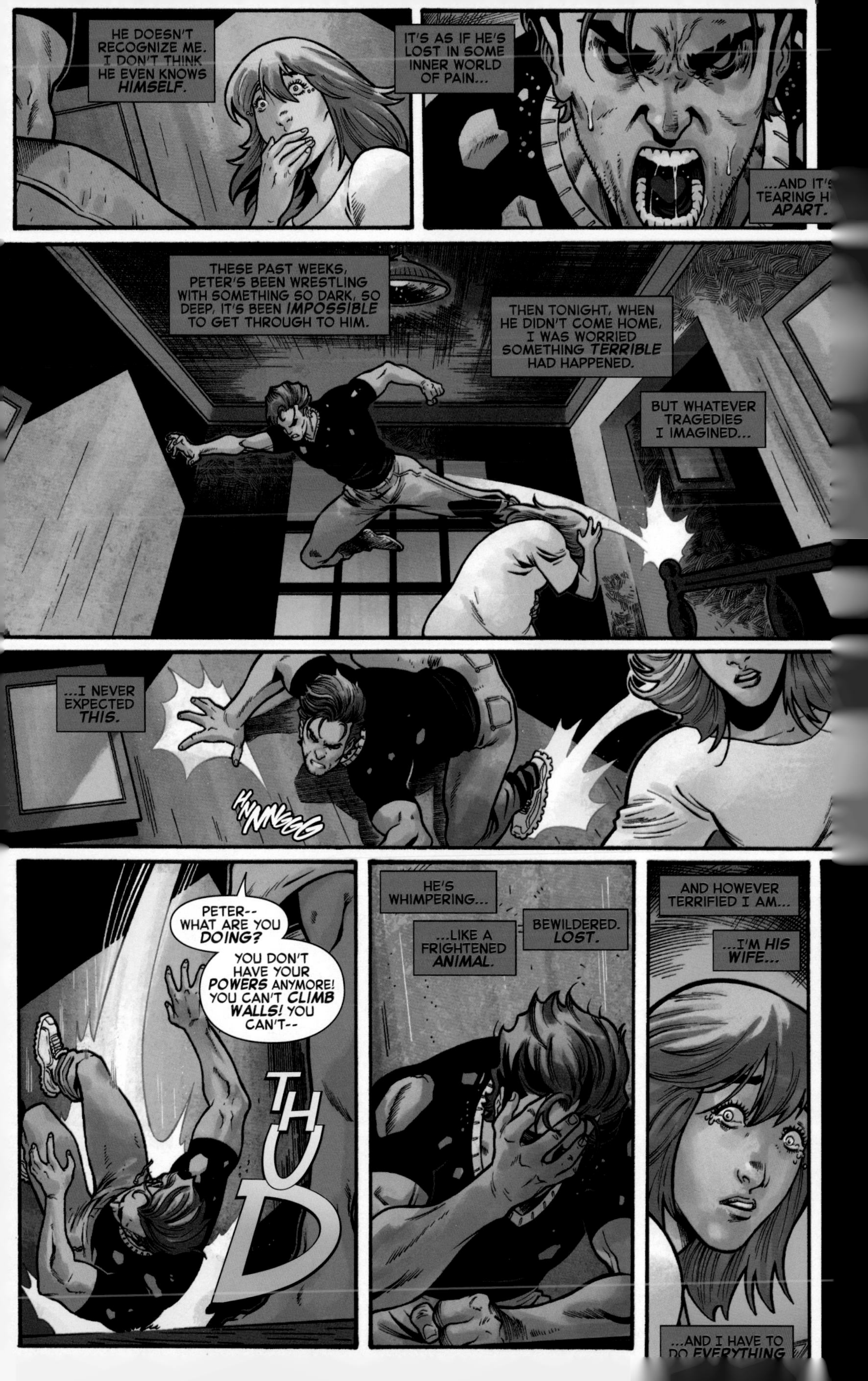
HE DOESN'T RECOGNIZE ME. I DON'T THINK HE EVEN KNOWS HIMSELF.
IT'S AS IF HE'S LOST IN SOME INNER WORLD OF PAIN...
...AND IT'S TEARING HI APART.
THESE PAST WEEKS, PETER'S BEEN WRESTLING WITH SOMETHING SO DARK, SO DEEP, IT'S BEEN IMPOSSIBLE TO GET THROUGH TO HIM.
THEN TONIGHT, WHEN HE DIDN'T COME HOME, I WAS WORRIED SOMETHING TERRIBLE HAD HAPPENED.
BUT WHATEVER TRAGEDIES I IMAGINED...
...I NEVER EXPECTED THIS.
HNNNGGG
PETER-- WHAT ARE YOU DOING?
YOU DON'T HAVE YOUR POWERS ANYMORE! YOU CAN'T CLIMB WALLS! YOU CAN'T--
THUD
HE'S WHIMPERING...
...LIKE A FRIGHTENED ANIMAL.
BEWILDERED. LOST.
AND HOWEVER TERRIFIED I AM...
...I'M HIS WIFE...
...AND I HAVE TO DO EVERYTHING

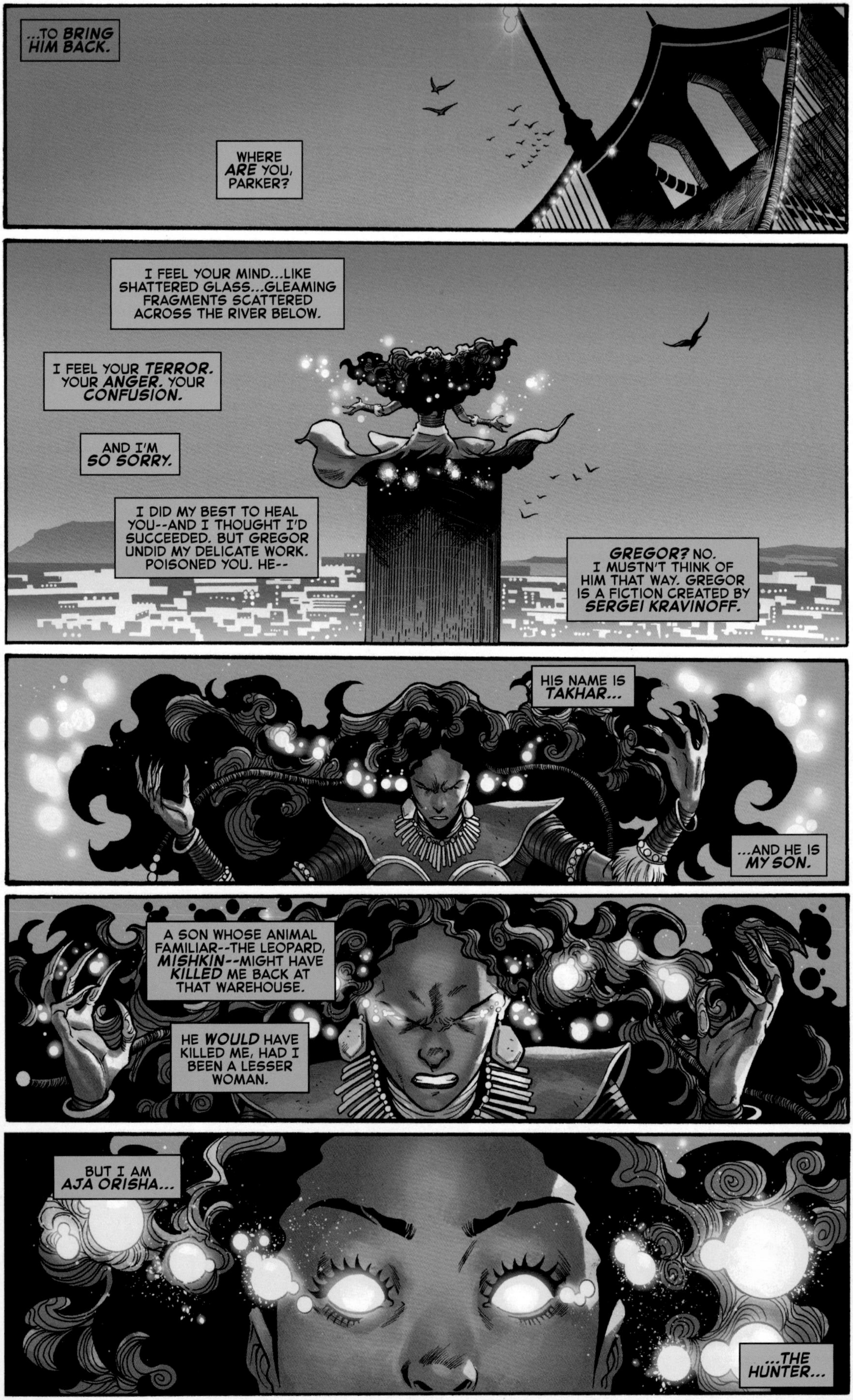
...TO BRING HIM BACK.
WHERE ARE YOU, PARKER?
I FEEL YOUR MIND...LIKE SHATTERED GLASS...GLEAMING FRAGMENTS SCATTERED ACROSS THE RIVER BELOW.
I FEEL YOUR TERROR. YOUR ANGER. YOUR CONFUSION.
AND I'M SO SORRY.
I DID MY BEST TO HEAL YOU--AND I THOUGHT I'D SUCCEEDED. BUT GREGOR UNDID MY DELICATE WORK. POISONED YOU. HE--
GREGOR? NO. I MUSTN'T THINK OF HIM THAT WAY. GREGOR IS A FICTION CREATED BY SERGEI KRAVINOFF.
HIS NAME IS TAKHAR...
...AND HE IS MY SON.
A SON WHOSE ANIMAL FAMILIAR--THE LEOPARD, MISHKIN--MIGHT HAVE KILLED ME BACK AT THAT WAREHOUSE.
HE WOULD HAVE KILLED ME, HAD I BEEN A LESSER WOMAN.
BUT I AM AJA ORISHA...
...THE HUNTER...

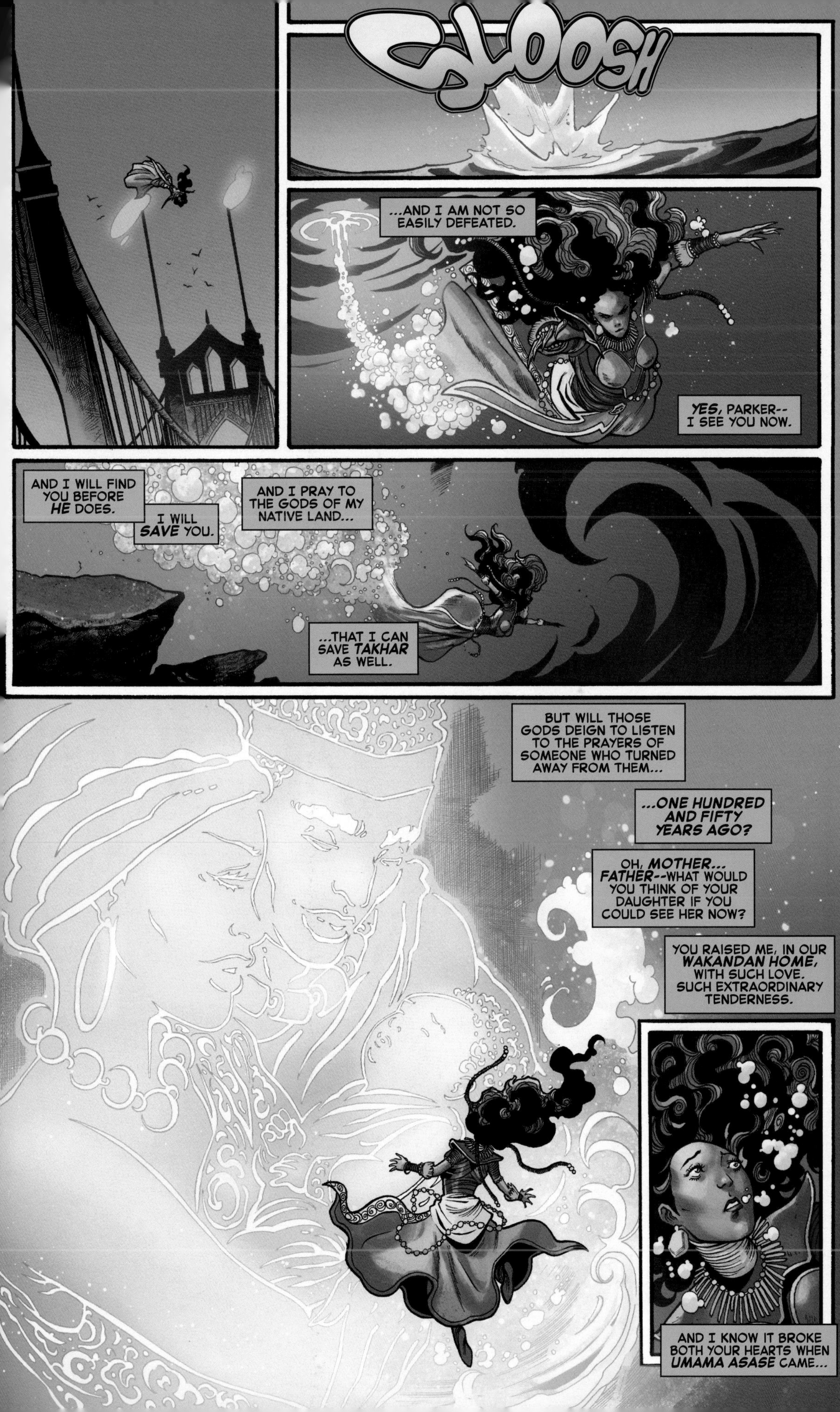
GLOOSH
...AND I AM NOT SO EASILY DEFEATED.
YES, PARKER-- I SEE YOU NOW.
AND I WILL FIND YOU BEFORE HE DOES.
I WILL SAVE YOU.
AND I PRAY TO THE GODS OF MY NATIVE LAND...
...THAT I CAN SAVE TAKHAR AS WELL.
BUT WILL THOSE GODS DEIGN TO LISTEN TO THE PRAYERS OF SOMEONE WHO TURNED AWAY FROM THEM...
...ONE HUNDRED AND FIFTY YEARS AGO?
OH, MOTHER... FATHER--WHAT WOULD YOU THINK OF YOUR DAUGHTER IF YOU COULD SEE HER NOW?
YOU RAISED ME, IN OUR WAKANDAN HOME, WITH SUCH LOVE. SUCH EXTRAORDINARY TENDERNESS.
AND I KNOW IT BROKE BOTH YOUR HEARTS WHEN UMAMA ASASE CAME...

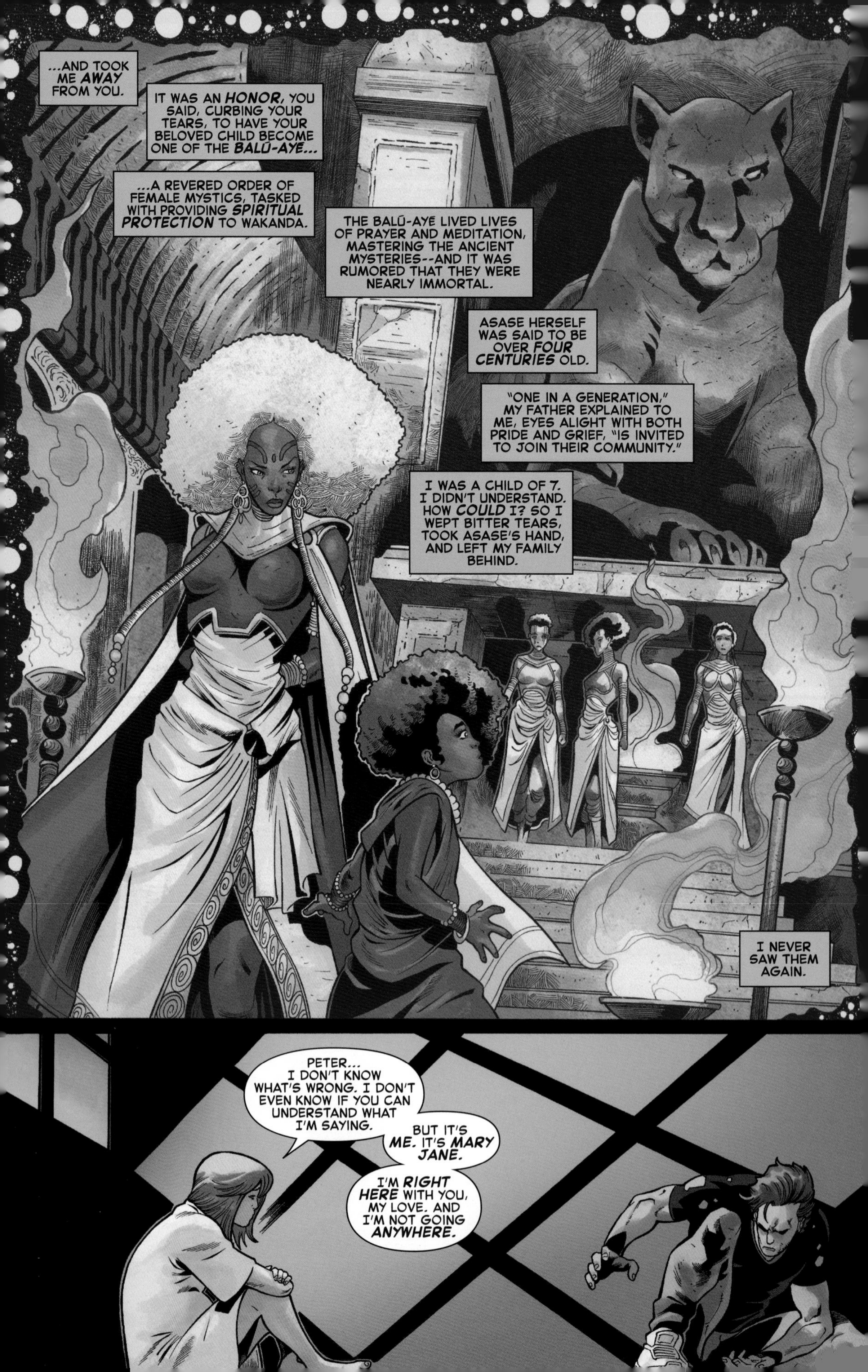
...AND TOOK ME AWAY FROM YOU.
IT WAS AN HONOR, YOU SAID, CURBING YOUR TEARS, TO HAVE YOUR BELOVED CHILD BECOME ONE OF THE BALŪ-AYE...
...A REVERED ORDER OF FEMALE MYSTICS, TASKED WITH PROVIDING SPIRITUAL PROTECTION TO WAKANDA.
THE BALŪ-AYE LIVED LIVES OF PRAYER AND MEDITATION, MASTERING THE ANCIENT MYSTERIES--AND IT WAS RUMORED THAT THEY WERE NEARLY IMMORTAL.
ASASE HERSELF WAS SAID TO BE OVER FOUR CENTURIES OLD.
"ONE IN A GENERATION," MY FATHER EXPLAINED TO ME, EYES ALIGHT WITH BOTH PRIDE AND GRIEF, "IS INVITED TO JOIN THEIR COMMUNITY."
I WAS A CHILD OF 7. I DIDN'T UNDERSTAND. HOW COULD I? SO I WEPT BITTER TEARS, TOOK ASASE'S HAND, AND LEFT MY FAMILY BEHIND.
I NEVER SAW THEM AGAIN.
PETER... I DON'T KNOW WHAT'S WRONG. I DON'T EVEN KNOW IF YOU CAN UNDERSTAND WHAT I'M SAYING.
BUT IT'S ME. IT'S MARY JANE.
I'M RIGHT HERE WITH YOU, MY LOVE. AND I'M NOT GOING ANYWHERE.

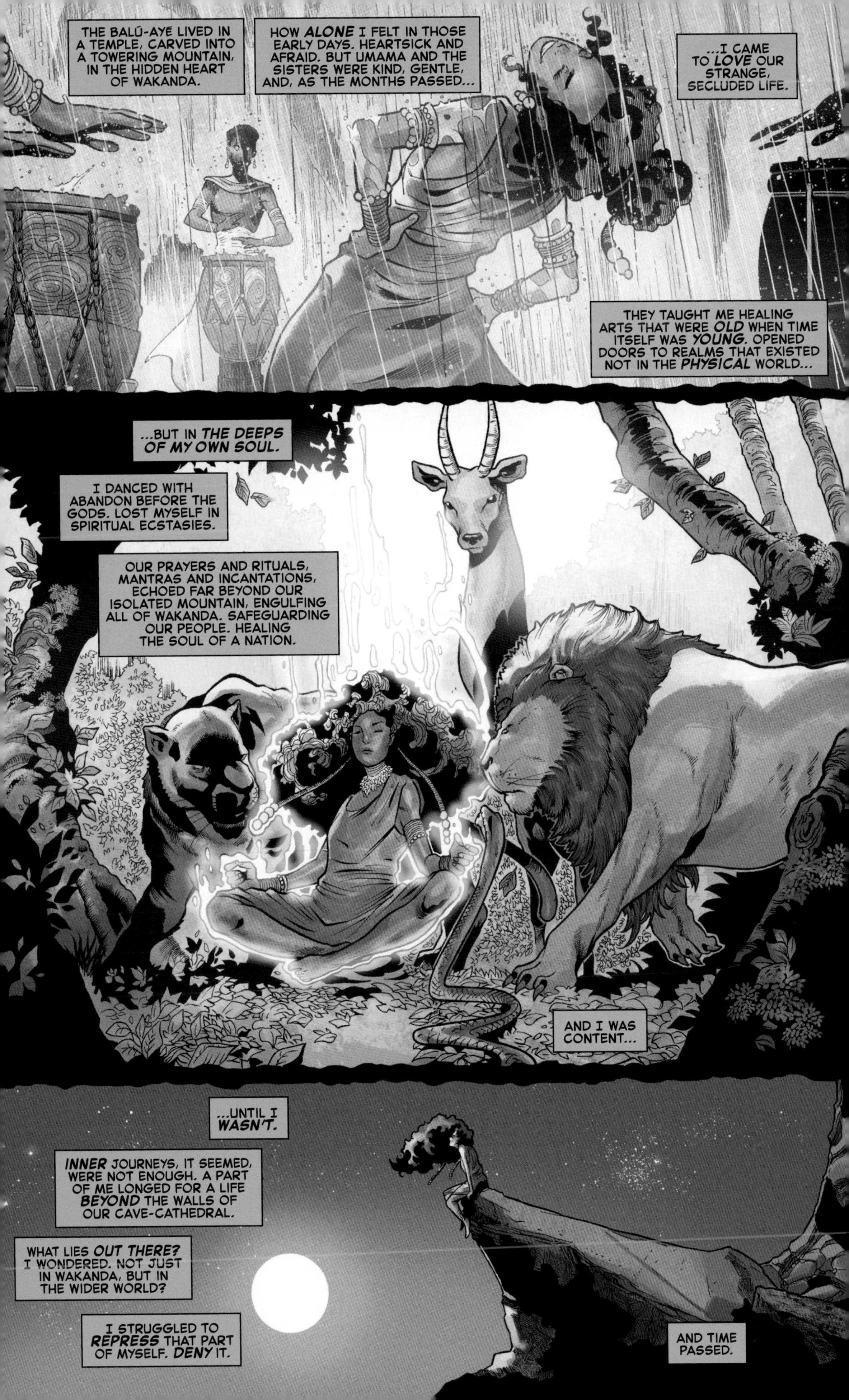
THE BALŪ-AYE LIVED IN A TEMPLE, CARVED INTO A TOWERING MOUNTAIN, IN THE HIDDEN HEART OF WAKANDA.
HOW ALONE I FELT IN THOSE EARLY DAYS. HEARTSICK AND AFRAID. BUT UMAMA AND THE SISTERS WERE KIND, GENTLE, AND, AS THE MONTHS PASSED...
...I CAME TO LOVE OUR STRANGE, SECLUDED LIFE.
THEY TAUGHT ME HEALING ARTS THAT WERE OLD WHEN TIME ITSELF WAS YOUNG. OPENED DOORS TO REALMS THAT EXISTED NOT IN THE PHYSICAL WORLD...
...BUT IN THE DEEPS OF MY OWN SOUL.
I DANCED WITH ABANDON BEFORE THE GODS. LOST MYSELF IN SPIRITUAL ECSTASIES.
OUR PRAYERS AND RITUALS, MANTRAS AND INCANTATIONS, ECHOED FAR BEYOND OUR ISOLATED MOUNTAIN, ENGULFING ALL OF WAKANDA. SAFEGUARDING OUR PEOPLE. HEALING THE SOUL OF A NATION.
AND I WAS CONTENT...
...UNTIL I WASN'T.
INNER JOURNEYS, IT SEEMED, WERE NOT ENOUGH. A PART OF ME LONGED FOR A LIFE BEYOND THE WALLS OF OUR CAVE-CATHEDRAL.
WHAT LIES OUT THERE? I WONDERED. NOT JUST IN WAKANDA, BUT IN THE WIDER WORLD?
I STRUGGLED TO REPRESS THAT PART OF MYSELF. DENY IT.
AND TIME PASSED.

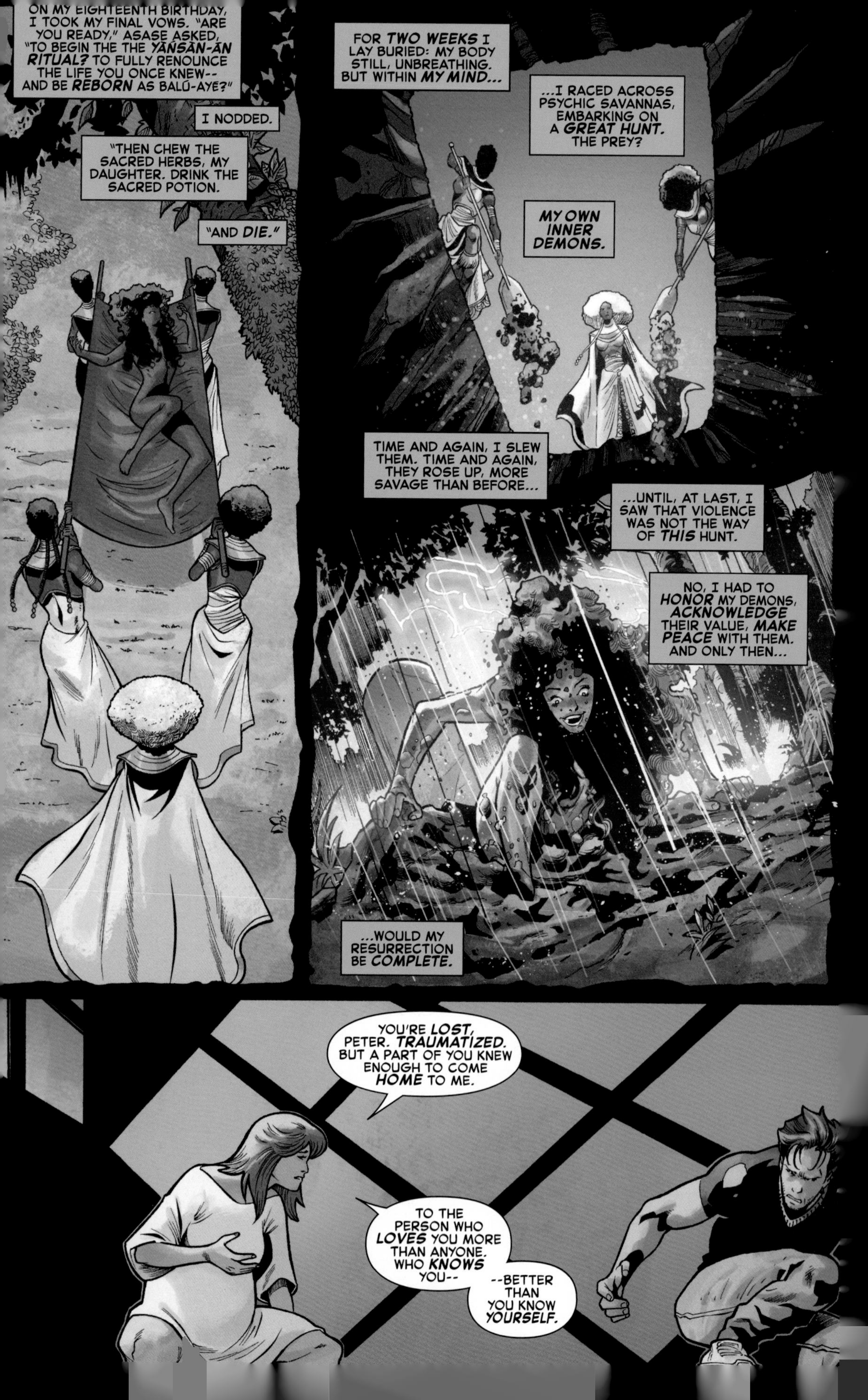
ON MY EIGHTEENTH BIRTHDAY, I TOOK MY FINAL VOWS. "ARE YOU READY," ASASE ASKED, "TO BEGIN THE THE YÀNSÀN-ÀN RITUAL? TO FULLY RENOUNCE THE LIFE YOU ONCE KNEW-- AND BE REBORN AS BALÚ-AYÉ?"
I NODDED.
"THEN CHEW THE SACRED HERBS, MY DAUGHTER. DRINK THE SACRED POTION.
"AND DIE."
FOR TWO WEEKS I LAY BURIED: MY BODY STILL, UNBREATHING. BUT WITHIN MY MIND...
...I RACED ACROSS PSYCHIC SAVANNAS, EMBARKING ON A GREAT HUNT. THE PREY?
MY OWN INNER DEMONS.
TIME AND AGAIN, I SLEW THEM. TIME AND AGAIN, THEY ROSE UP, MORE SAVAGE THAN BEFORE...
...UNTIL, AT LAST, I SAW THAT VIOLENCE WAS NOT THE WAY OF THIS HUNT.
NO, I HAD TO HONOR MY DEMONS, ACKNOWLEDGE THEIR VALUE, MAKE PEACE WITH THEM. AND ONLY THEN...
...WOULD MY RESURRECTION BE COMPLETE.
YOU'RE LOST, PETER. TRAUMATIZED. BUT A PART OF YOU KNEW ENOUGH TO COME HOME TO ME.
TO THE PERSON WHO LOVES YOU MORE THAN ANYONE. WHO KNOWS YOU--
--BETTER THAN YOU KNOW YOURSELF.

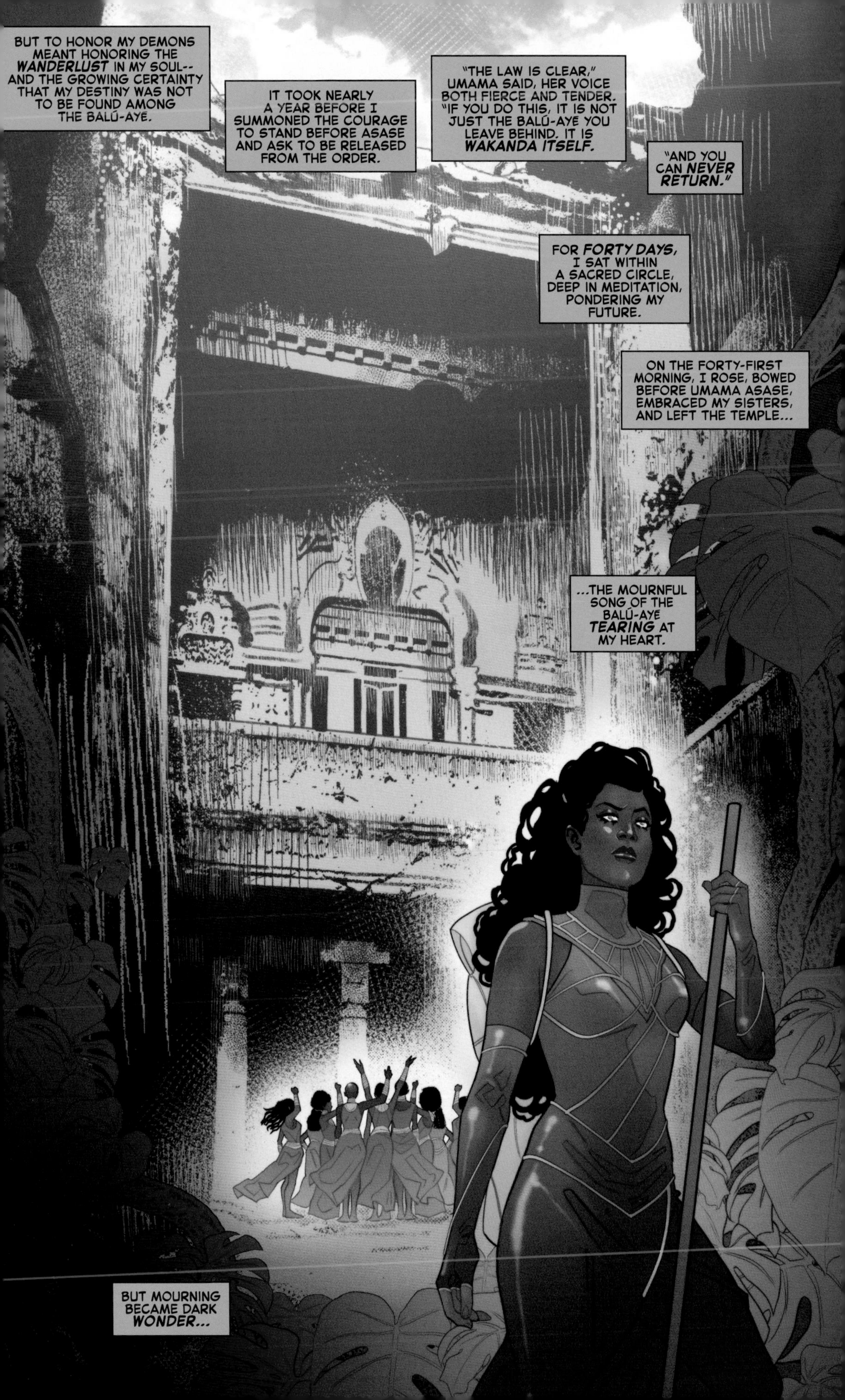
BUT TO HONOR MY DEMONS MEANT HONORING THE WANDERLUST IN MY SOUL--AND THE GROWING CERTAINTY THAT MY DESTINY WAS NOT TO BE FOUND AMONG THE BALÚ-AYE.
IT TOOK NEARLY A YEAR BEFORE I SUMMONED THE COURAGE TO STAND BEFORE ASASE AND ASK TO BE RELEASED FROM THE ORDER.
"THE LAW IS CLEAR," UMAMA SAID, HER VOICE BOTH FIERCE AND TENDER. "IF YOU DO THIS, IT IS NOT JUST THE BALÚ-AYE YOU LEAVE BEHIND. IT IS WAKANDA ITSELF.
"AND YOU CAN NEVER RETURN."
FOR FORTY DAYS, I SAT WITHIN A SACRED CIRCLE, DEEP IN MEDITATION, PONDERING MY FUTURE.
ON THE FORTY-FIRST MORNING, I ROSE, BOWED BEFORE UMAMA ASASE, EMBRACED MY SISTERS, AND LEFT THE TEMPLE...
...THE MOURNFUL SONG OF THE BALÚ-AYE TEARING AT MY HEART.
BUT MOURNING BECAME DARK WONDER...

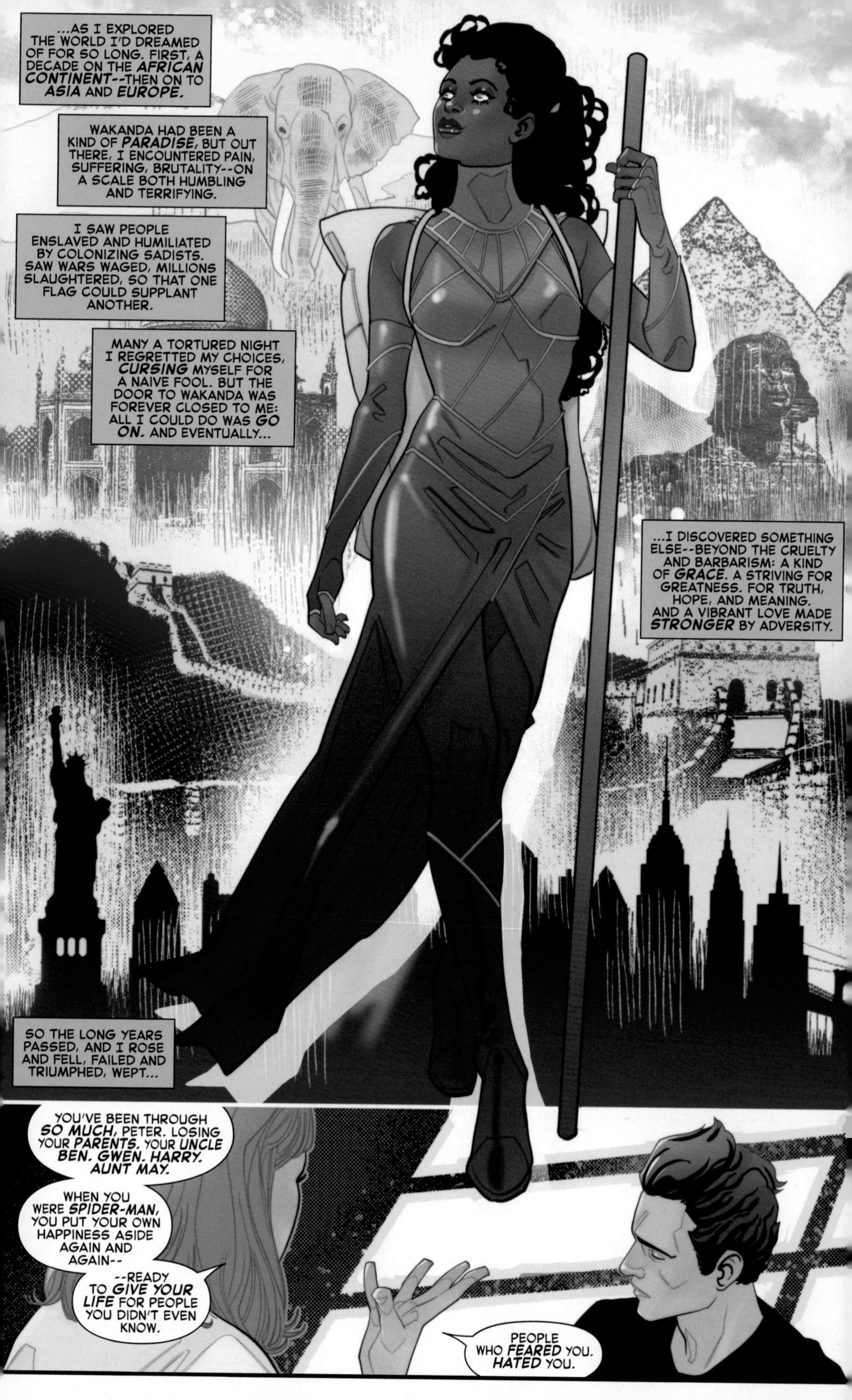
...AS I EXPLORED THE WORLD I'D DREAMED OF FOR SO LONG. FIRST, A DECADE ON THE AFRICAN CONTINENT--THEN ON TO ASIA AND EUROPE.
WAKANDA HAD BEEN A KIND OF PARADISE, BUT OUT THERE, I ENCOUNTERED PAIN, SUFFERING, BRUTALITY--ON A SCALE BOTH HUMBLING AND TERRIFYING.
I SAW PEOPLE ENSLAVED AND HUMILIATED BY COLONIZING SADISTS. SAW WARS WAGED, MILLIONS SLAUGHTERED, SO THAT ONE FLAG COULD SUPPLANT ANOTHER.
MANY A TORTURED NIGHT I REGRETTED MY CHOICES, CURSING MYSELF FOR A NAIVE FOOL. BUT THE DOOR TO WAKANDA WAS FOREVER CLOSED TO ME: ALL I COULD DO WAS GO ON. AND EVENTUALLY...
...I DISCOVERED SOMETHING ELSE--BEYOND THE CRUELTY AND BARBARISM: A KIND OF GRACE. A STRIVING FOR GREATNESS. FOR TRUTH, HOPE, AND MEANING. AND A VIBRANT LOVE MADE STRONGER BY ADVERSITY.
SO THE LONG YEARS PASSED, AND I ROSE AND FELL, FAILED AND TRIUMPHED, WEPT...
YOU'VE BEEN THROUGH SO MUCH, PETER. LOSING YOUR PARENTS. YOUR UNCLE BEN. GWEN. HARRY. AUNT MAY.
WHEN YOU WERE SPIDER-MAN, YOU PUT YOUR OWN HAPPINESS ASIDE AGAIN AND AGAIN--
--READY TO GIVE YOUR LIFE FOR PEOPLE YOU DIDN'T EVEN KNOW.
PEOPLE WHO FEARED YOU. HATED YOU.

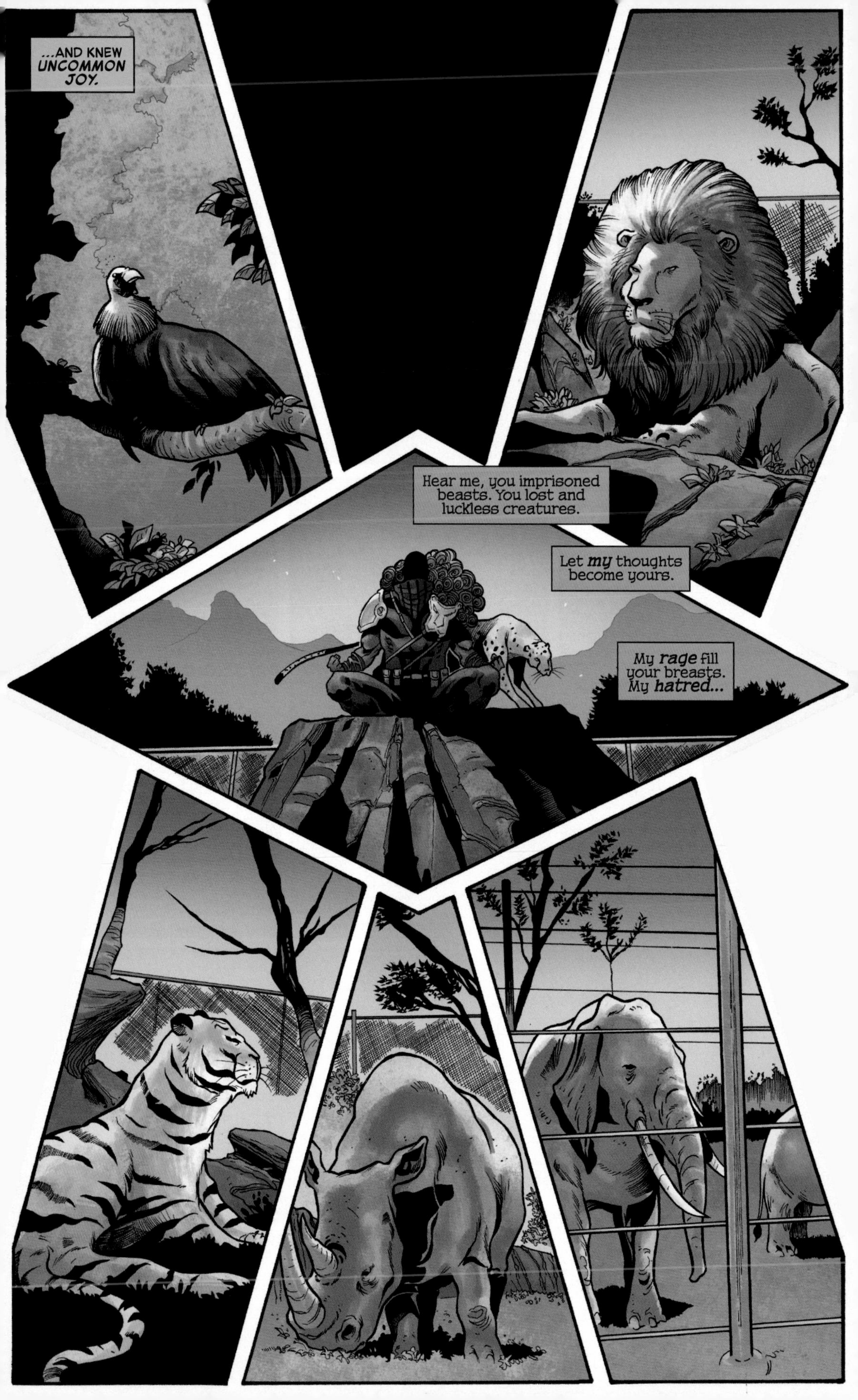
...AND KNEW UNCOMMON JOY.
Hear me, you imprisoned beasts. You lost and luckless creatures.
Let my thoughts become yours.
My rage fill your breasts. My hatred...

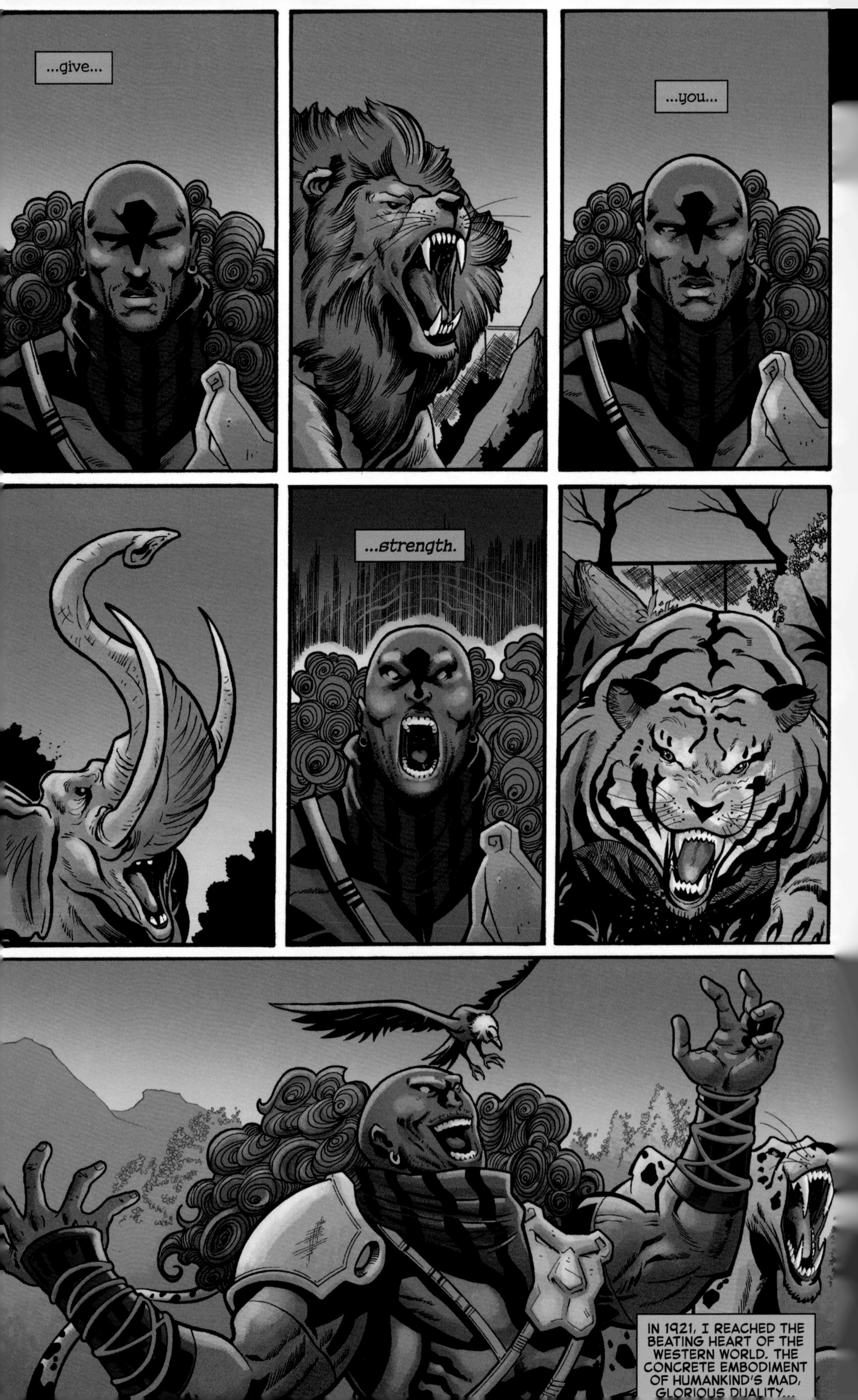
...give...
...you...
...strength.
IN 1921, I REACHED THE BEATING HEART OF THE WESTERN WORLD. THE CONCRETE EMBODIMENT OF HUMANKIND'S MAD, GLORIOUS DUALITY...

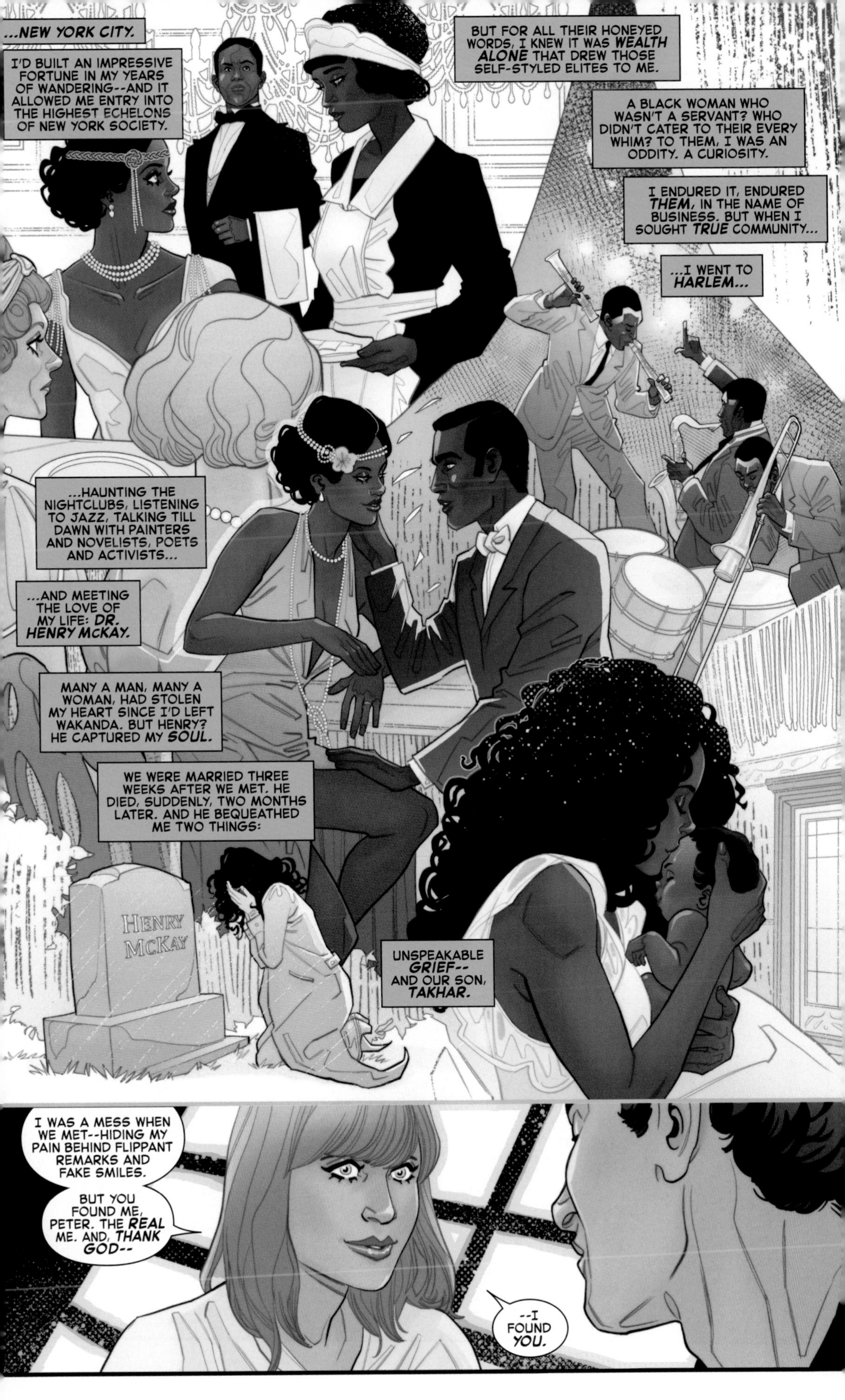

...NEW YORK CITY.
I'D BUILT AN IMPRESSIVE FORTUNE IN MY YEARS OF WANDERING--AND IT ALLOWED ME ENTRY INTO THE HIGHEST ECHELONS OF NEW YORK SOCIETY.
BUT FOR ALL THEIR HONEYED WORDS, I KNEW IT WAS WEALTH ALONE THAT DREW THOSE SELF-STYLED ELITES TO ME.
A BLACK WOMAN WHO WASN'T A SERVANT? WHO DIDN'T CATER TO THEIR EVERY WHIM? TO THEM, I WAS AN ODDITY. A CURIOSITY.
I ENDURED IT, ENDURED THEM, IN THE NAME OF BUSINESS. BUT WHEN I SOUGHT TRUE COMMUNITY...
...I WENT TO HARLEM...
...HAUNTING THE NIGHTCLUBS, LISTENING TO JAZZ, TALKING TILL DAWN WITH PAINTERS AND NOVELISTS, POETS AND ACTIVISTS...
...AND MEETING THE LOVE OF MY LIFE: DR. HENRY MCKAY.
MANY A MAN, MANY A WOMAN, HAD STOLEN MY HEART SINCE I'D LEFT WAKANDA. BUT HENRY? HE CAPTURED MY SOUL.
WE WERE MARRIED THREE WEEKS AFTER WE MET. HE DIED, SUDDENLY, TWO MONTHS LATER. AND HE BEQUEATHED ME TWO THINGS:
HENRY MCKAY
UNSPEAKABLE GRIEF--AND OUR SON, TAKHAR.
I WAS A MESS WHEN WE MET--HIDING MY PAIN BEHIND FLIPPANT REMARKS AND FAKE SMILES.
BUT YOU FOUND ME, PETER. THE REAL ME. AND, THANK GOD--
--I FOUND YOU.

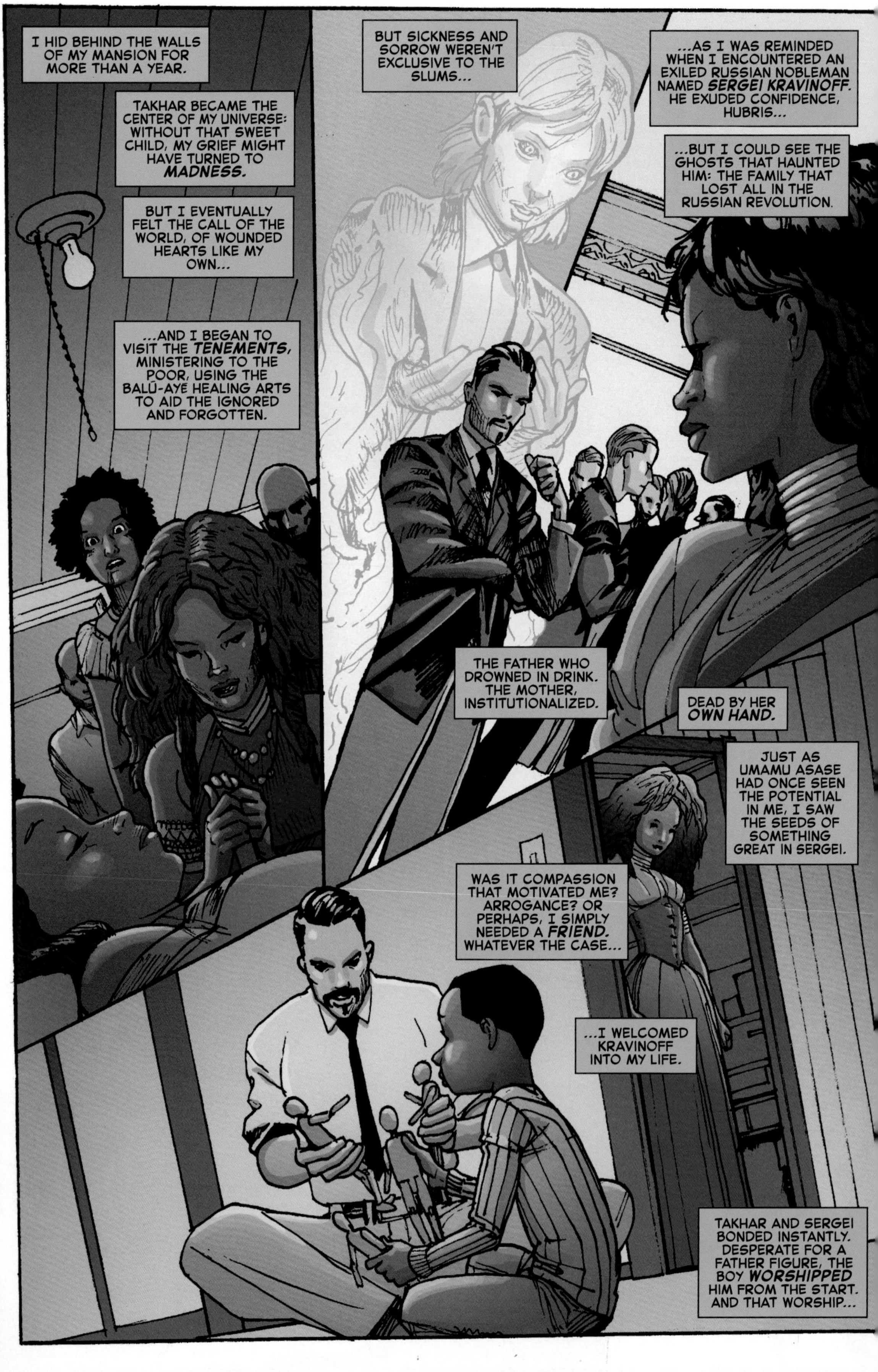
I HID BEHIND THE WALLS OF MY MANSION FOR MORE THAN A YEAR.
TAKHAR BECAME THE CENTER OF MY UNIVERSE: WITHOUT THAT SWEET CHILD, MY GRIEF MIGHT HAVE TURNED TO *MADNESS.*
BUT I EVENTUALLY FELT THE CALL OF THE WORLD, OF WOUNDED HEARTS LIKE MY OWN...
...AND I BEGAN TO VISIT THE *TENEMENTS,* MINISTERING TO THE POOR, USING THE BALŪ-AYÉ HEALING ARTS TO AID THE IGNORED AND FORGOTTEN.
BUT SICKNESS AND SORROW WEREN'T EXCLUSIVE TO THE SLUMS...
...AS I WAS REMINDED WHEN I ENCOUNTERED AN EXILED RUSSIAN NOBLEMAN NAMED *SERGEI KRAVINOFF.* HE EXUDED CONFIDENCE, HUBRIS...
...BUT I COULD SEE THE GHOSTS THAT HAUNTED HIM: THE FAMILY THAT LOST ALL IN THE RUSSIAN REVOLUTION.
THE FATHER WHO DROWNED IN DRINK. THE MOTHER, INSTITUTIONALIZED.
DEAD BY HER *OWN HAND.*
JUST AS UMAMU ASASE HAD ONCE SEEN THE POTENTIAL IN ME, I SAW THE SEEDS OF SOMETHING GREAT IN SERGEI.
WAS IT COMPASSION THAT MOTIVATED ME? ARROGANCE? OR PERHAPS, I SIMPLY NEEDED A *FRIEND.* WHATEVER THE CASE...
...I WELCOMED KRAVINOFF INTO MY LIFE.
TAKHAR AND SERGEI BONDED INSTANTLY. DESPERATE FOR A FATHER FIGURE, THE BOY *WORSHIPPED* HIM FROM THE START. AND THAT WORSHIP...

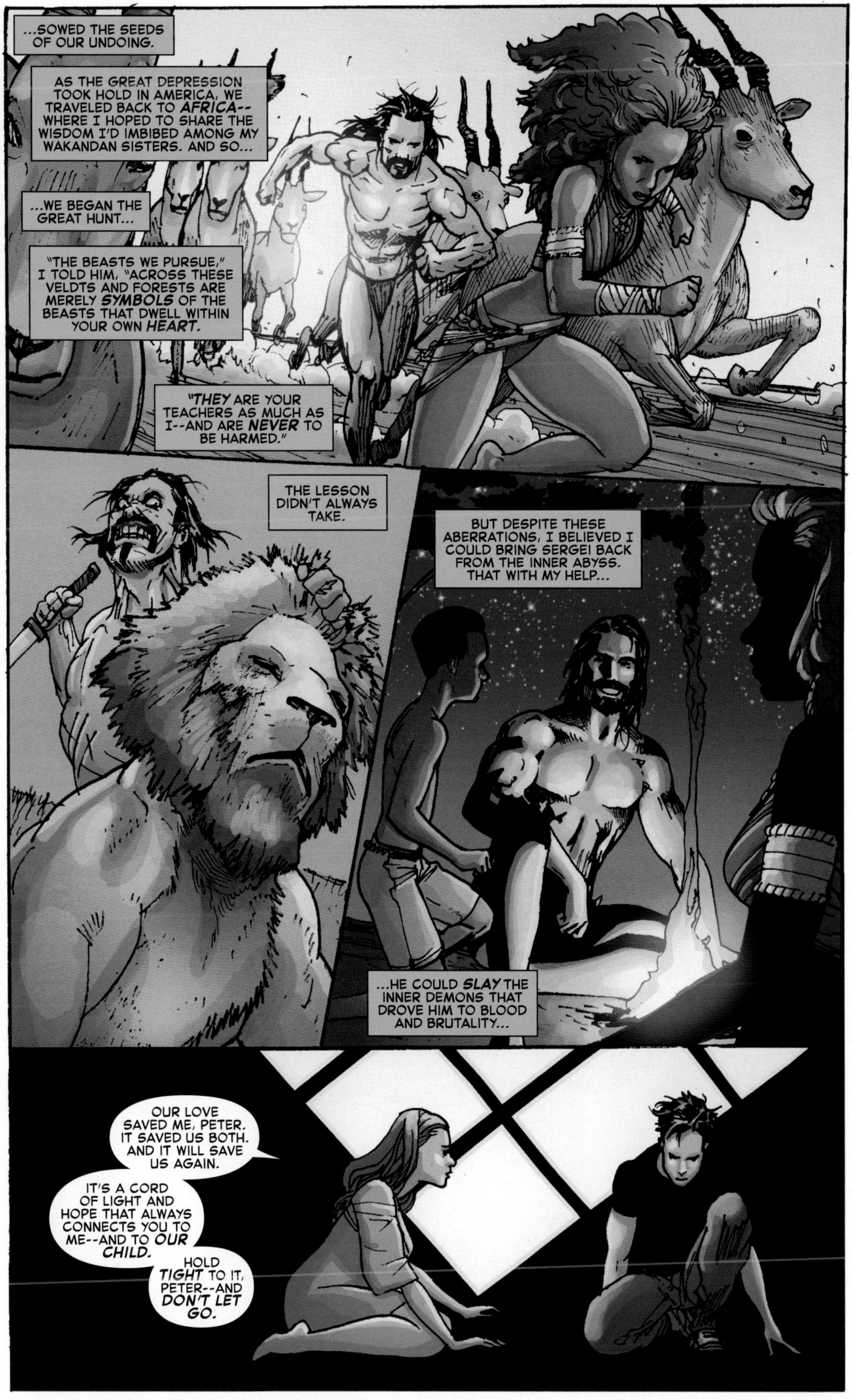
...SOWED THE SEEDS OF OUR UNDOING.
AS THE GREAT DEPRESSION TOOK HOLD IN AMERICA, WE TRAVELED BACK TO AFRICA-- WHERE I HOPED TO SHARE THE WISDOM I'D IMBIBED AMONG MY WAKANDAN SISTERS. AND SO...
...WE BEGAN THE GREAT HUNT...
"THE BEASTS WE PURSUE," I TOLD HIM, "ACROSS THESE VELDTS AND FORESTS ARE MERELY SYMBOLS OF THE BEASTS THAT DWELL WITHIN YOUR OWN HEART.
"THEY ARE YOUR TEACHERS AS MUCH AS I--AND ARE NEVER TO BE HARMED."
THE LESSON DIDN'T ALWAYS TAKE.
BUT DESPITE THESE ABERRATIONS, I BELIEVED I COULD BRING SERGEI BACK FROM THE INNER ABYSS. THAT WITH MY HELP...
...HE COULD SLAY THE INNER DEMONS THAT DROVE HIM TO BLOOD AND BRUTALITY...
OUR LOVE SAVED ME, PETER. IT SAVED US BOTH. AND IT WILL SAVE US AGAIN.
IT'S A CORD OF LIGHT AND HOPE THAT ALWAYS CONNECTS YOU TO ME--AND TO OUR CHILD.
HOLD TIGHT TO IT, PETER--AND DON'T LET GO.

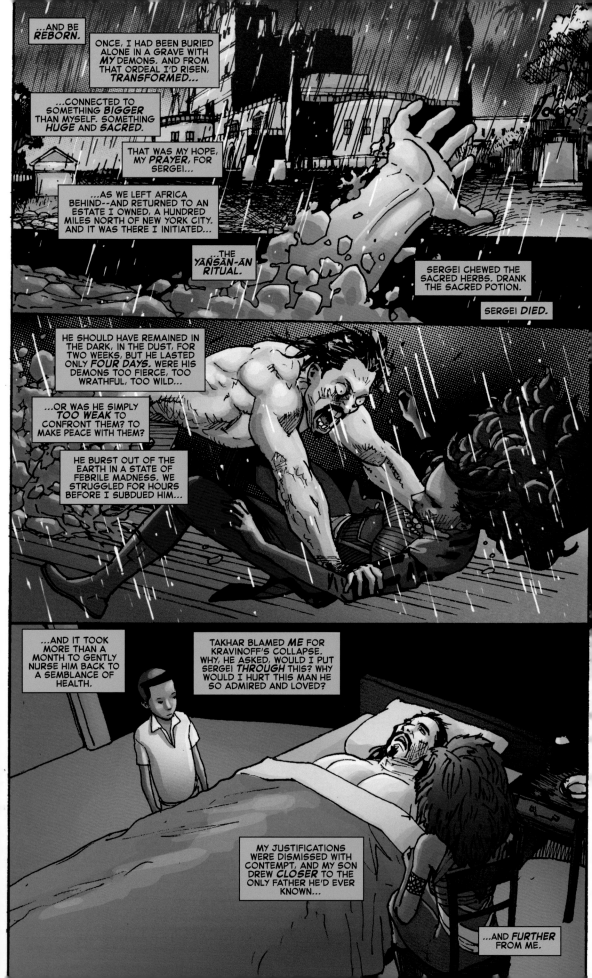

...AND BE *REBORN*.

ONCE, I HAD BEEN BURIED ALONE IN A GRAVE WITH *MY* DEMONS. AND FROM THAT ORDEAL I'D RISEN, *TRANSFORMED*...

...CONNECTED TO SOMETHING *BIGGER* THAN MYSELF. SOMETHING *HUGE* AND *SACRED*.

THAT WAS MY HOPE, MY *PRAYER*, FOR SERGEI...

...AS WE LEFT AFRICA BEHIND--AND RETURNED TO AN ESTATE I OWNED, A HUNDRED MILES NORTH OF NEW YORK CITY. AND IT WAS THERE I INITIATED...

...THE *YAÑSÁN-ÁN* RITUAL.

SERGEI CHEWED THE SACRED HERBS. DRANK THE SACRED POTION.

SERGEI *DIED*.

HE SHOULD HAVE REMAINED IN THE DARK, IN THE DUST, FOR TWO WEEKS, BUT HE LASTED ONLY *FOUR DAYS*. WERE HIS DEMONS TOO FIERCE, TOO WRATHFUL, TOO WILD...

...OR WAS HE SIMPLY *TOO WEAK* TO CONFRONT THEM? TO MAKE PEACE WITH THEM?

HE BURST OUT OF THE EARTH IN A STATE OF FEBRILE MADNESS. WE STRUGGLED FOR HOURS BEFORE I SUBDUED HIM...

...AND IT TOOK MORE THAN A MONTH TO GENTLY NURSE HIM BACK TO A SEMBLANCE OF HEALTH.

TAKHAR BLAMED *ME* FOR KRAVINOFF'S COLLAPSE. WHY, HE ASKED, WOULD I PUT SERGEI *THROUGH* THIS? WHY WOULD I HURT THIS MAN HE SO ADMIRED AND LOVED?

MY JUSTIFICATIONS WERE DISMISSED WITH CONTEMPT, AND MY SON DREW *CLOSER* TO THE ONLY FATHER HE'D EVER KNOWN...

...AND *FURTHER* FROM ME.

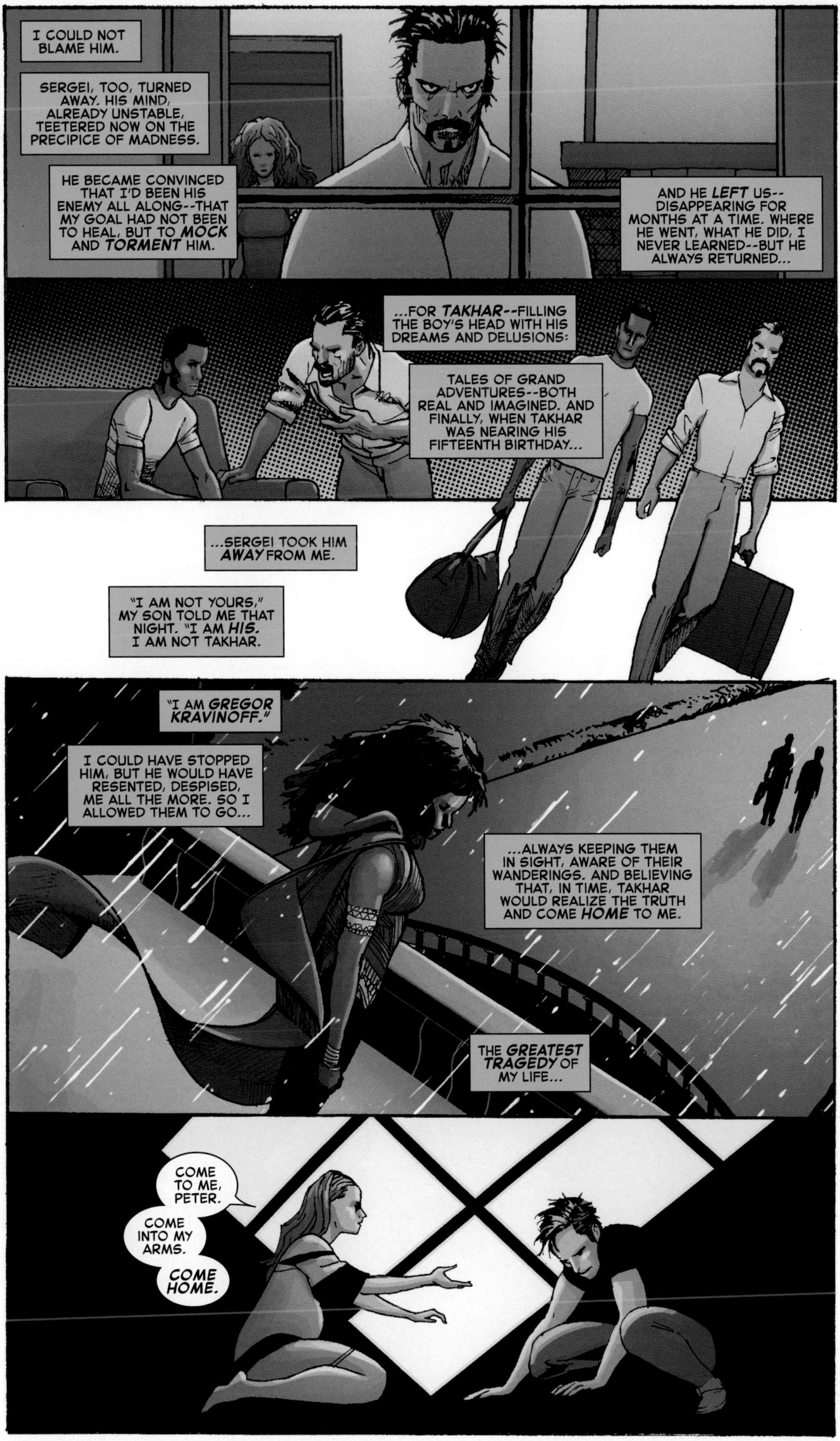
I COULD NOT BLAME HIM.
SERGEI, TOO, TURNED AWAY. HIS MIND, ALREADY UNSTABLE, TEETERED NOW ON THE PRECIPICE OF MADNESS.
HE BECAME CONVINCED THAT I'D BEEN HIS ENEMY ALL ALONG--THAT MY GOAL HAD NOT BEEN TO HEAL, BUT TO MOCK AND TORMENT HIM.
AND HE LEFT US--DISAPPEARING FOR MONTHS AT A TIME. WHERE HE WENT, WHAT HE DID, I NEVER LEARNED--BUT HE ALWAYS RETURNED...
...FOR TAKHAR--FILLING THE BOY'S HEAD WITH HIS DREAMS AND DELUSIONS:
TALES OF GRAND ADVENTURES--BOTH REAL AND IMAGINED. AND FINALLY, WHEN TAKHAR WAS NEARING HIS FIFTEENTH BIRTHDAY...
...SERGEI TOOK HIM AWAY FROM ME.
"I AM NOT YOURS," MY SON TOLD ME THAT NIGHT. "I AM HIS. I AM NOT TAKHAR.
"I AM GREGOR KRAVINOFF."
I COULD HAVE STOPPED HIM, BUT HE WOULD HAVE RESENTED, DESPISED, ME ALL THE MORE. SO I ALLOWED THEM TO GO...
...ALWAYS KEEPING THEM IN SIGHT, AWARE OF THEIR WANDERINGS. AND BELIEVING THAT, IN TIME, TAKHAR WOULD REALIZE THE TRUTH AND COME HOME TO ME.
THE GREATEST TRAGEDY OF MY LIFE...
COME TO ME, PETER.
COME INTO MY ARMS.
COME HOME.

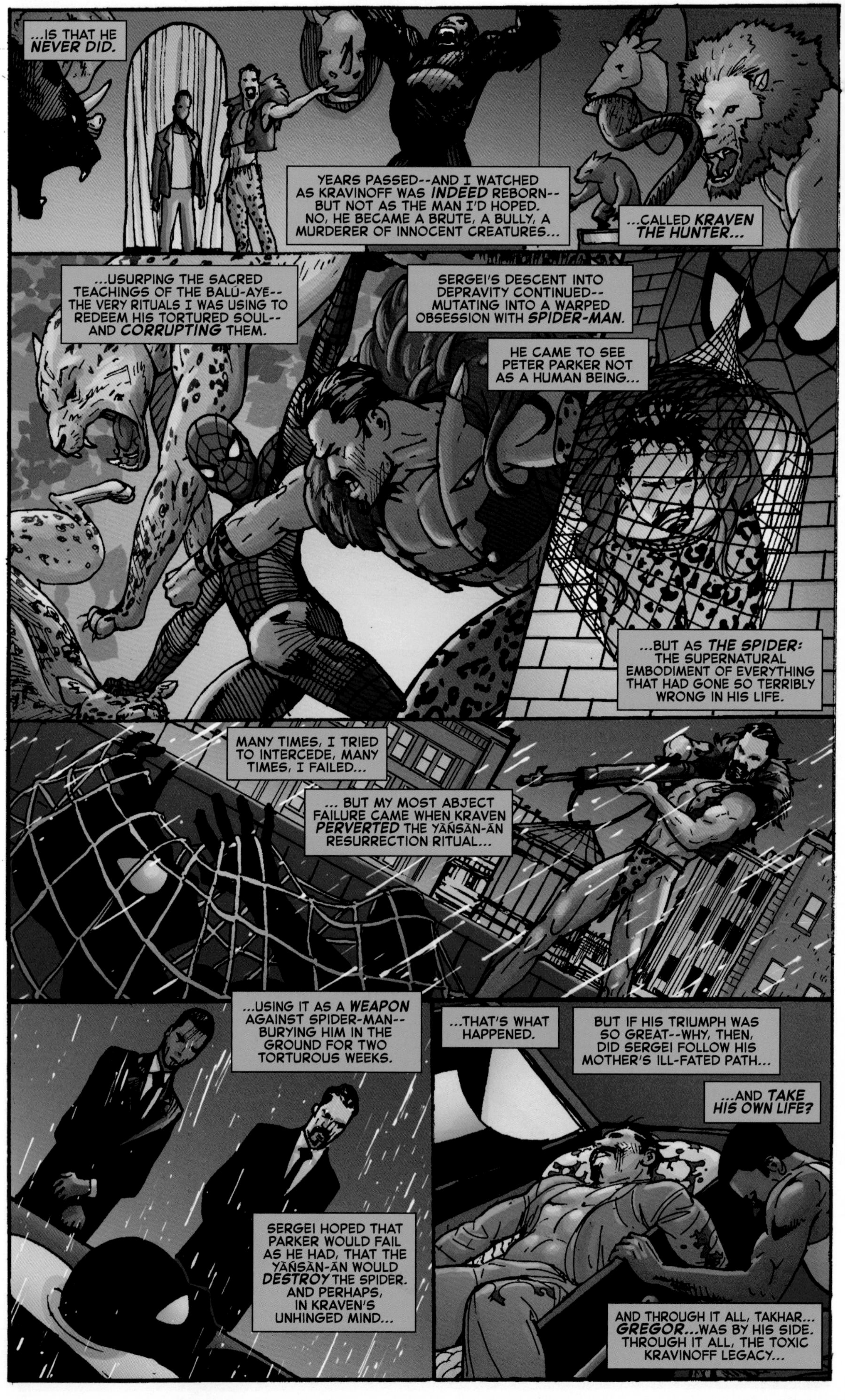
...IS THAT HE NEVER DID.
YEARS PASSED--AND I WATCHED AS KRAVINOFF WAS INDEED REBORN--BUT NOT AS THE MAN I'D HOPED. NO, HE BECAME A BRUTE, A BULLY, A MURDERER OF INNOCENT CREATURES...
...CALLED KRAVEN THE HUNTER...
...USURPING THE SACRED TEACHINGS OF THE BALÚ-AYE--THE VERY RITUALS I WAS USING TO REDEEM HIS TORTURED SOUL--AND CORRUPTING THEM.
SERGEI'S DESCENT INTO DEPRAVITY CONTINUED--MUTATING INTO A WARPED OBSESSION WITH SPIDER-MAN.
HE CAME TO SEE PETER PARKER NOT AS A HUMAN BEING...
...BUT AS THE SPIDER: THE SUPERNATURAL EMBODIMENT OF EVERYTHING THAT HAD GONE SO TERRIBLY WRONG IN HIS LIFE.
MANY TIMES, I TRIED TO INTERCEDE, MANY TIMES, I FAILED...
... BUT MY MOST ABJECT FAILURE CAME WHEN KRAVEN PERVERTED THE YĀŃSĀN-ĀN RESURRECTION RITUAL...
...USING IT AS A WEAPON AGAINST SPIDER-MAN--BURYING HIM IN THE GROUND FOR TWO TORTUROUS WEEKS.
SERGEI HOPED THAT PARKER WOULD FAIL AS HE HAD, THAT THE YĀŃSĀN-ĀN WOULD DESTROY THE SPIDER. AND PERHAPS, IN KRAVEN'S UNHINGED MIND...
...THAT'S WHAT HAPPENED.
BUT IF HIS TRIUMPH WAS SO GREAT--WHY, THEN, DID SERGEI FOLLOW HIS MOTHER'S ILL-FATED PATH...
...AND TAKE HIS OWN LIFE?
AND THROUGH IT ALL, TAKHAR... GREGOR...WAS BY HIS SIDE. THROUGH IT ALL, THE TOXIC KRAVINOFF LEGACY...

...INFECTED MY CHILD'S SOUL.
THAT IS A BURDEN I MUST BEAR. THAT...
SLOOOSH
...AND SO MUCH MORE.
I SOUGHT ONLY TO HEAL A FRIEND, BUT MY OWN NEEDS BLINDED ME. AND FOR THE REST OF MY DAYS I'LL WONDER:
IF I'D UNDERSTOOD SOONER HOW DEEP SERGEI'S MADNESS RAN--COULD I HAVE SAVED HIM?
SAVED THEM BOTH?
...MMMM...
...MARY...
MARY JANE.
YOU DID IT.

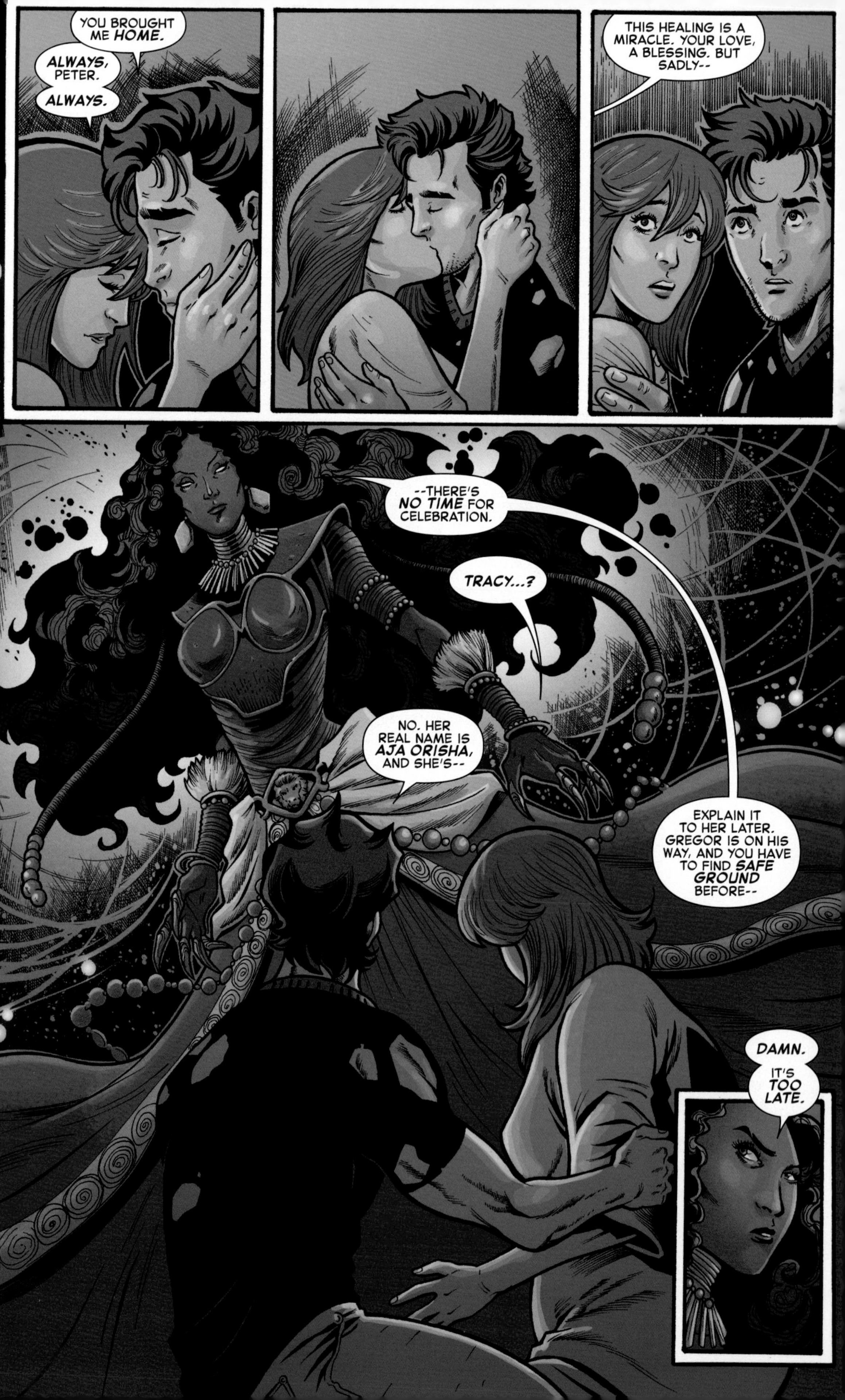
YOU BROUGHT ME HOME.
ALWAYS, PETER.
ALWAYS.
THIS HEALING IS A MIRACLE. YOUR LOVE, A BLESSING. BUT SADLY--
--THERE'S NO TIME FOR CELEBRATION.
TRACY...?
NO. HER REAL NAME IS AJA ORISHA, AND SHE'S--
EXPLAIN IT TO HER LATER. GREGOR IS ON HIS WAY, AND YOU HAVE TO FIND SAFE GROUND BEFORE--
DAMN.
IT'S TOO LATE.

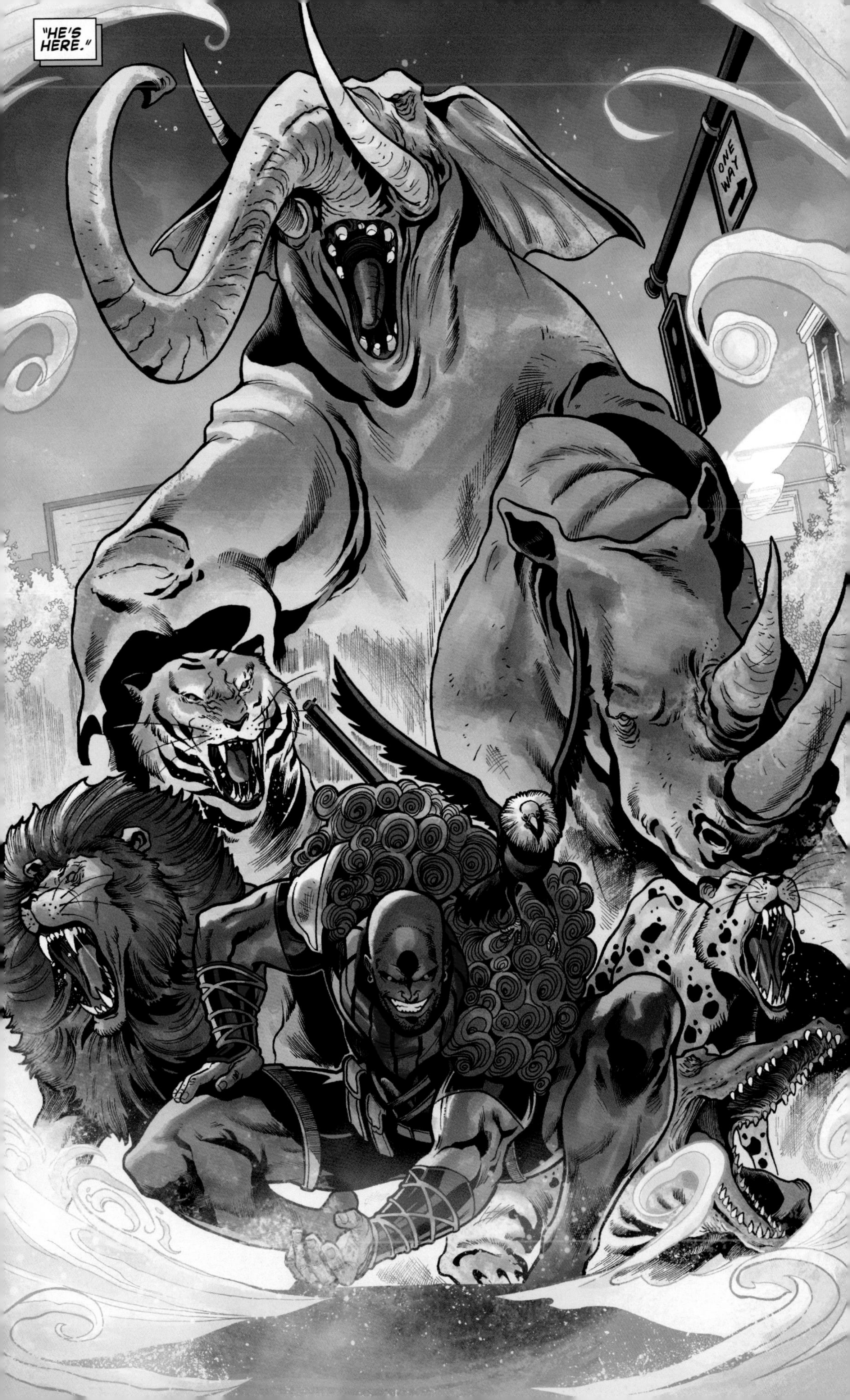
"HE'S HERE."
ONE WAY

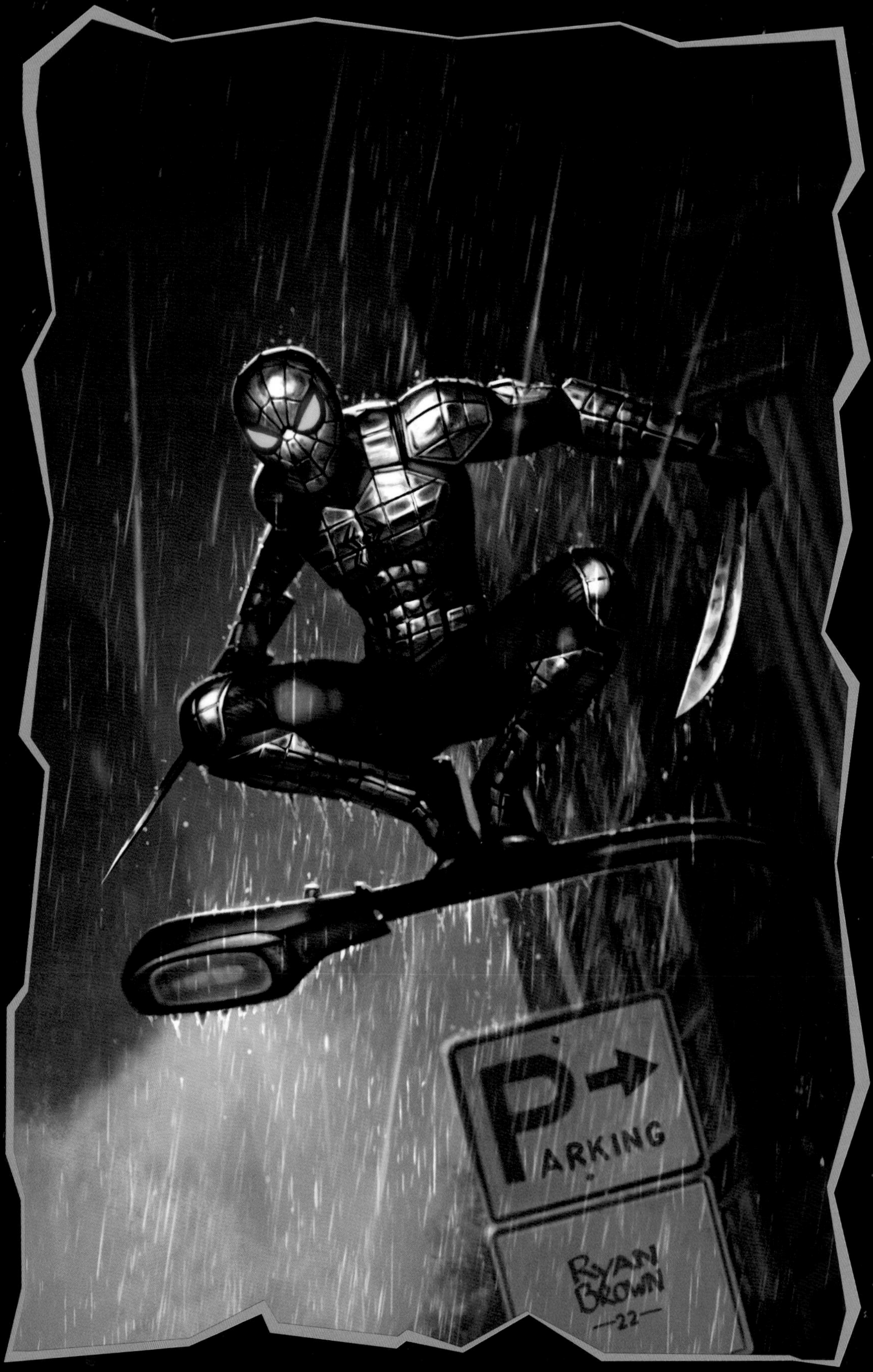
PARKING
RYAN BROWN
-22-

5

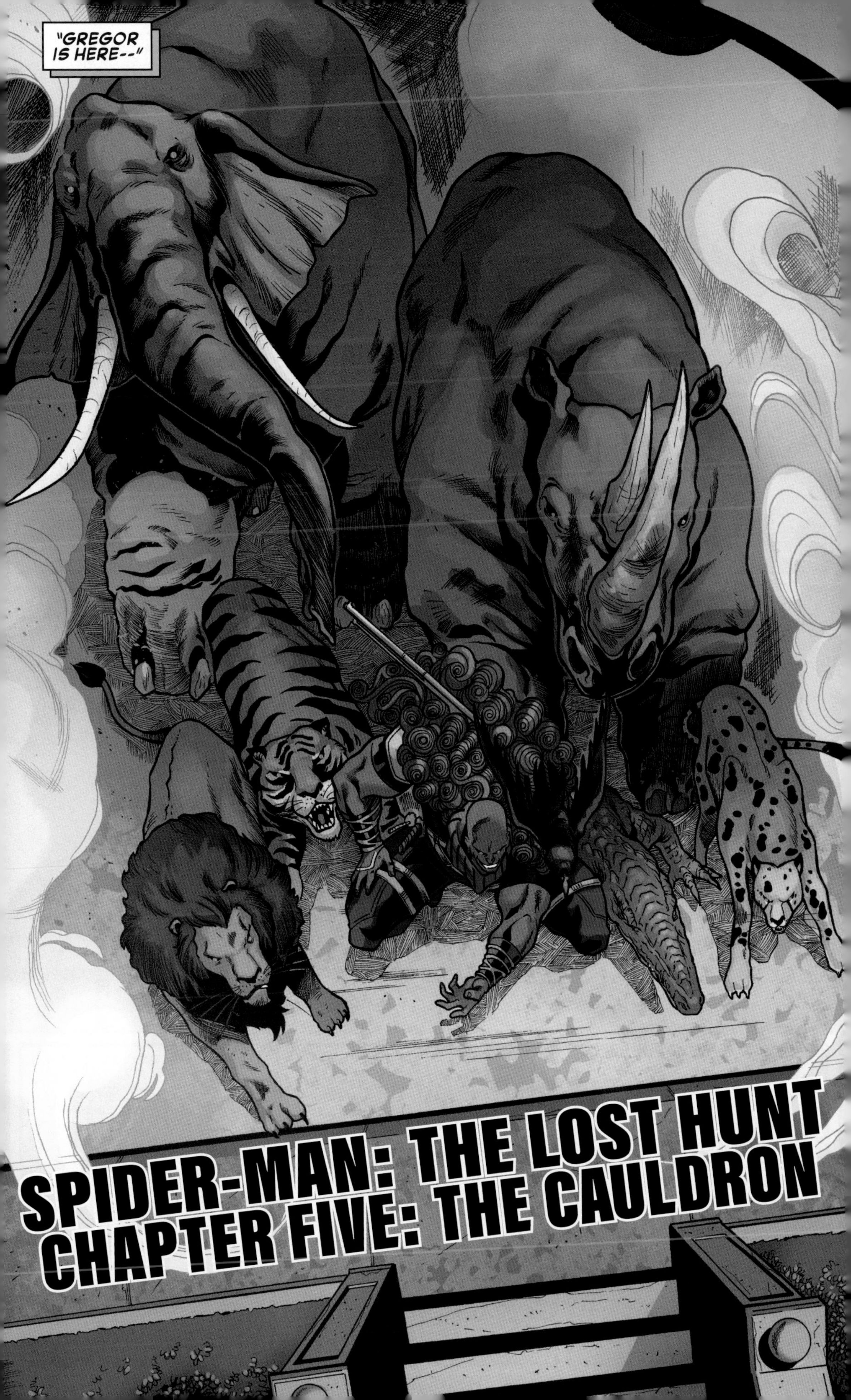
"GREGOR IS HERE--"
SPIDER-MAN: THE LOST HUNT
CHAPTER FIVE: THE CAULDRON

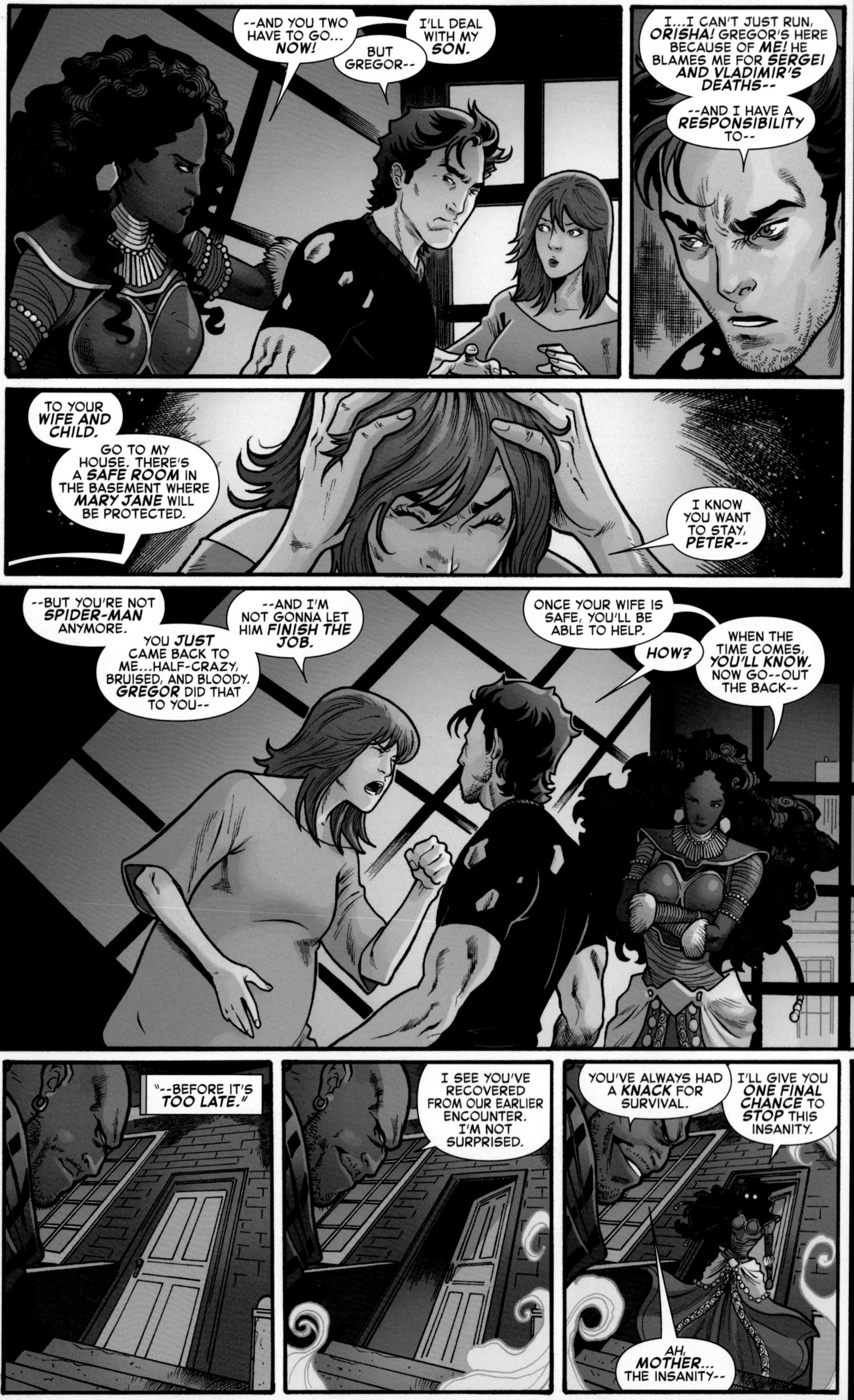
--AND YOU TWO HAVE TO GO... NOW!
BUT GREGOR--
I'LL DEAL WITH MY SON.
I...I CAN'T JUST RUN, ORISHA! GREGOR'S HERE BECAUSE OF ME! HE BLAMES ME FOR SERGEI AND VLADIMIR'S DEATHS--
--AND I HAVE A RESPONSIBILITY TO--
TO YOUR WIFE AND CHILD.
GO TO MY HOUSE. THERE'S A SAFE ROOM IN THE BASEMENT WHERE MARY JANE WILL BE PROTECTED.
I KNOW YOU WANT TO STAY, PETER--
--BUT YOU'RE NOT SPIDER-MAN ANYMORE.
YOU JUST CAME BACK TO ME...HALF-CRAZY, BRUISED, AND BLOODY. GREGOR DID THAT TO YOU--
--AND I'M NOT GONNA LET HIM FINISH THE JOB.
ONCE YOUR WIFE IS SAFE, YOU'LL BE ABLE TO HELP.
HOW?
WHEN THE TIME COMES, YOU'LL KNOW. NOW GO--OUT THE BACK--
"--BEFORE IT'S TOO LATE."
I SEE YOU'VE RECOVERED FROM OUR EARLIER ENCOUNTER. I'M NOT SURPRISED.
YOU'VE ALWAYS HAD A KNACK FOR SURVIVAL.
I'LL GIVE YOU ONE FINAL CHANCE TO STOP THIS INSANITY.
AH, MOTHER... THE INSANITY--

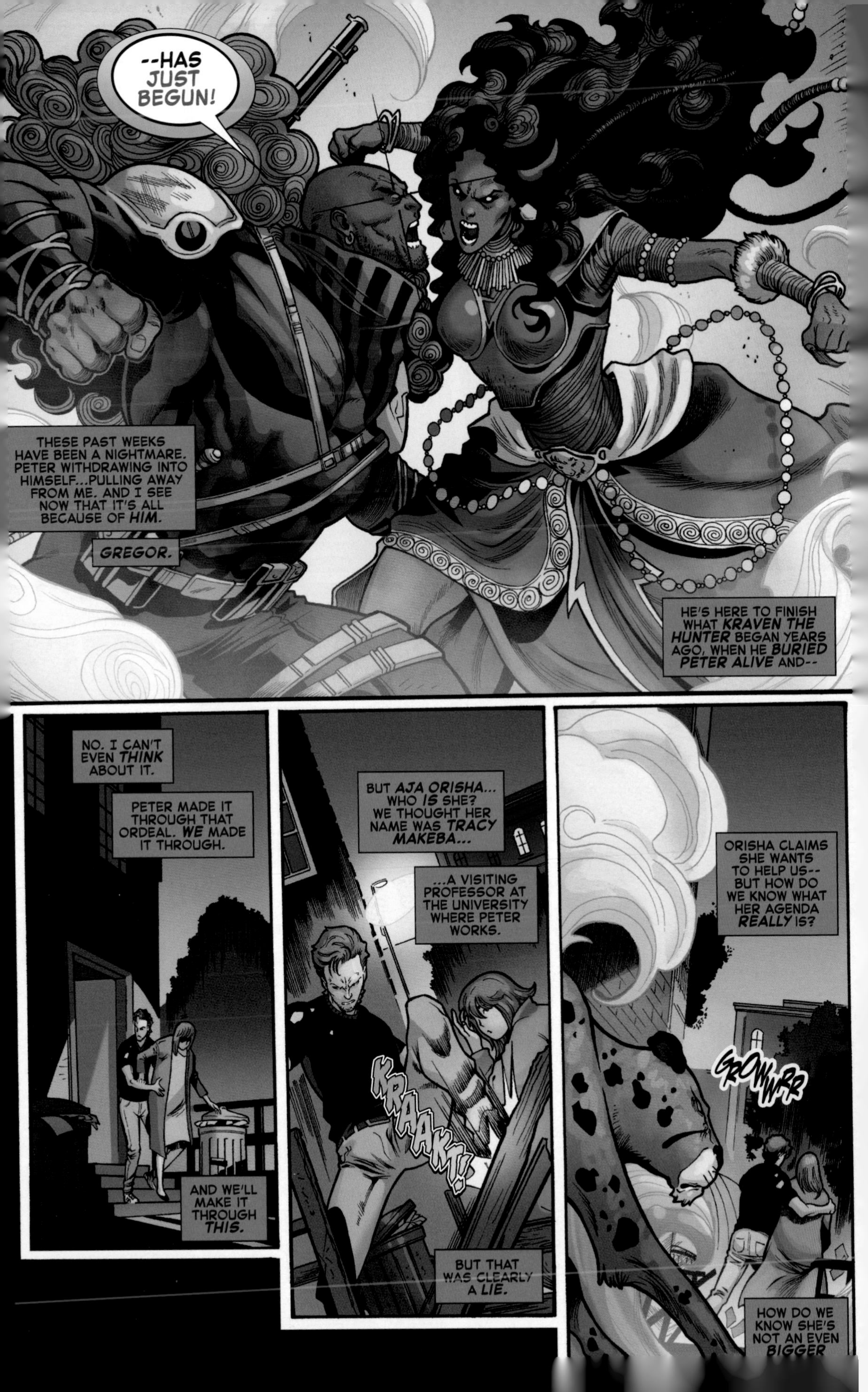
--HAS JUST BEGUN!
THESE PAST WEEKS HAVE BEEN A NIGHTMARE. PETER WITHDRAWING INTO HIMSELF...PULLING AWAY FROM ME. AND I SEE NOW THAT IT'S ALL BECAUSE OF HIM.
GREGOR.
HE'S HERE TO FINISH WHAT KRAVEN THE HUNTER BEGAN YEARS AGO, WHEN HE BURIED PETER ALIVE AND--
NO. I CAN'T EVEN THINK ABOUT IT.
PETER MADE IT THROUGH THAT ORDEAL. WE MADE IT THROUGH.
AND WE'LL MAKE IT THROUGH THIS.
BUT AJA ORISHA... WHO IS SHE? WE THOUGHT HER NAME WAS TRACY MAKEBA...
...A VISITING PROFESSOR AT THE UNIVERSITY WHERE PETER WORKS.
KRAAAKT!
BUT THAT WAS CLEARLY A LIE.
ORISHA CLAIMS SHE WANTS TO HELP US--BUT HOW DO WE KNOW WHAT HER AGENDA REALLY IS?
GROWWRR
HOW DO WE KNOW SHE'S NOT AN EVEN BIGGER

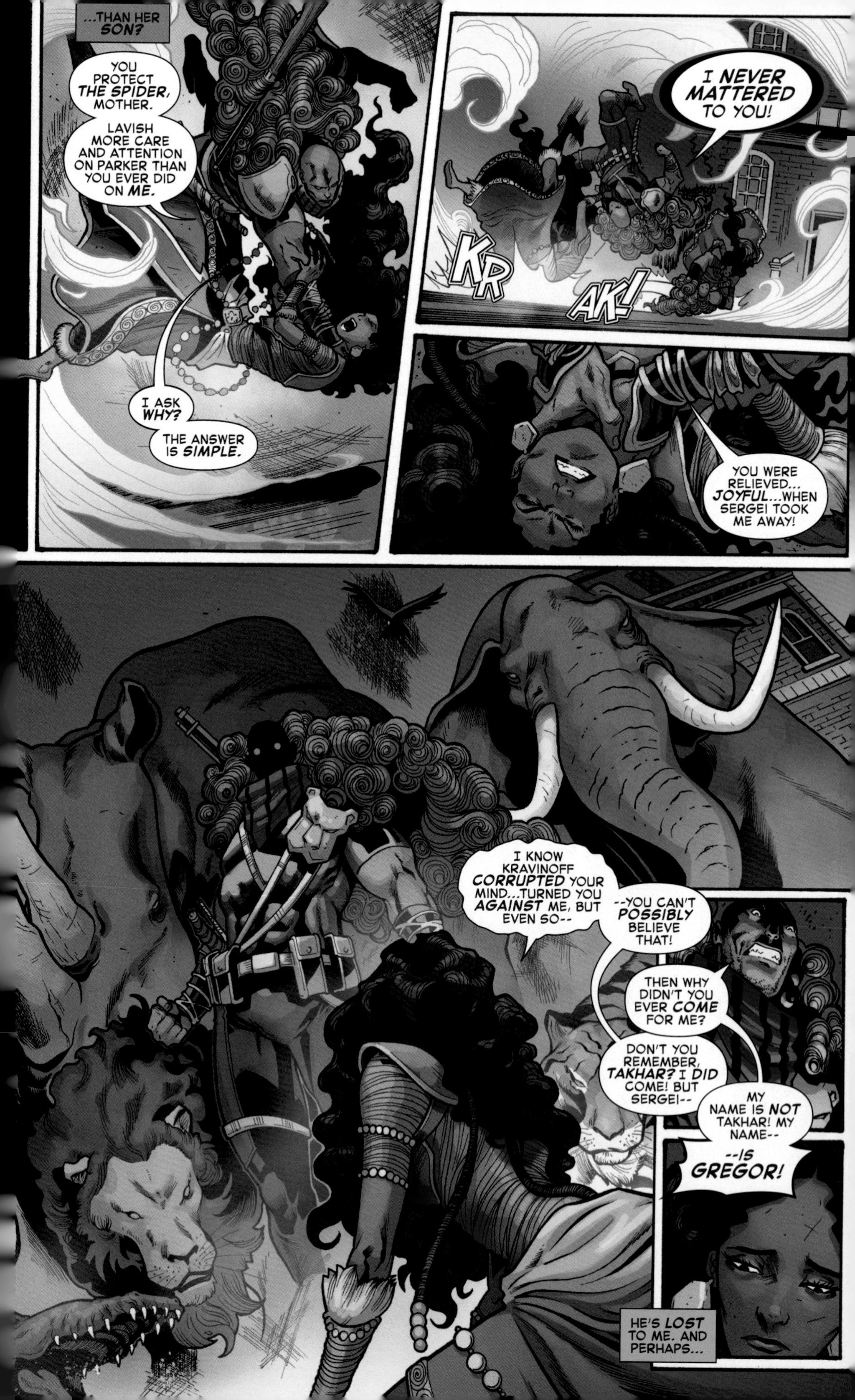
...THAN HER SON?
YOU PROTECT THE SPIDER, MOTHER.
LAVISH MORE CARE AND ATTENTION ON PARKER THAN YOU EVER DID ON ME.
I ASK WHY?
THE ANSWER IS SIMPLE.
I NEVER MATTERED TO YOU!
KRAK!
YOU WERE RELIEVED... JOYFUL...WHEN SERGEI TOOK ME AWAY!
I KNOW KRAVINOFF CORRUPTED YOUR MIND...TURNED YOU AGAINST ME, BUT EVEN SO--
--YOU CAN'T POSSIBLY BELIEVE THAT!
THEN WHY DIDN'T YOU EVER COME FOR ME?
DON'T YOU REMEMBER, TAKHAR? I DID COME! BUT SERGEI--
MY NAME IS NOT TAKHAR! MY NAME--
--IS GREGOR!
HE'S LOST TO ME. AND PERHAPS...

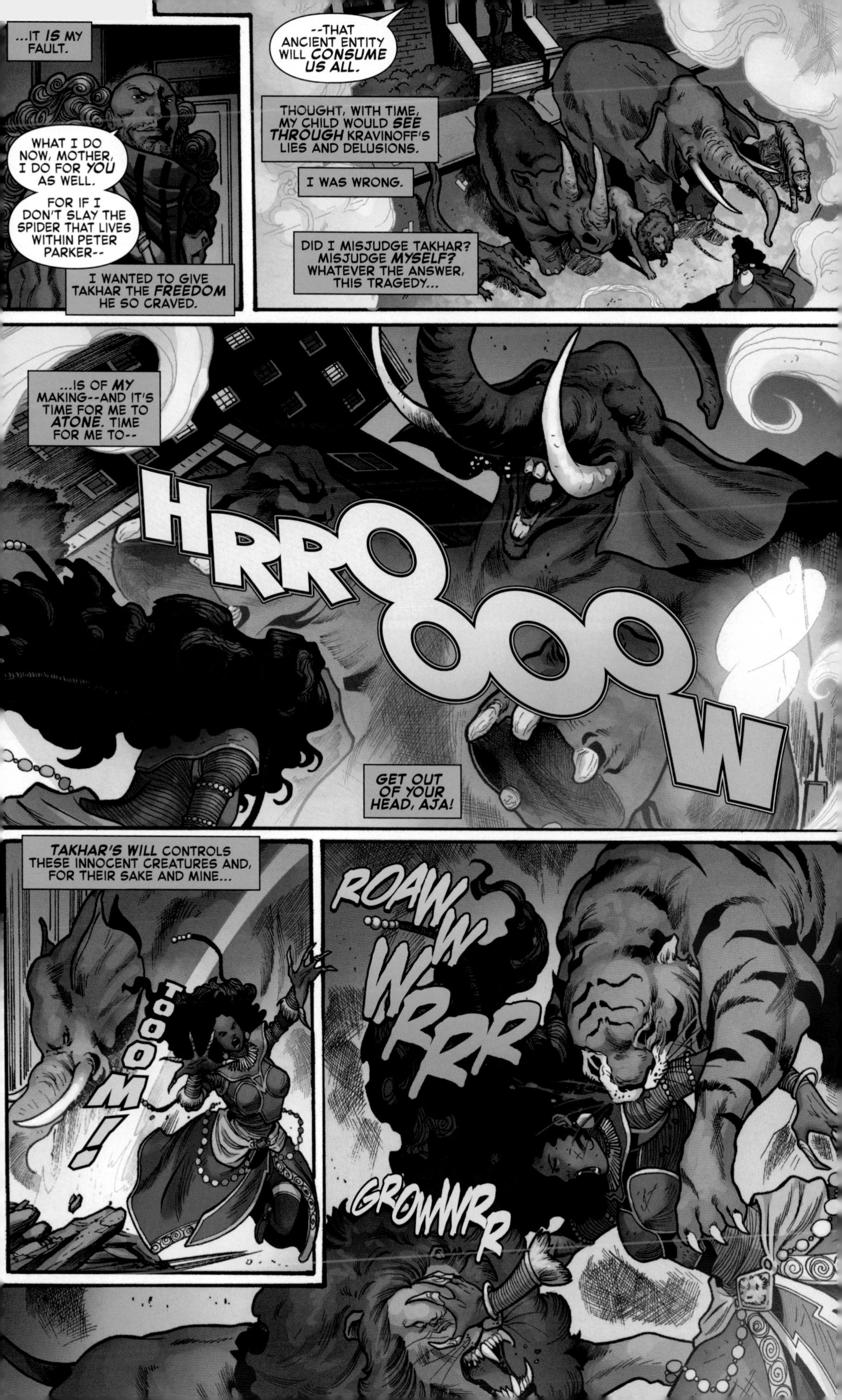

...IT IS MY FAULT.
WHAT I DO NOW, MOTHER, I DO FOR YOU AS WELL.
FOR IF I DON'T SLAY THE SPIDER THAT LIVES WITHIN PETER PARKER--
I WANTED TO GIVE TAKHAR THE FREEDOM HE SO CRAVED.
--THAT ANCIENT ENTITY WILL CONSUME US ALL.
THOUGHT, WITH TIME, MY CHILD WOULD SEE THROUGH KRAVINOFF'S LIES AND DELUSIONS.
I WAS WRONG.
DID I MISJUDGE TAKHAR? MISJUDGE MYSELF? WHATEVER THE ANSWER, THIS TRAGEDY...
...IS OF MY MAKING--AND IT'S TIME FOR ME TO ATONE. TIME FOR ME TO--
HRROOOOW
GET OUT OF YOUR HEAD, AJA!
TAKHAR'S WILL CONTROLS THESE INNOCENT CREATURES AND, FOR THEIR SAKE AND MINE...
TOOOOM!
ROAWWWRRR
GROWWRR

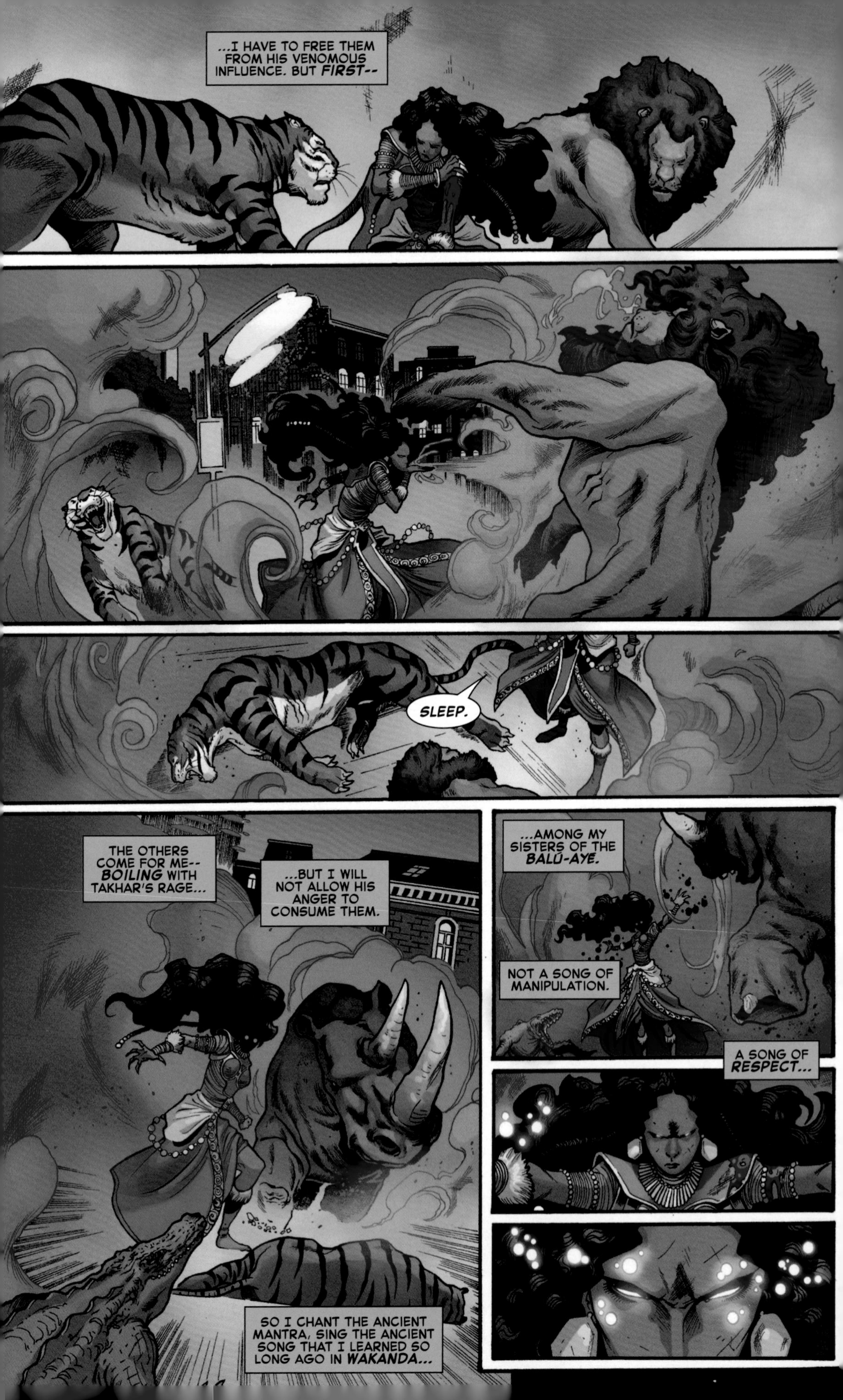
...I HAVE TO FREE THEM FROM HIS VENOMOUS INFLUENCE. BUT FIRST--
SLEEP.
THE OTHERS COME FOR ME-- BOILING WITH TAKHAR'S RAGE...
...BUT I WILL NOT ALLOW HIS ANGER TO CONSUME THEM.
SO I CHANT THE ANCIENT MANTRA, SING THE ANCIENT SONG THAT I LEARNED SO LONG AGO IN WAKANDA...
...AMONG MY SISTERS OF THE BALÚ-AYE.
NOT A SONG OF MANIPULATION.
A SONG OF RESPECT...

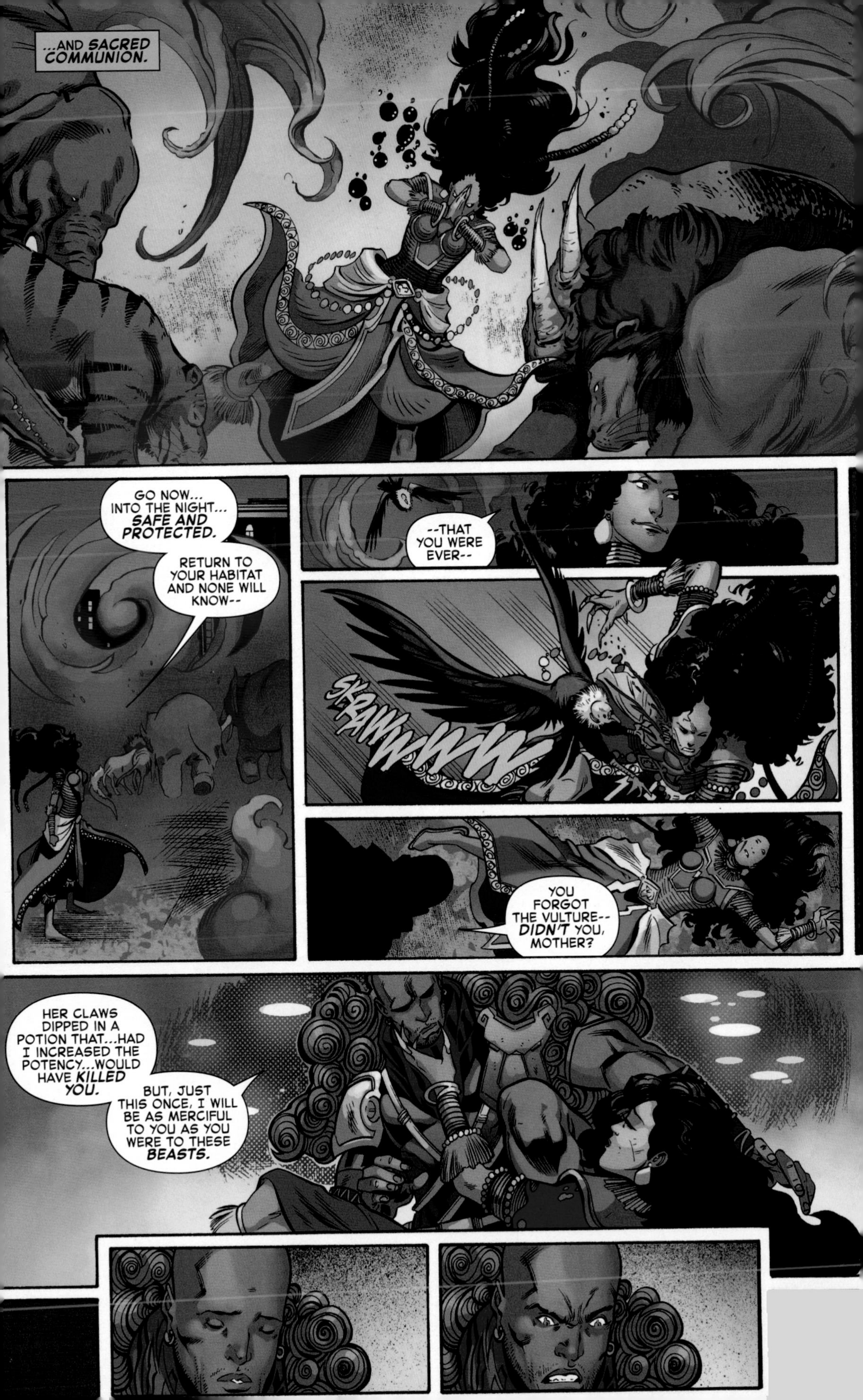
...AND SACRED COMMUNION.
GO NOW... INTO THE NIGHT... SAFE AND PROTECTED.
RETURN TO YOUR HABITAT AND NONE WILL KNOW--
--THAT YOU WERE EVER--
SKRAWWWWW
YOU FORGOT THE VULTURE-- DIDN'T YOU, MOTHER?
HER CLAWS DIPPED IN A POTION THAT...HAD I INCREASED THE POTENCY...WOULD HAVE KILLED YOU.
BUT, JUST THIS ONCE, I WILL BE AS MERCIFUL TO YOU AS YOU WERE TO THESE BEASTS.

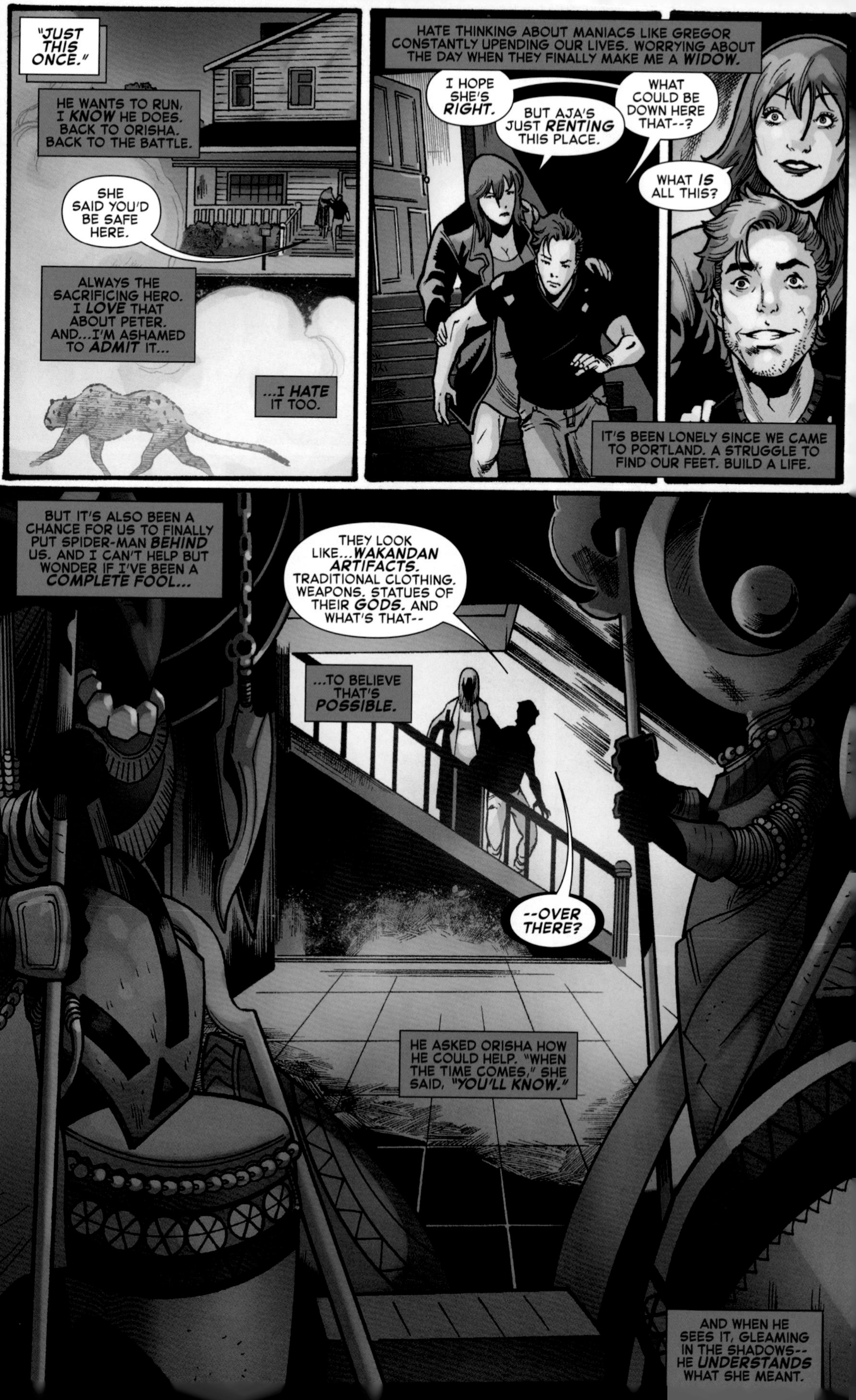
"JUST THIS ONCE."
HE WANTS TO RUN, I KNOW HE DOES. BACK TO ORISHA. BACK TO THE BATTLE.
SHE SAID YOU'D BE SAFE HERE.
ALWAYS THE SACRIFICING HERO. I LOVE THAT ABOUT PETER. AND...I'M ASHAMED TO ADMIT IT...
...I HATE IT TOO.
HATE THINKING ABOUT MANIACS LIKE GREGOR CONSTANTLY UPENDING OUR LIVES. WORRYING ABOUT THE DAY WHEN THEY FINALLY MAKE ME A WIDOW.
I HOPE SHE'S RIGHT.
BUT AJA'S JUST RENTING THIS PLACE.
WHAT COULD BE DOWN HERE THAT--?
WHAT IS ALL THIS?
IT'S BEEN LONELY SINCE WE CAME TO PORTLAND. A STRUGGLE TO FIND OUR FEET. BUILD A LIFE.
BUT IT'S ALSO BEEN A CHANCE FOR US TO FINALLY PUT SPIDER-MAN BEHIND US. AND I CAN'T HELP BUT WONDER IF I'VE BEEN A COMPLETE FOOL...
THEY LOOK LIKE...WAKANDAN ARTIFACTS. TRADITIONAL CLOTHING. WEAPONS. STATUES OF THEIR GODS. AND WHAT'S THAT--
...TO BELIEVE THAT'S POSSIBLE.
--OVER THERE?
HE ASKED ORISHA HOW HE COULD HELP. "WHEN THE TIME COMES," SHE SAID, "YOU'LL KNOW."
AND WHEN HE SEES IT, GLEAMING IN THE SHADOWS--HE UNDERSTANDS WHAT SHE MEANT.

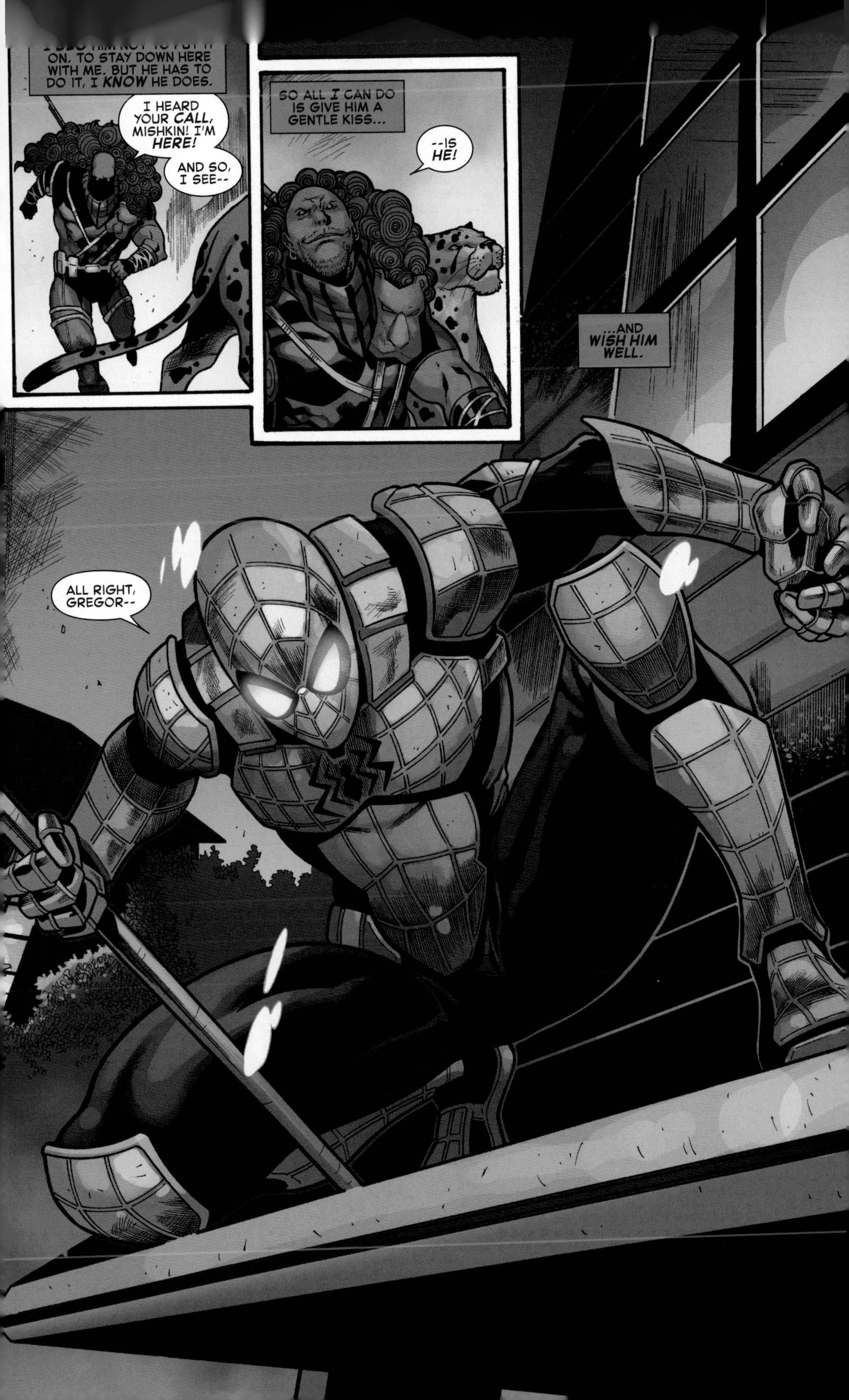
ON. TO STAY DOWN HERE WITH ME. BUT HE HAS TO DO IT. I KNOW HE DOES.
I HEARD YOUR CALL, MISHKIN! I'M HERE!
AND SO, I SEE--
SO ALL I CAN DO IS GIVE HIM A GENTLE KISS...
--IS HE!
...AND WISH HIM WELL.
ALL RIGHT, GREGOR--

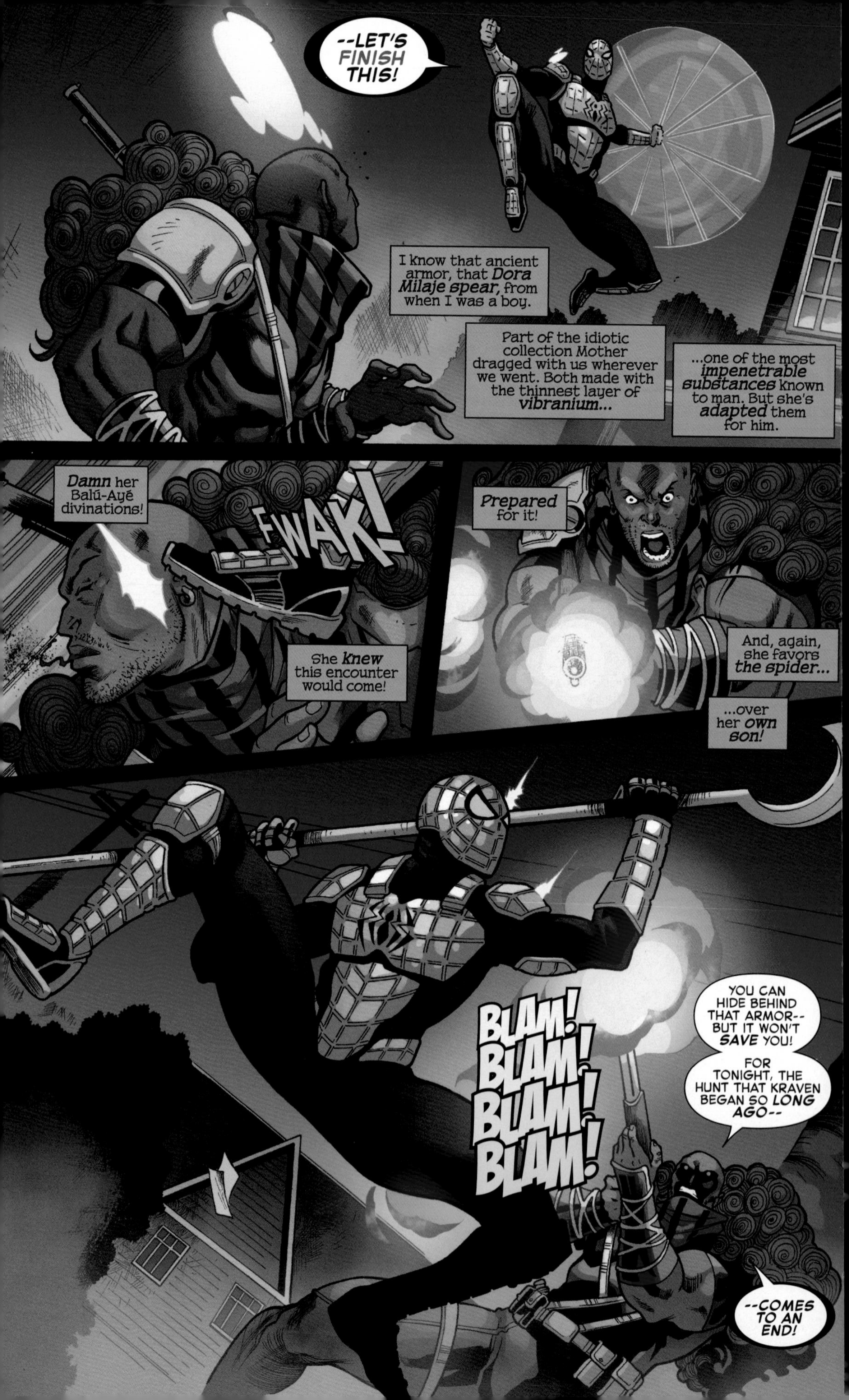

--LET'S FINISH THIS!
I know that ancient armor, that Dora Milaje spear, from when I was a boy.
Part of the idiotic collection Mother dragged with us wherever we went. Both made with the thinnest layer of vibranium...
...one of the most impenetrable substances known to man. But she's adapted them for him.
Damn her Balú-Ayé divinations!
FWAK!
She knew this encounter would come!
Prepared for it!
And, again, she favors the spider...
...over her own son!
BLAM! BLAM! BLAM! BLAM!
YOU CAN HIDE BEHIND THAT ARMOR-- BUT IT WON'T SAVE YOU!
FOR TONIGHT, THE HUNT THAT KRAVEN BEGAN SO LONG AGO--
--COMES TO AN END!

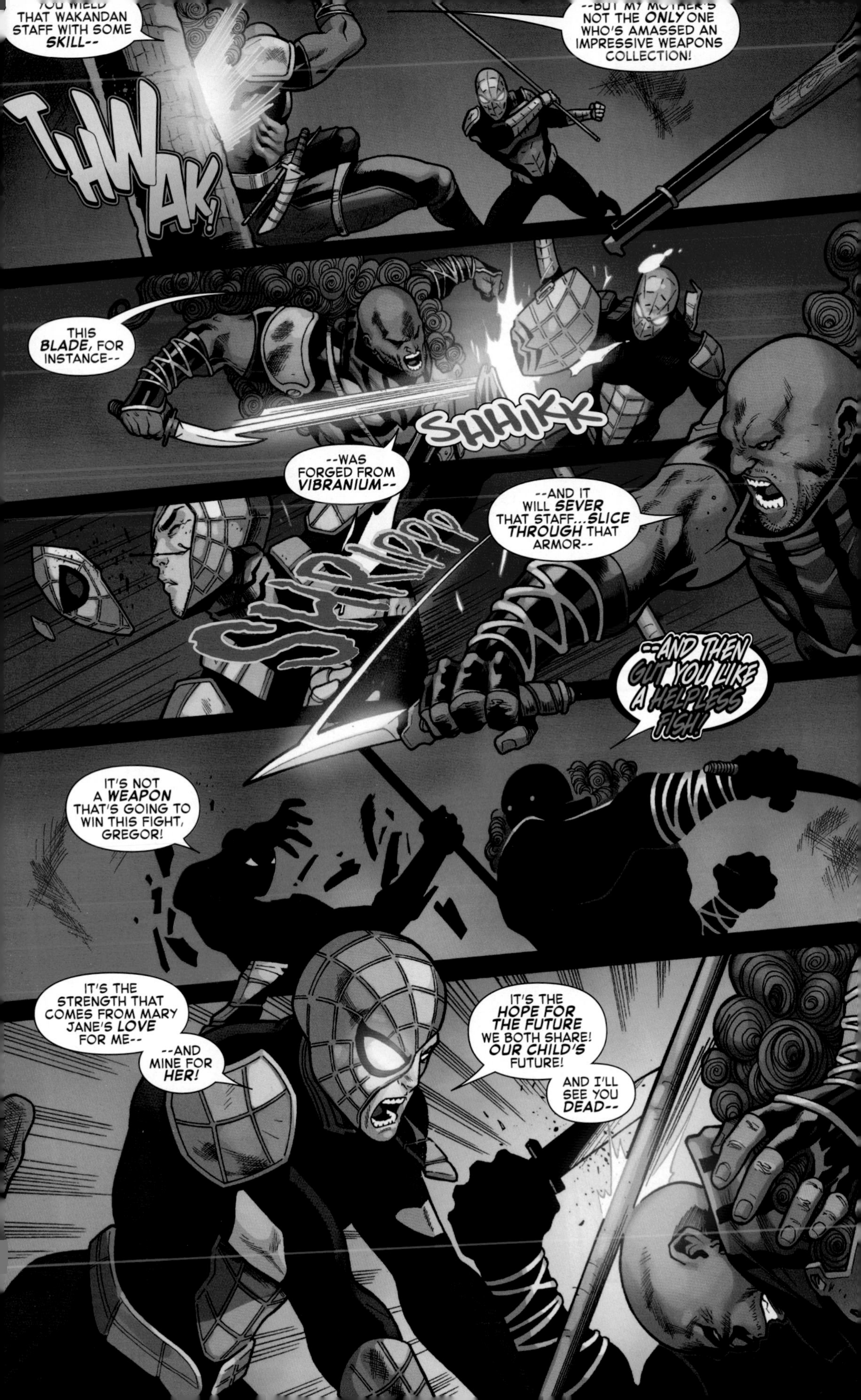

YOU WIELD THAT WAKANDAN STAFF WITH SOME SKILL--
--BUT MY MOTHER'S NOT THE ONLY ONE WHO'S AMASSED AN IMPRESSIVE WEAPONS COLLECTION!
THWAK!
THIS BLADE, FOR INSTANCE--
SHHIKK
--WAS FORGED FROM VIBRANIUM--
SHRPP
--AND IT WILL SEVER THAT STAFF...SLICE THROUGH THAT ARMOR--
--AND THEN GUT YOU LIKE A HELPLESS FISH!
IT'S NOT A WEAPON THAT'S GOING TO WIN THIS FIGHT, GREGOR!
IT'S THE STRENGTH THAT COMES FROM MARY JANE'S LOVE FOR ME--
--AND MINE FOR HER!
IT'S THE HOPE FOR THE FUTURE WE BOTH SHARE! OUR CHILD'S FUTURE!
AND I'LL SEE YOU DEAD--

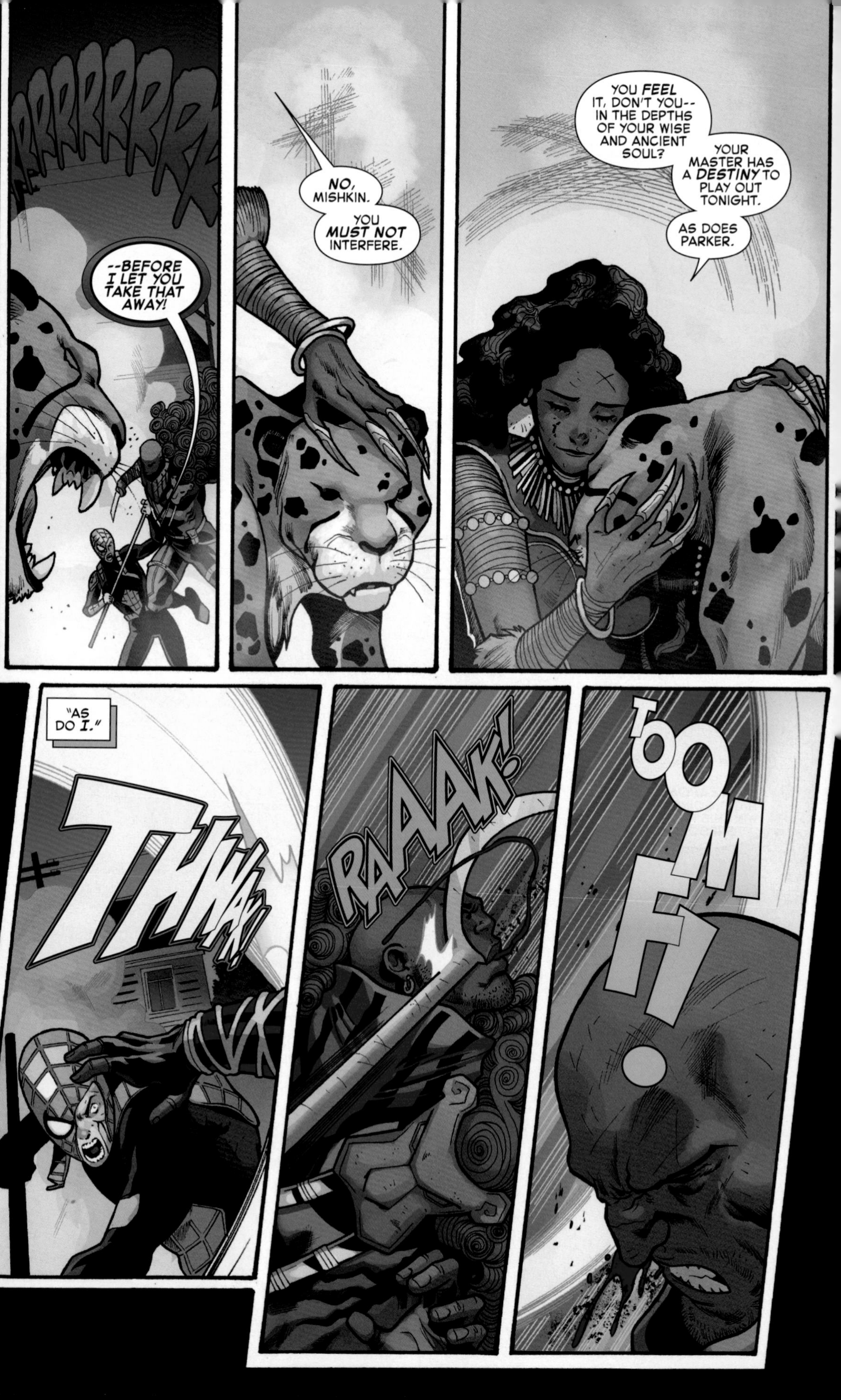
RRRRRRRR
--BEFORE I LET YOU TAKE THAT AWAY!
NO, MISHKIN.
YOU MUST NOT INTERFERE.
YOU FEEL IT, DON'T YOU-- IN THE DEPTHS OF YOUR WISE AND ANCIENT SOUL?
YOUR MASTER HAS A DESTINY TO PLAY OUT TONIGHT.
AS DOES PARKER.
"AS DO I."
THWAK!
RAAAK!
TOOOMFF!

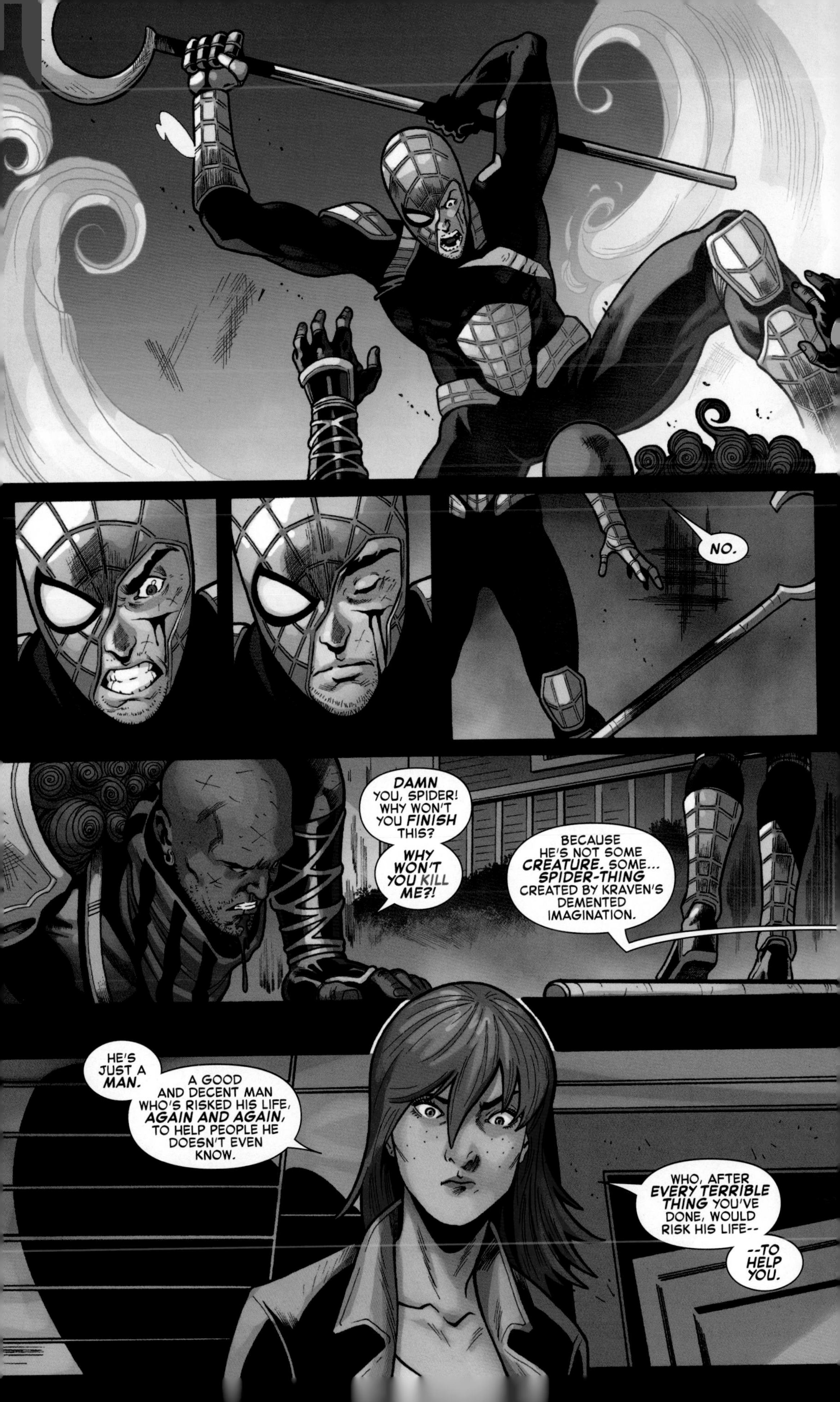
NO.
DAMN YOU, SPIDER! WHY WON'T YOU FINISH THIS?
WHY WON'T YOU KILL ME?!
BECAUSE HE'S NOT SOME CREATURE. SOME... SPIDER-THING CREATED BY KRAVEN'S DEMENTED IMAGINATION.
HE'S JUST A MAN.
A GOOD AND DECENT MAN WHO'S RISKED HIS LIFE, AGAIN AND AGAIN, TO HELP PEOPLE HE DOESN'T EVEN KNOW.
WHO, AFTER EVERY TERRIBLE THING YOU'VE DONE, WOULD RISK HIS LIFE--
--TO HELP YOU.

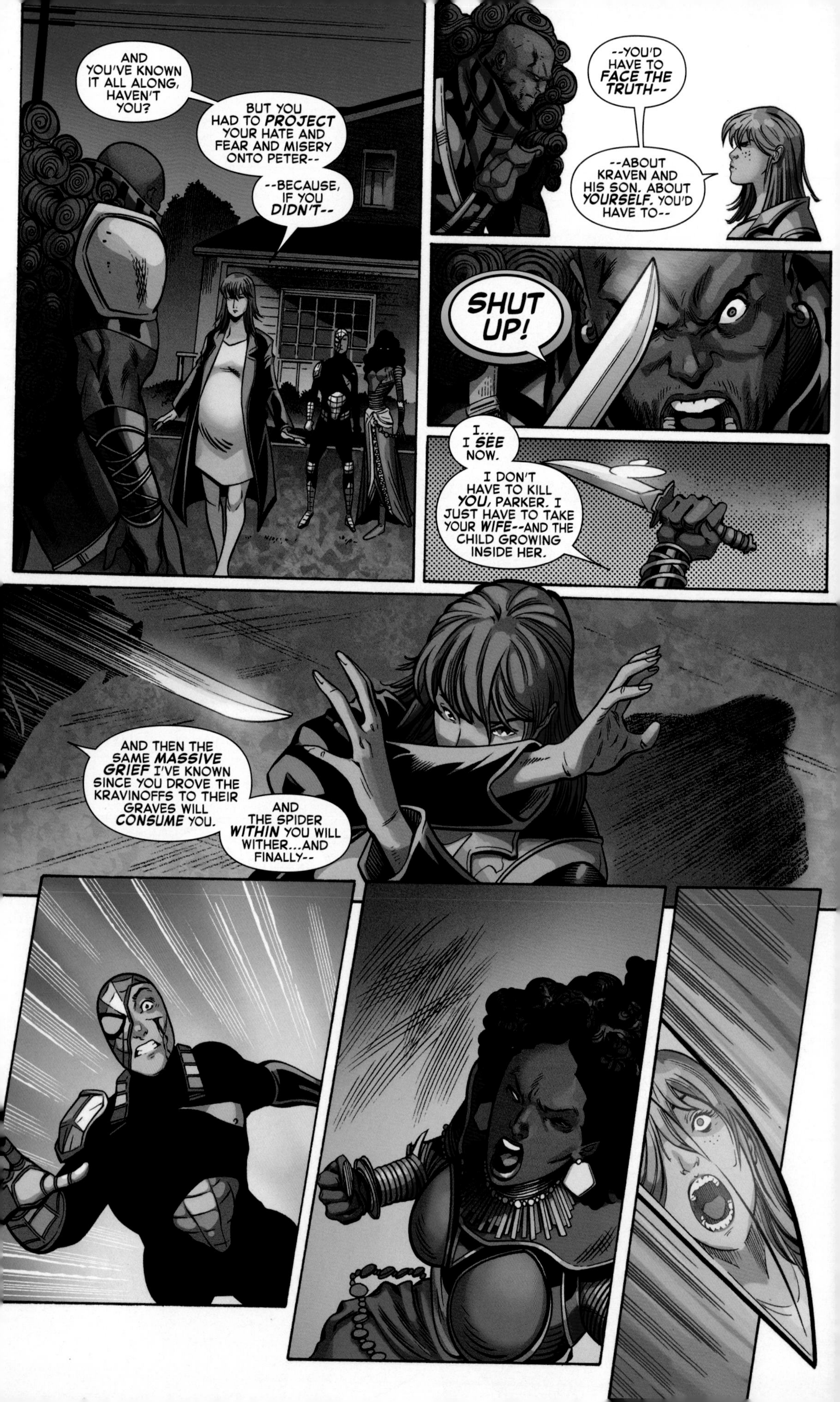

AND YOU'VE KNOWN IT ALL ALONG, HAVEN'T YOU?
BUT YOU HAD TO PROJECT YOUR HATE AND FEAR AND MISERY ONTO PETER--
--BECAUSE, IF YOU DIDN'T--
--YOU'D HAVE TO FACE THE TRUTH--
--ABOUT KRAVEN AND HIS SON. ABOUT YOURSELF. YOU'D HAVE TO--
SHUT UP!
I... I SEE NOW.
I DON'T HAVE TO KILL YOU, PARKER. I JUST HAVE TO TAKE YOUR WIFE--AND THE CHILD GROWING INSIDE HER.
AND THEN THE SAME MASSIVE GRIEF I'VE KNOWN SINCE YOU DROVE THE KRAVINOFFS TO THEIR GRAVES WILL CONSUME YOU.
AND THE SPIDER WITHIN YOU WILL WITHER...AND FINALLY--

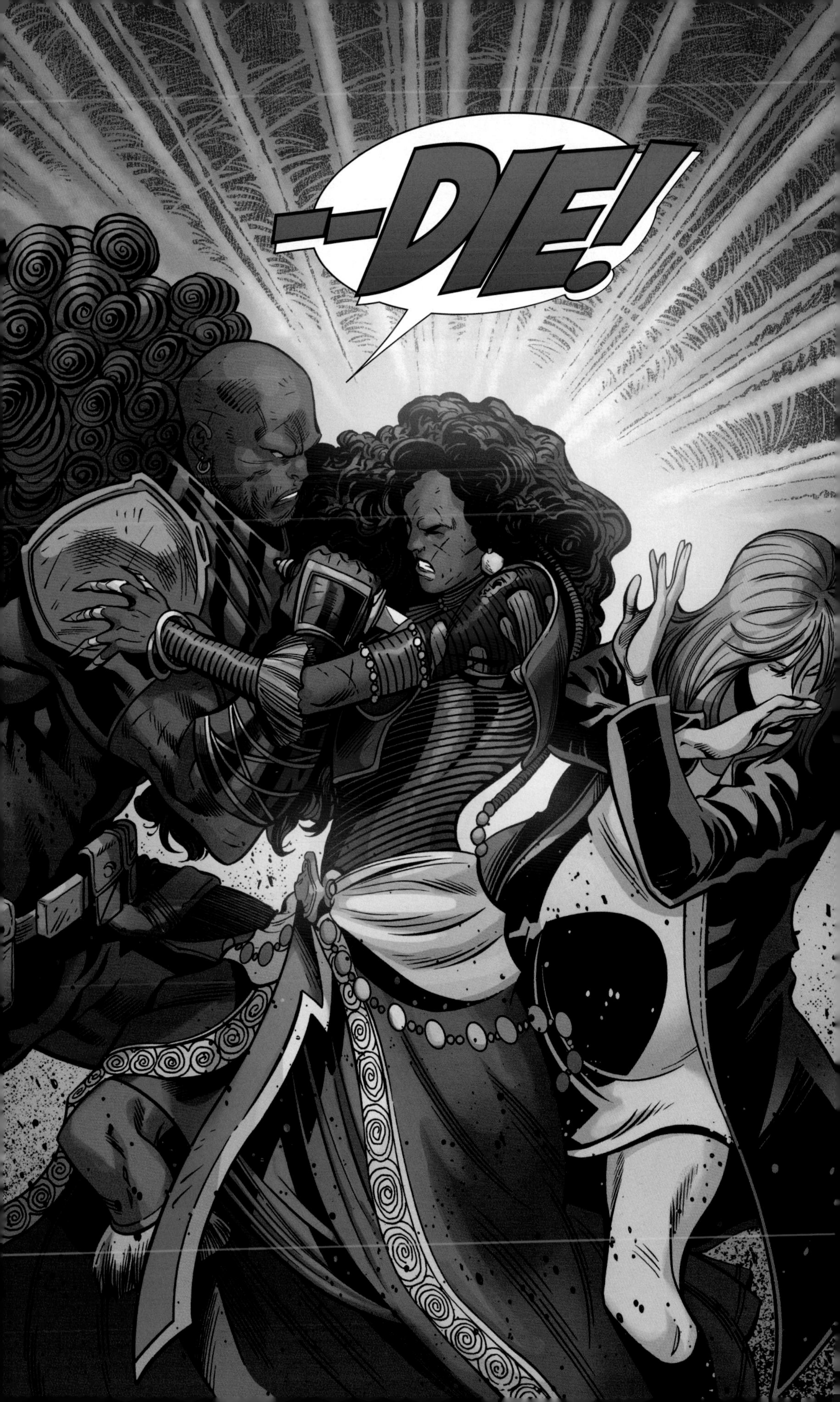
--DIE!

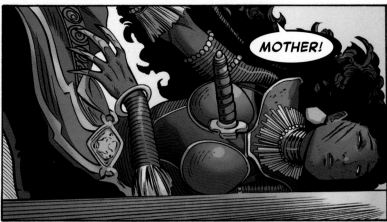

MOTHER!

MOTHER... I DIDN'T MEAN--

I KNOW. THIS WAS DESTINY'S WORK...NOT YOURS.

IT WAS THE ONLY WAY TO DISPEL THE DEMONS IN YOUR HEART--

--AND BRING MY BELOVED SON--

--BACK TO ME...

I...I'M SO SORRY, GREGOR.

MY NAME--IS TAKHAR!

And, at last, with painful clarity, I see myself...

THWAK!

...and my wasted life.

I betrayed my mother. My heritage.

And like that tortured madman I once worshipped...

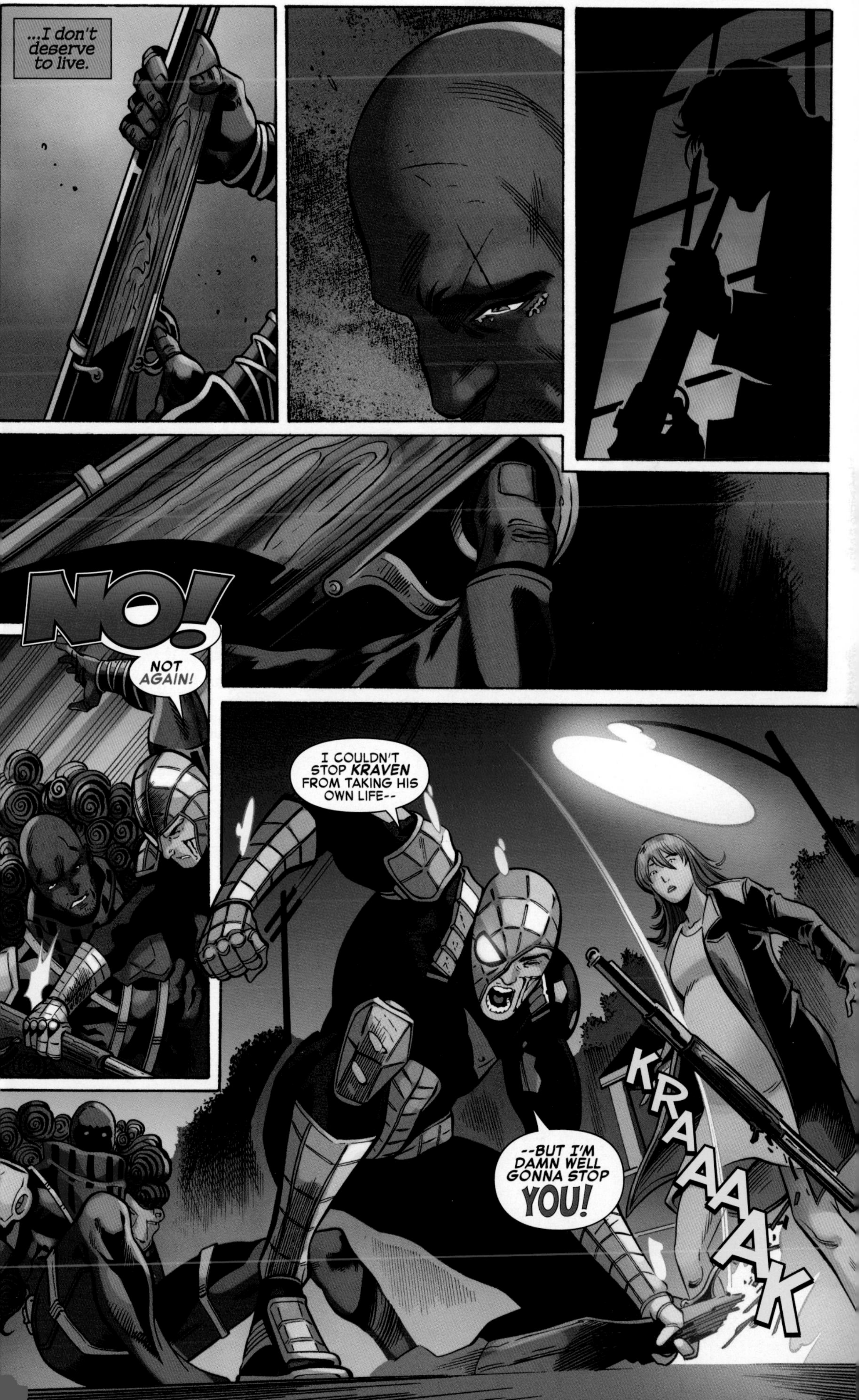
...I don't deserve to live.
NO!
NOT AGAIN!
I COULDN'T STOP KRAVEN FROM TAKING HIS OWN LIFE--
--BUT I'M DAMN WELL GONNA STOP YOU!
KRAAAAK

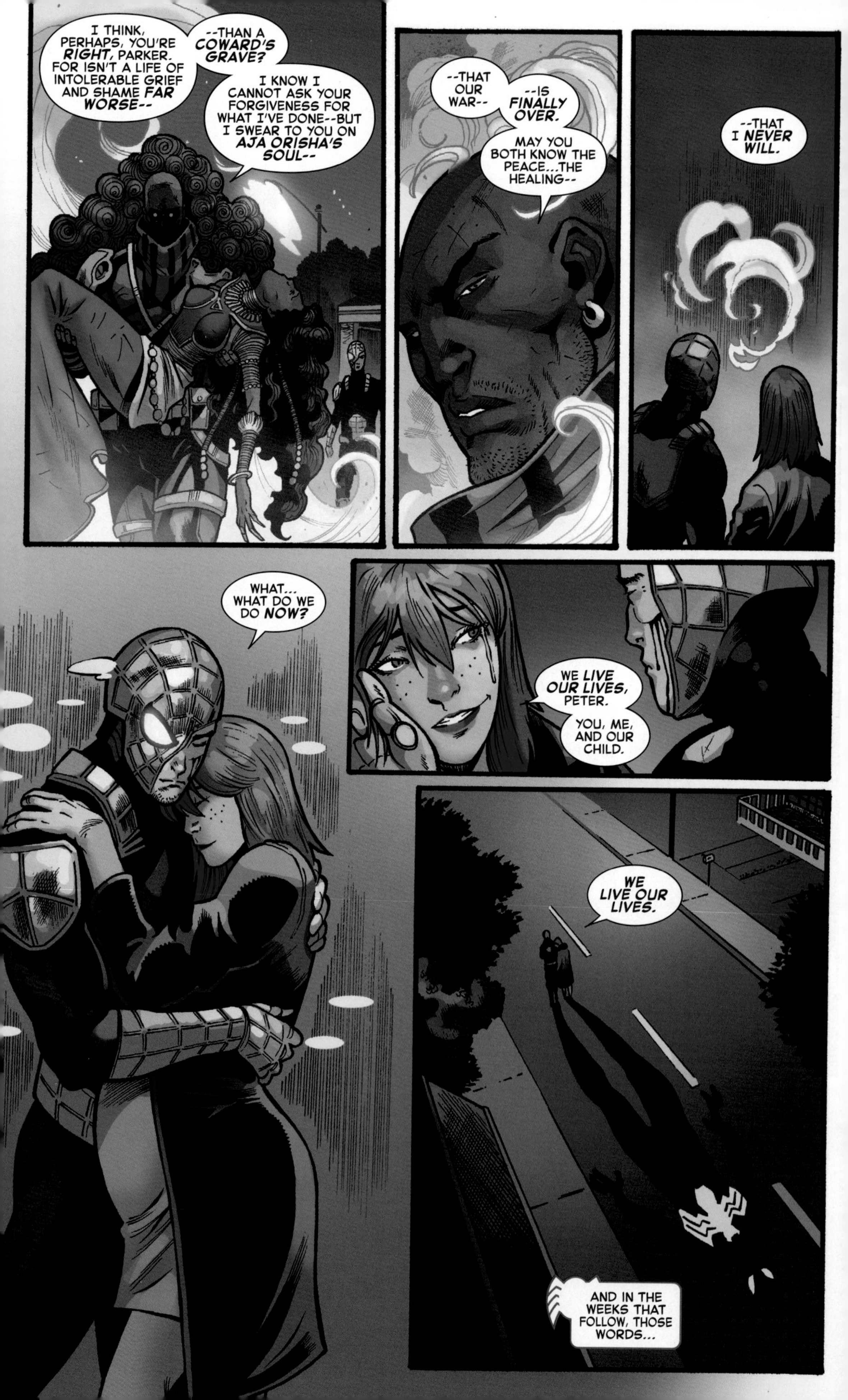
I THINK, PERHAPS, YOU'RE RIGHT, PARKER. FOR ISN'T A LIFE OF INTOLERABLE GRIEF AND SHAME FAR WORSE--
--THAN A COWARD'S GRAVE?
I KNOW I CANNOT ASK YOUR FORGIVENESS FOR WHAT I'VE DONE--BUT I SWEAR TO YOU ON AJA ORISHA'S SOUL--
--THAT OUR WAR--
--IS FINALLY OVER.
MAY YOU BOTH KNOW THE PEACE...THE HEALING--
--THAT I NEVER WILL.
WHAT... WHAT DO WE DO NOW?
WE LIVE OUR LIVES, PETER.
YOU, ME, AND OUR CHILD.
WE LIVE OUR LIVES.
AND IN THE WEEKS THAT FOLLOW, THOSE WORDS...

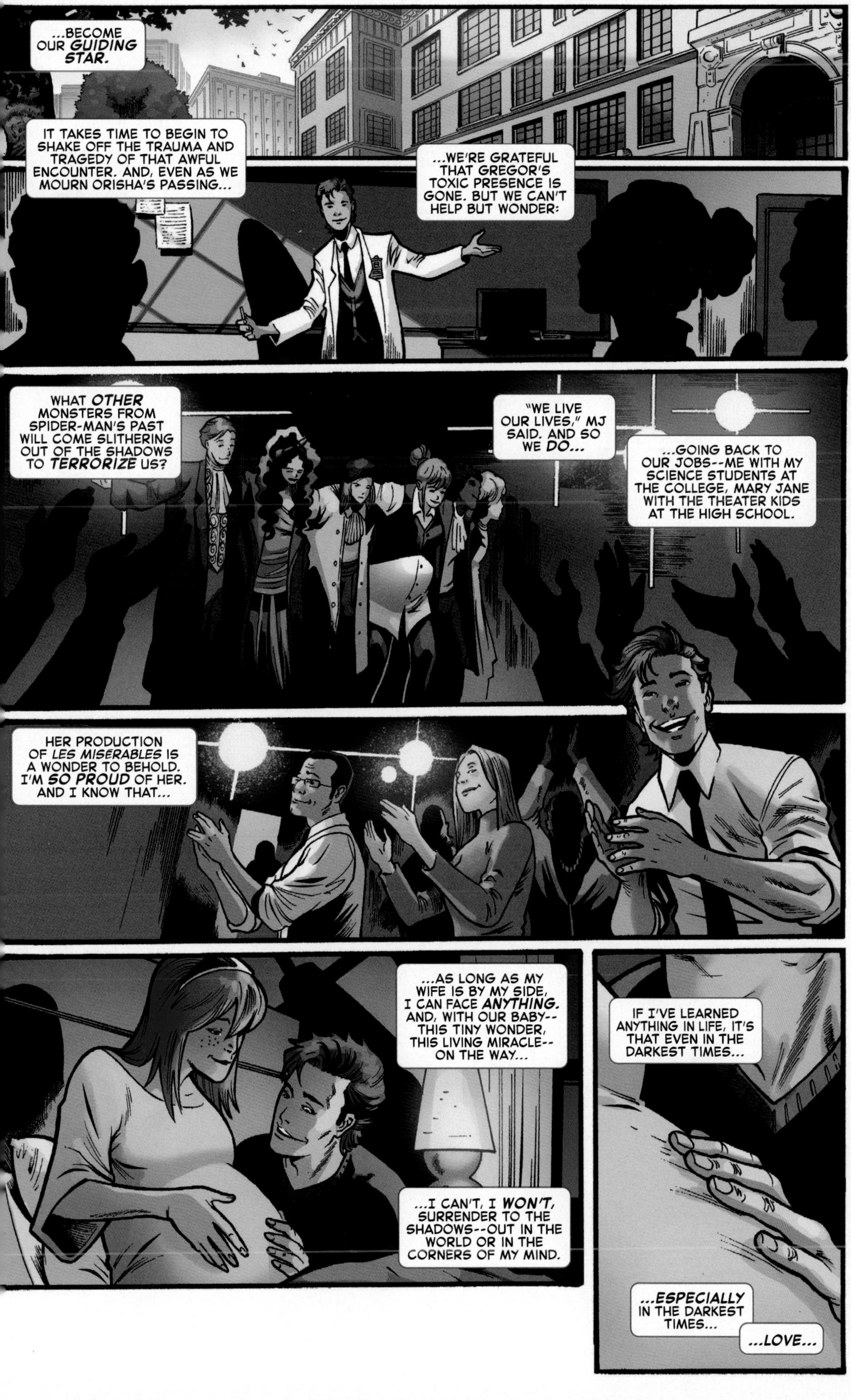
...BECOME OUR GUIDING STAR.
IT TAKES TIME TO BEGIN TO SHAKE OFF THE TRAUMA AND TRAGEDY OF THAT AWFUL ENCOUNTER. AND, EVEN AS WE MOURN ORISHA'S PASSING...
...WE'RE GRATEFUL THAT GREGOR'S TOXIC PRESENCE IS GONE. BUT WE CAN'T HELP BUT WONDER:
WHAT OTHER MONSTERS FROM SPIDER-MAN'S PAST WILL COME SLITHERING OUT OF THE SHADOWS TO TERRORIZE US?
"WE LIVE OUR LIVES," MJ SAID. AND SO WE DO...
...GOING BACK TO OUR JOBS--ME WITH MY SCIENCE STUDENTS AT THE COLLEGE, MARY JANE WITH THE THEATER KIDS AT THE HIGH SCHOOL.
HER PRODUCTION OF LES MISERABLES IS A WONDER TO BEHOLD. I'M SO PROUD OF HER. AND I KNOW THAT...
...AS LONG AS MY WIFE IS BY MY SIDE, I CAN FACE ANYTHING. AND, WITH OUR BABY--THIS TINY WONDER, THIS LIVING MIRACLE--ON THE WAY...
...I CAN'T, I WON'T, SURRENDER TO THE SHADOWS--OUT IN THE WORLD OR IN THE CORNERS OF MY MIND.
IF I'VE LEARNED ANYTHING IN LIFE, IT'S THAT EVEN IN THE DARKEST TIMES...
...ESPECIALLY IN THE DARKEST TIMES...
...LOVE...

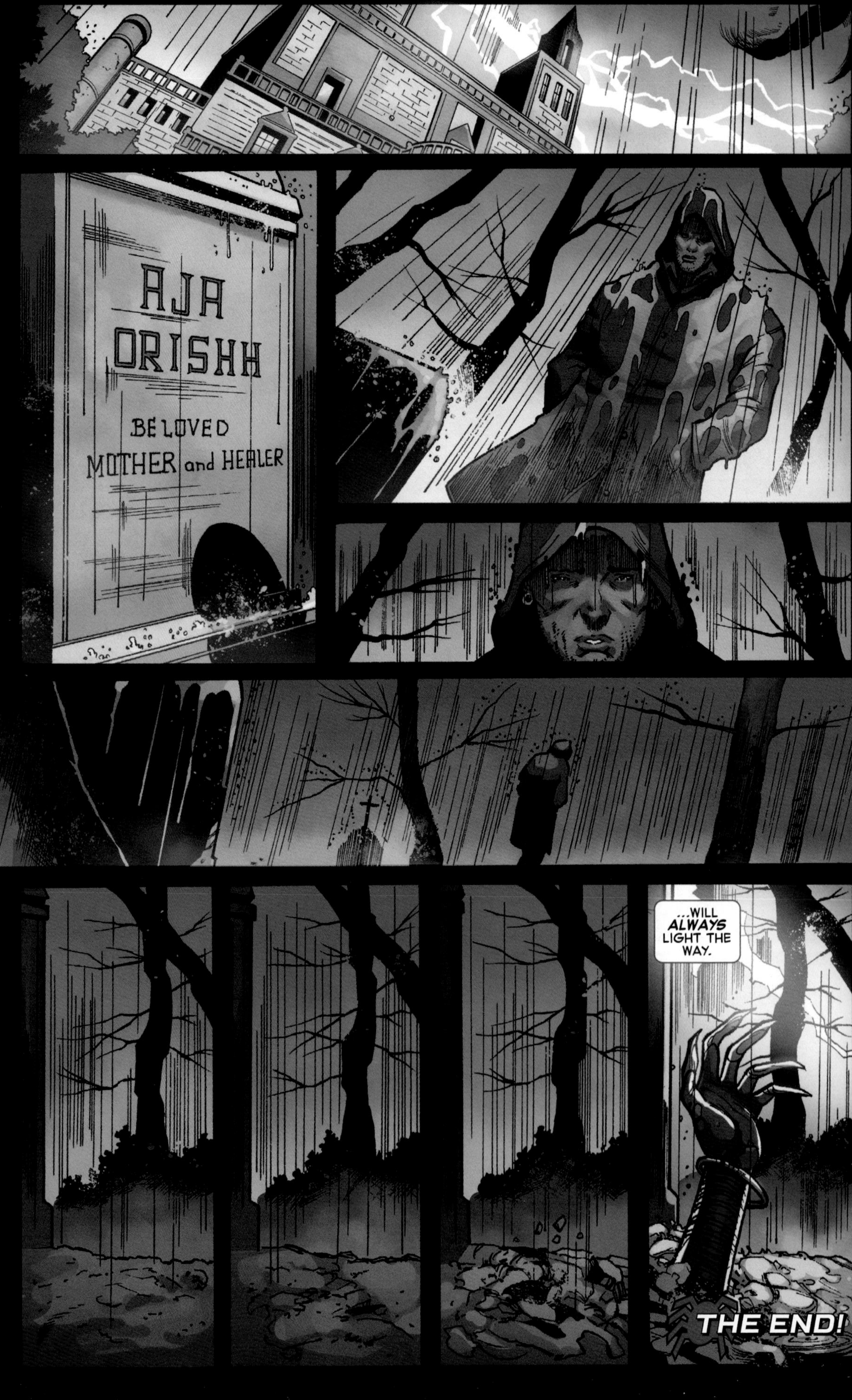
AJA
ORISHA
BELOVED
MOTHER and HEALER
...WILL ALWAYS LIGHT THE WAY.
THE END!

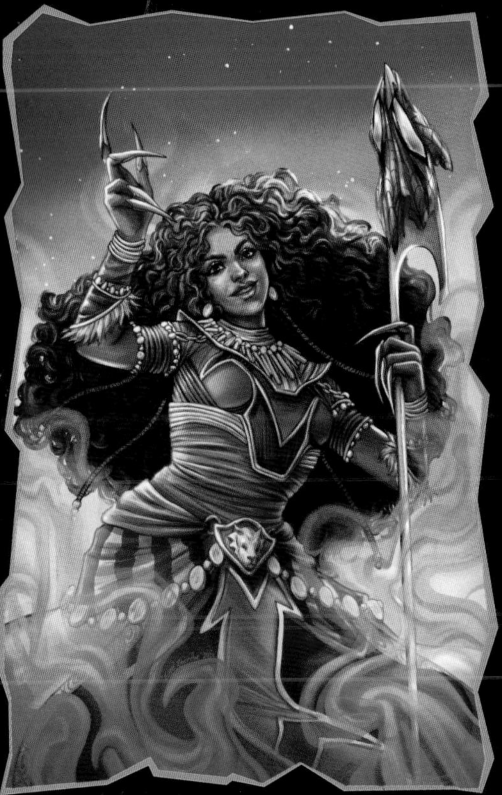

#1 VARIANT BY EJIWA "EDGE" EBENEBE

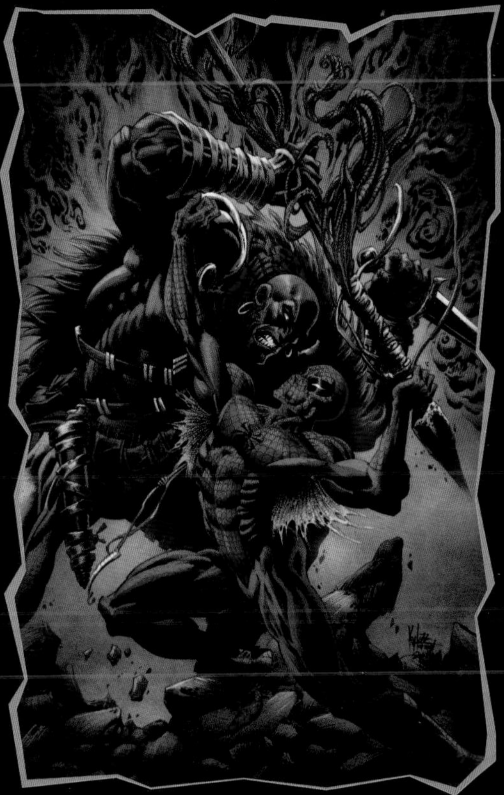

#1 VARIANT BY
KYLE HOTZ & RACHELLE ROSENBERG

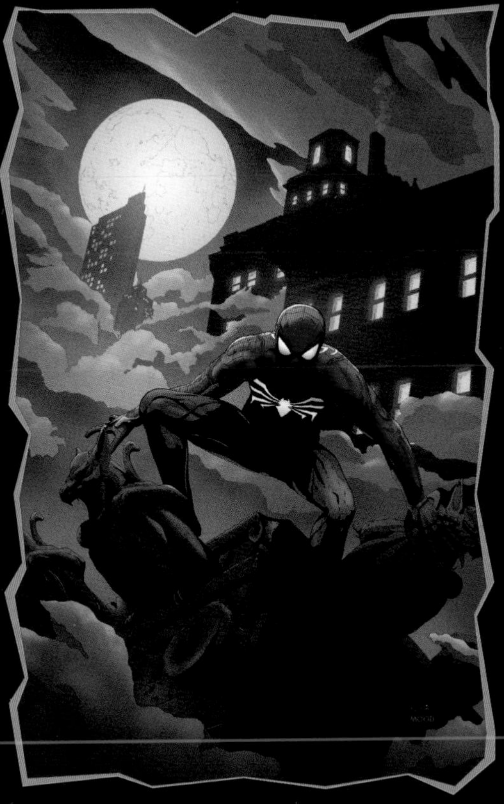

#2 BEYOND AMAZING SPIDER-MAN
VARIANT BY OSCAR FETSCHER

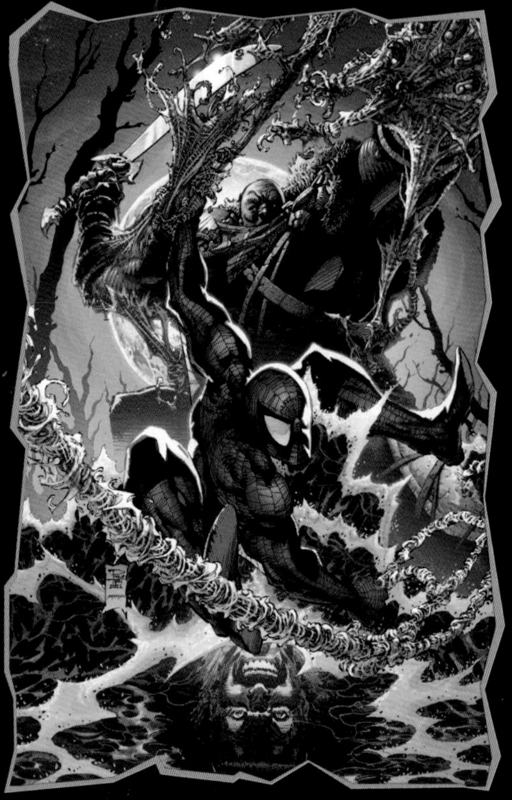

#2 VARIANT BY
PHILIP TAN & BRAD ANDERSON

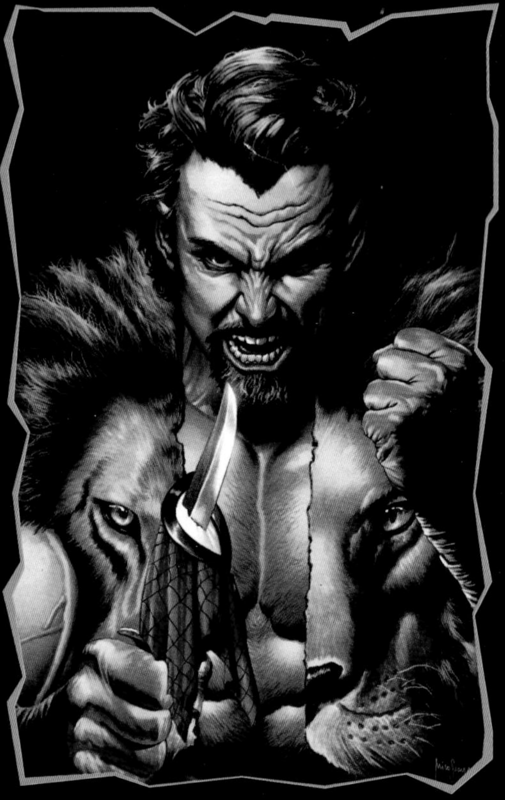

#3 VARIANT BY
MICO SUAYAN & BRIAN REBER

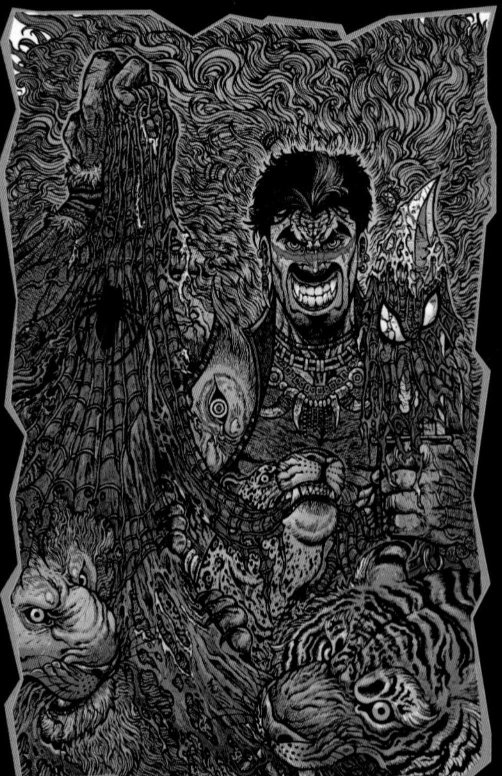

#4 VARIANT BY
MARIA WOLF & MIKE SPICER